Islam

the text of this book is printed on 100% recycled paper

A volume
in
DOCUMENTARY HISTORY
of
WESTERN CIVILIZATION

Islam

from the Prophet Muhammad to the Capture of Constantinople

Edited and translated by
BERNARD LEWIS

I: Politics and War

Harper & Row, Publishers
New York, Evanston, San Francisco, London

ISLAM: FROM THE PROPHET MUHAMMAD TO THE CAPTURE OF CONSTANTINOPLE
 For information address Harper & Row, Publishers, Inc., 10 East 53d Street, New York, N.Y. 10022. Published simultaneously in Canada by Fitzhenry & Whiteside Limited, Toronto.

First HARPER & ROW edition published 1974

LIBRARY OF CONGRESS CATALOG CARD NUMBER: 72–7229

STANDARD BOOK NUMBER: 06–138924–2

Designed by Ann Scrimgeour

History is a science of fine principles, manifold uses, and noble purpose. It informs us about the people of the past—the characters of nations, the lives of prophets, the kingdoms and policies of kings—thus usefully providing example for the emulation of those who desire it in religious and worldly affairs. The writer of history requires many sources and varied knowledge; he also requires keen judgment and careful scrutiny to lead him to the truth and away from lapses and errors. If reliance is placed on simple narrative as transmitted, without studying the roots of custom, the foundations of politics, the nature of civilization, and the circumstances of human society, and without comparing far with near and past with present—then there will often be danger of slipping and stumbling and straying from the right road.

Ibn Khaldūn, *Al-Muqaddima*

Contents

Preface

The following pages contain a selection, in English translation, from the original sources for the history of Islam in the Middle Ages. The excerpts have been arranged in two volumes. The first is concerned with politics and war and consists, in part, of narratives of events and, in part, of theoretical and descriptive statements on these two themes. In the second volume attention is transferred from the state to society and is focused on the religious, cultural, and social life of the medieval Muslim world. With so vast a subject, comprehensive coverage is clearly impossible. In choosing passages for translation, I have tried to give representative examples of the different periods and regions with which the work is concerned and of the different kinds of evidence on which it is based. Some stress, however, has been laid on the central lands of Islam and on the central, formative period.

It was my original intention to conform to the usual pattern and compile this book, in the main, from material already translated. I soon found myself obliged to abandon this plan. For one thing, reliance on the sources which by accident or caprice have become available in English would have produced a very unbalanced picture; for another, the existing translations vary unacceptably in quality and manner. It therefore seemed best to start afresh. All the passages in these two volumes have been newly translated by the editor, most of them for the first time into English. The majority are from Arabic; smaller numbers are from Persian and Turkish, and two are from Hebrew.

My thanks are due to Professor Claude Cahen for permission to reproduce the illustrations on pages 220–222, first published by him; to Professor S. D. Goitein for permission to use two Geniza documents edited by him and for advice on translating them; and to Professor E. Kedourie and Dr. H. M. Rabie, for reading and commenting on parts of my manuscript. I am most grateful to them for the trouble they took and the help they gave. I should also like to express my thanks to Mr. and Mrs. R. M. Burrell for reading and correcting a set of proofs.

B.L.

Introduction

The theme of this work is the history of Islam from the advent of the Prophet Muḥammad to the capture of Constantinople by Sultan Meḥmed, the Conqueror. It is concerned with a period that extends from the beginning of the seventh century to 1453; with a region that expands from Western Arabia to embrace the Middle East and North Africa, as well as parts of Asia, of tropical Africa, and southern and eastern Europe; with peoples and states which, amid many diversities, shared a common acceptance of the faith and law of Islam and professed to live by them, and, finally, with the civilization which they created.

Classical Islamic civilization is expressed in three major languages, the first of which is Arabic. It was among the Arabs of the Ḥijāz that Muḥammad was born, lived, and died, and in their language that his sacred book was written. Under his successors, the Caliphs, a great wave of Arab conquest and migration carried his faith and his book out of Arabia into the fertile crescent, eastward across Iran to the borders of India and China, and westward across Egypt and North Africa to Sicily and Spain. In the vast empire which they founded, Arabic was, for a long time, the language not only of religion, but also of government, commerce, and culture.

Most of the peoples conquered by the Arabs forgot their previous history and identity and were merged into Arabic-speaking Islam. Not all, however; the Persians, sustained both by recent memories of imperial greatness and by current awareness of their immense contribution to Islamic civilization, recovered and reasserted their separate identity. Arabic remained a scriptural and classical language in Iran, which had become a profoundly Islamic country, but from the eleventh century onward, the principal medium of expression was a new form of Persian—written in the Arabic script, full of Arabic loanwords, yet unmistakably Persian, not Arabic. The Persian cultural awakening was helped by a political revival in Iran and by the emergence of Persian dynasties and courts which used and fostered the new language. Persian became the second classical language of Islam; Persian influence was dominant in the eastern lands and powerful even in the western lands of the Islamic Caliphate.

The Persian renaissance forms a kind of overlapping interlude between the decline of the Arabs and the rise of the Turks. Medieval Islamic history begins with the irruption into the Middle East of Arab invaders from the south; it ends with the triumph of another group of newcomers, the steppe peoples from the north. The Turks, after their conversion to Islam, established an ascendancy which lasted a thousand years; they created new patterns of government and society and made Turkish the third major language of Islamic civilization.

They also brought to Islam, at a time of great weakness, the strength to survive new and terrible dangers that threatened to overwhelm it and to resist the enemies advancing from both east and west. It was Turkish rulers and armies that halted the Mongol invaders, saving Egypt and all western Islam from their rule; it was Turks again who took over the leadership of Islam in its millennial struggle with Christian Europe.

From its birth the Islamic religion was the chief contender with Christianity for the hearts of men; Islamic civilization was the nearest neighbor and deadliest rival of European Christendom. Between the two there was almost permanent conflict. Islam arose outside the Christian world, in pagan Arabia, and much of its expansion was among non-Christians. A major part, perhaps the most important part, of the victories of Islam were at Christian expense. The Arab warriors brought their religion and their dominion to the old Christian lands of the Levant and North Africa and even to Sicily, Spain, and parts of southern Italy and France, establishing an Islamic supremacy in most of the former Roman-Mediterranean world. For a while Arab Islam seemed to threaten the very existence of Christian Europe.

The advance of the Arabs in France and Italy was halted and reversed, and during the eleventh century Western Christendom launched a great counterattack which recovered Sicily and much of Spain and culminated in the arrival of the Crusaders in Syria and Palestine. Here the Crusaders encountered the new champions of Islam—the Turks—who by now governed most of the Middle East and had conquered even the great Byzantine stronghold of Anatolia. The Turks and their associates[1] held and eventually threw back the Christian invaders and began a new advance which once again

[1] Saladin, the most famous opponent of the Crusaders, was a Kurd, not a Turk. The first and last leaders of the countercrusade were all Turks, however, and even Saladin's dynasty relied largely on Turkish forces and was rapidly Turkicized.

brought Islam into Europe—this time at the eastern end and in a Turkish form. It was not until much later that the powers of Europe were able to launch a counterattack into the lands of Islam and establish European imperial domination in old Islamic territories, in Central Asia, North Africa, and finally in some of the heartlands of the Middle East.

During the centuries of confrontation and conflict, Muslims and Christians alike were more conscious of their differences than of their similarities. Yet these similarities are very great, for the two religions and the two cultures had much in common: Both shared the inheritance of the ancient civilizations of the Middle East; both had adopted the Jewish religious tradition of ethical monotheism, prophetic mission, and revelation preserved in scripture; both were disciples of Greek thought and science and heirs, in different ways, of the societies and institutions that had grown up in the Middle East and around the Mediterranean under the rule of Alexander, his successors, and the Romans. However much Christians and Muslims may have argued with one another, the very fact that they were able to do so, using a common logic and common concepts, shows the degree of kinship that existed between them. This becomes more apparent when either is compared with the remoter civilizations of Asia, in China and India. Muslims and Christians could dispute the relative merits of the Qur'ān and the Bible and the missions of Muḥammad and Christ, for both shared a common universe of discourse. Neither could have conducted a meaningful dialogue with a Hindu or a Confucian.

These inherent resemblances were confirmed and extended by their long cohabitation across the whole length of the Mediterranean world and by the mutual influences between them.

An appreciation of the affinities between Christianity and Islam, however, should not lead us to overlook the very real differences which divide them or to try and describe Islam by false analogies. Muḥammad is not the Muslim Christ, the Qur'ān is not the Muslim Bible, the mosque is not the Muslim church. One might add that Friday is not the Muslim sabbath, the ulema are not the Muslim clergy, and Sunnism is not the Muslim orthodoxy. These popular analogies, though they obviously contain a certain element of truth, nevertheless distort and conceal more than they explain.

Muḥammad, like Jesus, was the founder of a great world religion. Unlike Jesus, he achieved worldly success in his own lifetime. At first he too, like other prophets, was a humble, persecuted teacher and preacher. But instead of martyrdom he attained power. In Mecca he had been a proscribed critic of the existing order; in Medina he created his own order. As head of the *umma*, the community of his converts and adherents, he governed, dispensed justice, collected taxes, and made peace and war. In Mecca he preached; in Medina he practiced. The scope of his revelation was extended from religious and moral principles to a wide range of mundane matters; its form changed from precept to law. This change is clearly reflected in the Qur'ān.

The Qur'ān may be called the Muslim scripture; it cannot be called the Muslim Bible. For Muslims it is a single book, in the most literal sense the word of God, dictated to the Prophet by the angel Gabriel. Most historians consider it an authentic contemporary record of the teaching and activities of Muḥammad, dating from his lifetime in a recension compiled very shortly after his death. Unlike the Old and New Testaments, it is not a collection of texts assembled from works written over a long period of time; it is the work of a single author, arising from a single career.[2] The development from the earlier Meccan chapters to the later Medinan chapters illustrates very clearly the change in the Prophet's status and preoccupations.

Islam was thus involved with political power from the start. Medina was a state and, as it turned out, the nucleus of an empire with the Prophet as its first magistrate. The true and sole sovereign in the Muslim view was God, from whose mandate the Prophet derived his authority and whose will, made known by revelation, was the sole source of law. The *umma* thus expressed from its inception the fusion of politics and religion characteristic of the later Islamic states. The founder of Christianity had enjoined his followers to "render unto Caesar the things which are Caesar's, and unto God the things which are God's," and three centuries of suffering and persecution were to pass before Christianity captured the Roman empire, with the conversion of the Roman emperor Constantine, and in a sense was captured by it. Muḥammad was his own Constantine and founded his own empire. The dichotomy of *regnum* and *sacerdotium*, deeply rooted in Western Christendom, does not exist in Islam, and, indeed, such pairs of words as spiritual and temporal, lay and ecclesiastical, and religious and secular have no equivalents in the classical languages of the Muslim peoples.

[2] Most Western scholars have accepted the Qur'ān as historically authentic, in the sense of preserving what was promulgated by Muḥammad during his lifetime. Some modern scholars, however, chiefly in the Soviet Union, have argued that the text was not merely edited but actually composed under the Caliphs.

Under Muḥammad's successors, the Caliphs, the community of Medina was transformed by conquest into a vast empire, and Muḥammad's Arab creed became a world religion. In the experience of the first Muslims, religious truth and political power were inextricably linked: the first sanctified the second; the second confirmed and sustained the first. This experience gave rise to a firm belief in God's concern with politics and in the manifestation of God's favor by success—that is, by the victory and dominion in this world of those who obeyed His law.

In the Islamic world, therefore, there could be no conflict between Pope and Emperor, for the powers which these two represented were one and the same. The Caliph was at once head of the state, the community, and the faith. In the sense of a building, a place of daily and weekly public worship, the mosque is the equivalent of the church; but in the sense of an institution, an organized corporate body, the church has no equivalent in Islam, for the institution over which the Caliph presided was church and state at once.

For the same reason, Islam has no clergy and no orthodoxy in the Christian sense. There is no pope, no bishops or bishoprics, no hierarchy, and no councils or synods to determine and impose an approved creed and to condemn deviations from it as heterodoxy. Such authorities were never constituted in Islam, and the few attempts to do so failed utterly. The ulema are men of religious learning, not priests; they receive no ordination, have no parishes, and perform no sacraments. The nearest Islamic equivalent to orthodoxy is the *Sunna,* the custom and practice of the Prophet, his Companions, and his immediate successors, as preserved by the historic memory of the community as a whole. The basic Muslim creed is that God is one and Muḥammad is His prophet, and no one who rejects either of these propositions can be considered a Muslim. Beyond that, loyalty to Islam is expressed, first and foremost, not by correct belief but by correct behavior—that is, by acceptance of the norms and patterns of Islamic life, loyalty to the Islamic community, and obedience to the head of the Islamic state. Consequently, it is deviation from custom, withdrawal from the community, and disobedience to authority, rather than incorrect belief, which constitute the nearest Islamic equivalents of heresy. What a man believes, beyond the basic minimum, is his own concern. Authority is concerned only with his behavior, and God alone can judge a man's sincerity.

Because of this, knowledge of the past was from the start of immense, indeed, of transcendent, importance for Muslims. The mission of the Prophet was itself an event in history; its circumstances and meaning could be known to later generations of believers only through memory and record—through the work of preservation, transmission, and explanation of the first Muslim historians. The *Sunna,* too, was essentially historical. The doctrine of consensus, according to which divine guidance passed to the Muslim community as a whole after the death of the Prophet, gave a religious significance to the acts and experiences of that community, in which could be seen the revelation of God's will on earth. God, it was believed, would not allow His community to fall into sin. What the community as a whole accepted and did was right and was an expression of God's purpose. *Sunna* was defined by consensus, and past consensus was known from tradition. The study of tradition was therefore necessary for theology and holy law—that is, for salvation.

Interest in the past soon became a distinguishing characteristic of Muslim civilization. Since early times Muslim entities—states, dynasties, cities, even professions—have been conscious of their place in history; they have been interested in the deeds of those who went before them and anxious to record their own for those who came after. Almost every dynasty that ruled in Muslim lands has left annals or chronicles of some kind; in many countries, including some of high civilization, serious historical writing begins with the coming of Islam.

The earliest historical record of Islam is, of course, the Qur'ān itself. For Muslims this is a work of religion—that is, scripture, not history. However, it also provides important historical information concerning the career of the Prophet and the community which he founded. The beginnings of Islamic historical writing, in the proper sense, must be sought in the collections of *ḥadīth,* that is, traditions purporting to preserve the decisions, actions, and utterances of the Prophet. According to Muslim belief, the Prophet was the inspired bearer of God's commands, not only when he was repeating the divine text dictated to him, but also in everything that he said and did. And so in addition to the Qur'ān (the word of God), the *ḥadīths* (the word of the Prophet) came to be treated as a second source of revelation.

There was, however, an important difference between the two. The Qur'ān was edited and promulgated in a standard text not long after Muḥammad's death. Regarded as of divine authorship, it could not be increased or diminished in any way; its authenticity, textual accuracy, and authority were beyond question. *Ḥadīth,* on the other hand, was a vast and heterogeneous assemblage of individual traditions, each relating some detail of the precept and practice of the Prophet and varying greatly in provenance, content, and plausibility.

Much of it was of dubious origin. For three generations or more it was orally transmitted—and this during a period of rapid change, and of bitter conflicts and rivalries. Whether to justify an action or to promote a cause, there could be no better argument than to adduce a *ḥadīth* citing a Prophetic precedent. Even in medieval times Muslim jurists were well aware of the problems of distortion and fabrication, and of the innumerable *ḥadīths* in circulation, they chose a more limited number; these came to be accepted as authentic and constitute, after the Qur'ān, the main base of Muslim law and doctrine. Modern critical scholarship has dismissed many of these as spurious and has called most of the remainder into doubt. But, although a fabricated *ḥadīth* tells us nothing about the Prophet, it may tell us a great deal about the time, circumstances, and purpose of its fabrication.

Certain categories of *ḥadīths* are of particular interest to the historian—for example, the numerous polemic *ḥadīths* directed against one tribe, faction, or sect, in the interest of another. Some, in the form of direct prophecy of future events, are palpable fakes. Others are clever fabrications in which Muḥammad is alleged to say something about events in his own time; these are not overtly prophetic but nevertheless have a direct bearing on subsequent conflicts.

A second important group are legal traditions which state a principle or establish a precedent regarded as legally binding. Some of these may be genuine, but a large proportion represent the untheoretical response of early Islamic rulers and governors to immediate needs. Such *ḥadīths* include principles of Roman and other legal systems encountered in the conquered provinces and ad hoc decisions based on usage, political or administrative necessity, or simple common sense.

Another class of *ḥadīths,* also of great interest, consists of pronouncements, admonitory rather than prescriptive, on what were obviously matters of current controversy and concern. One such theme is racial conflict. There are traditions which condemn racial hostility or arrogance; there are also traditions which express them by condemning or extolling individual races.

Another matter of concern was inflation. There is, for example, a small group of traditions in which the Prophet is quoted as saying that "Only God can fix prices." It is obvious that the Prophet said no such thing, for such a question could hardly have arisen in western Arabia during his lifetime. It did, however, arise after his death. Muslim rulers in the Middle East, like their Roman and Byzantine predecessors, were troubled by the continuous rise in prices and attempted from time to time to halt and fix them by decree. "Only God can fix prices" is a theological statement of laissez-faire economics. This seems to have been the predominant view among the professional men of religion, since virtually all the traditions dealing with prices take this line.

One other group of traditions has a special interest—those of messianic or eschatological equality, which purport to relate the events at the end of time when the kingdom of tyranny will be overthrown and the Mahdī, the rightly guided one sent by God for the purpose, will establish the kingdom of heaven on earth. These traditions reflect the successive messianic revolts which occurred in the early formative period of Islam; they also reflect the expectations which were aroused and show what the believers hoped that the Mahdī would do.

The development of historical enquiry and exposition among Muslims was shaped by many influences, including the heroic sagas of pagan Arabia, the narrative books of the Bible, and the Iranian book of Kings. But the most important source of inspiration and example was the religious tradition. Muslim historiography grew out of *ḥadīth*. The first Caliphs obviously did not enjoy the same authority as the Prophet himself in Muslim eyes. Nevertheless, they had a certain sanctity, and the precedents established by the first heads of the Islamic community could be and were cited as authoritative in government and law. And so we find a continuation of the *ḥadīth* type of narrative in the earliest historical writings; actions and utterances attributed to the early Caliphs and their officers were handed down and attested in much the same way as the *ḥadīths*. These, too, are subject to the same suspicion of having been fabricated, or at least adjusted, to serve some interest or purpose.

The early books are simple collections of narratives, each supported by a chain of authorities purporting to go back to an eyewitness or participant. With the growing complexity and sophistication of Islamic politics and culture, more varied and more elaborate forms of historiography developed. They include universal and imperial histories, dynastic annals, regional and local chronicles, collections of biographies, and a wide range of works dealing with specific topics, groups, or periods.

There is a fundamental difference in the origins and aims of medieval Western Christian and Muslim historical writing. Latin Christian historiography began in the chaos of the barbarian invasions and was dominated by two overwhelming facts: the rise of the Church and the fall of the Roman Empire. For St. Augustine, the body politic was the work of man and was evil, a punishment or a remedy for sin. (Had not Cain founded the first city?) Echoing the Hebrew prophets, St. Augustine and his pupil Orosius saw in defeat and ruin the instruments of God's purpose: that the peoples might throng to the churches and thereby be brought to a salvation which they would otherwise never have attained.

Islamic historiography begins not with defeat, but with victory; not with the fall, but with the rise of empire. For the Muslim historian, political authority is not a human evil, or even a lesser evil, but a divine good, established to maintain and promote God's faith and law. Like the Christian, he sees God in history and believes in God's involvement in human affairs, but he sees God as helping rather than testing His people, as desiring their supremacy in this world. For the Muslim historian, therefore, the state and its affairs are not external or secondary to the true purpose of history; they are its essential theme. Even in the age of decline, when he observed that power corrupts—the equivalent Muslim dictum might be rendered as "You can't have both power and paradise"—he still believed that Muslim authority, however obtained and however exercised, was a divinely ordained necessity and that the Sunnī community, which that power was needed to maintain, was the continuing medium of God's guidance to mankind.

This conviction is reflected in a number of ways in Islamic historiography: in the careful concern for detail and accuracy, in the sharp perception and calm acceptance of the realities of power, in the ability to conceive and present events over large areas and long periods, and, finally, in the pervading belief in the rightness, and therefore the significance, of the world as it is and as it has been.

Medieval Islamic historical literature is of immense richness and variety–incomparably greater, for example, than that of medieval Europe. From this literature it is possible to construct, with considerable detail and reasonable confidence, a narrative history of events in the Islamic world. But the modern historian is no longer satisfied merely with the surface movement of events. He seeks to penetrate to the deeper levels of the historic process, to the slower, heavier movement of societies and cultures, of institutions and structures, of groups and ideas.

For this kind of history, too, the chronicles have much to offer, far more than has yet been exploited. But the historian need not confine his attention to works of consciously historical intention. In a sense the whole literature of Islam is his source, including books on religion and sects, politics and economics, philosophy and science, travel, biography, and literary works of every kind. Of particular value are the specialized works arising from the exercise of certain professions. These include the administrative literature of the bureaucracy, the geographical literature of the postal service, the juridical literature of the ulema, and, in a different sense, the eulogies and satires of the poets—the media men and public relations men of medieval Islam.

All these works, however varied in form and content, have one feature in common: they are all books, literary compositions written by an author for a reader. But for the historian, books alone are not enough. In addition, he requires documents—the contemporary and direct evidence or traces of historical events in their original form, not as transmitted and therefore necessarily transformed by the mind of a literary intermediary.

For the history of Islam between the advent of Muḥammad and the rise of the Ottoman Empire, documents are very few indeed. Record offices and archives certainly existed in medieval Islam, as is attested by numerous references in the literary sources. Unfortunately, they were destroyed and the documents they contained have disappeared. The most important groups of surviving documents are inscriptions and coins—documents written on stone and metal. These are of great value but inevitably are rather limited in scope. Some documents survive in quotation, in histories, and in collections of model letters. These may be valuable, but they are not original and must, therefore, be treated with caution.

From medieval times only two groups of documents of any significance have been discovered, both of them in Egypt. One group consists of papyri, mostly of administrative content, written between the seventh and tenth centuries; the other consists of miscellaneous papers accumulated in a repository for litter in a synagogue in old Cairo and dates mostly from the tenth to the thirteenth centuries. These are discards, not archives. Both are fortuitous groupings—unconnected documents and fragments surviving by chance, discovered by accident, and distributed haphazard, with no cohesion other than that imposed on them by curators and historians. A few documents have been found here and there in Middle Eastern and European collections, but it is not until Ottoman times that we have genuine archives which have survived as such to our own day.

The student of Islamic history enters a field where much—one might even say most—of the basic research still remains to be done. He will have at his disposal few of the tools of research that are taken for granted by his classicist or Western medievalist colleagues. Faced with the need to read sources in several oriental languages, he will find that there are no historical grammars or dictionaries for any of them, and that even the general dictionaries are few and inadequate. Most of the historical ancillary sciences are in their infancy, and there are only two or three substantial works of reference. Translation remains a hazardous enterprise, and the writing of general surveys, whether narrative or analytical, requires a measure of reliance on earlier scholarship which, all too often, reflects the findings and judgments of a time when the critical study of Islamic history was only just beginning, when few historians knew Islamic sources, and few Islamicists cared for historical method. Their evaluations, therefore, and even their simple statements of what purports to be accepted fact, need rigorous scrutiny.

In recent years, despite, and perhaps to some extent because of, such difficulties, there has been increased activity in this field. Studies of growing value and interest have been published, dealing with specific aspects of Islamic history, and there are now even a few general works of real historical quality. A brief selection follows.

A readable short introduction to medieval Islamic history will be found in J. J. Saunders, *A History of Medieval Islam* (London: Routledge, 1965). More detailed introductory accounts, based on an intimate knowledge of the sources, are given in G. E. von Grunebaum, *Classical Islam; A History, 600–1258,* translated from the German (London: Allen & Unwin, 1970), and Claude Cahen, *L'Islam des origines au début de l'empire ottoman* (Paris: Bordas, 1970). The first gives special attention to cultural history, the second, to economic history.

The civilization of medieval Islam is assessed and presented by G. E. von Grunebaum, *Medieval Islam; A Study in Cultural Orientation,* revised edition (Chicago: University of Chicago Press, 1953, and by D. and J. Sourdel, *La civilisation de l'Islam classique* (Paris: Arthaud, 1968). An earlier work, still of great value, is Adam Mez, *The Renaissance of Islam,* translated from the German (London: Luzac, 1937).

The Cambridge History of Islam, 2 vols. (Cambridge: 1970), surveys the whole field of Islamic history and civilization, though with the inevitable unevenness of a syndicated work. For further guidance, reference may be made to *Jean Sauvaget's Introduction to the History of the Muslim East: A Bibliographical Guide,* recast by Claude Cahen, translated from the French (Berkeley and Los Angeles: University of California Press, 1965).

Chronological Table

c.570	Birth of Muḥammad
c.612	Beginning of Muḥammad's mission
622	The Hijra of Muḥammad from Mecca to Medina
630	Muḥammad conquers Mecca
632	Death of Muḥammad; appointment of Abū Bakr as first Caliph
634	Accession of 'Umar as Caliph
637–644	Conquest of Syria, Palestine, Iraq, Mesopotamia, Armenia, Egypt; invasion of Iran
644	Murder of 'Umar; accession of 'Uthmān
647	First Arab raids in North Africa
650–651	Establishment of standard text of Qur'ān; most of Iran conquered
656	Murder of 'Uthmān; accession of 'Alī; beginning of first civil war
657	Battle of Ṣiffīn
661	Murder of 'Alī; accession of Mu'āwiya; establishment of Umayyad Caliphate
670	Foundation of Qayrawān
673–678	Arabs besiege Constantinople
680	Massacre of al-Ḥusayn, his family, and supporters at Karbalā'
683–690	Second civil war
685–687	Shi'ite revolt in Iraq
690–696	'Abd al-Malik strikes first Muslim gold coins and orders the introduction of Arabic in government offices
691	Foundation of the Dome of the Rock in Jerusalem
705	Foundation of great Mosque of Damascus
705–715	Arab general Qutayba captures Bukhārā and Samarqand and establishes Muslim supremacy in Central Asia
710	Completion of conquest of North Africa; first Arab landing in Spain
711–714	Arabs conquer most of Spain; cross Jaxartes and raid Kāshgar; invade Indus valley and capture Multān

719	Cordova becomes seat of Arab governor
732	Battle of Tours; Franks halt Arab advance
750	Third civil war; fall of Umayyads; accession of 'Abbasids
751	Battle on the Talas; Arabs defeat Chinese army in Central Asia and capture Chinese paper makers; manufacture of paper at Samarqand
756	Foundation of Umayyad amirate of Cordova
c.757	Death of the author and translator Ibn al-Muqaffa'
762	Foundation of Baghdad
767	Death of the jurist Abū Ḥanīfa
785	Foundation of Great Mosque of Cordova
786–809	Caliphate of Hārūn al-Rashīd
789–	Rise of Idrisid amirs in Morocco; foundation of Fez
795	Death of the jurist Mālik
800	Rise of Aghlabid amirs in Tunisia; Arab merchants in Canton
820	Death of the jurist al-Shāfi'ī
821–	Rise of Tahirid amirs in Khurāsān
827	Arabs begin conquest of Sicily
831	Capture of Palermo; raids in Southern Italy
832	Foundation of "House of Wisdom" in Baghdad
836	Foundation of Sāmarrā—cantonments for Turkish slave guard
after 847	Death of the mathematician al-Khwārizmī
855	Death of the jurist Aḥmad ibn Ḥanbal
867–	Rise of Saffarid amirs in Eastern Iran
868	Death of the Arabic author al-Jāḥiẓ
868–	Rise of Tulunid amirs in Egypt
869–883	Revolt of black slaves in Iraq
875–	Rise of Samanid amirs in Transoxania, later also Khurāsān
877	Death of Ḥunayn ibn Isḥāq, translator of Greek works into Arabic
c.879	Disappearance of the twelfth Shi'ite Imam
889	Death of the author and scholar Ibn Qutayba
c.904	First Arabic treatise on agronomy
909–	Rise of the Fatimid Caliphate in Tunisia
923	Death of the Arabic historian al-Ṭabarī
925	Death of the physician al-Rāzī (Rhases)
929	'Abd al-Raḥmān III of Cordova adopts the title of Caliph; death of the astronomer al-Battānī

929–	Rise of Hamdanid amirs of Mesopotamia and Syria
c.935	Death of the theologian al-Ash'arī
945	Buyids in Iraq
950	Death of the philosopher al-Fārābī
960	Conversion of Qarakhanid Turks to Islam
969	Fatimids conquer Egypt and found Cairo
c.970	Seljuqs enter Islamic lands from the East
972–	Rise of (Berber) Zirid amirs in Tunisia
998–	Rise of Ghaznavid amirs in Eastern Iran
1001–1021	Maḥmūd of Ghaznī conquers the Panjāb
c.1020	Death of the Persian poet Firdawsī
1031	Fall of the Caliphate of Cordova
1037	Death of Ibn Sīnā (Avicenna)
1040	Battle of Dandānqān; Seljuqs defeat Ghaznavids and establish supremacy in Iran
1052	Banū Hilāl in North Africa
1055	Seljuq Prince Tughrul enters Baghdad; consolidation of the great Seljuq Sultanate
1065–1072	Famine in Egypt
1071	Battle of Manzikert; Seljuq Turks defeat Byzantines and occupy much of Anatolia
1072–1091	Normans conquer Sicily
1075	Seljuqs capture Nicaea (Iznik) and make it their capital in Anatolia
1085	Christians take Toledo
1097	Crusaders take Iznik; Seljuqs transfer capital to Konya
1099	Crusaders capture Jerusalem
1111	Death of the theologian al-Ghazālī
1141	Battle of the Qatvān steppe; Seljuq Sultan Sanjar defeated by Qara-Khitay invaders from the East
1144	Zangī captures Edessa
1154	Nūr al-Dīn ibn Zangī takes Damascus; Idrīsī completes his geography of the world; Fatimid Caliph grants commercial privileges to Pisa
1157	Death of Sanjar; breakup of great Seljuq Sultanate
1171	End of the Fatimid Caliphate; Egypt restored to Sunnī Islam
1173	Pisa obtains commercial privileges in Alexandria
1174–1193	Reign of Saladin
1187	Saladin takes Jerusalem
1198	Death of Ibn Rushd (Averroes)

1204	Death of the Jewish physician and philosopher Maimonides
1208	Sultan of Egypt accords commercial privileges to Venice
1212	Christian victory at Las Navas de Tolosa
1215	Jenghiz Khan takes Peking
1219	Jenghiz Khan crosses Jaxartes and invades Islamic lands
1220	Mongols conquer eastern territories of the Caliphate
1229	Al-Malik al-Kāmil, ruler of Egypt, reaches agreement with Frederick II and hands over Jerusalem
1233	Death of the Arabic historian Ibn al-Athīr
1236	Christians take Cordova
1237	Rise of Hafsids in Tunisia
1240	Death of the mystic Ibn al-ʿArabī
1242–1243	Mongols invade Anatolia; defeat Seljuqs at battle of Kösedagh
1244	Muslims recapture Jerusalem
1248	Christians take Seville
1249–1250	Crusade of St. Louis to Egypt; emergence of Mamlūk Sultanate
c.1250+	Khan of the Golden Horde converted to Islam
1254	Alphonso X (the Wise) establishes a school of Latin and Arabic studies in Seville
1256–	Hülegü, grandson of Jenghiz Khan, leads Mongol army westward
1258	Mongols capture Baghdad; end of Abbasid Caliphate
1260	Mamlūks defeat Mongols at ʿAyn Jālūt
1273	Death of the poet and mystic Jalāl al-Dīn Rūmī
1289	Mamlūks capture Tripoli from the Crusaders
1291	Fall of Acre; Crusaders finally expelled from Palestine
1292	Death of the Persian poet Saʿdī
1294	Ghāzān Khan, Mongol Il-Khan of Persia, converted to Islam
c.1299–1300	Breakup of Seljuq Sultanate of Anatolia into independent principalities; emergence of Ottoman amirate in Bithynia
1303	Last Mongol invasion of Syria defeated by Mamlūks
1318	Death of the Persian historian Rashīd al-Dīn
1326	Ottomans take Brusa (Bursa)
1331	Ottomans take Iznik
1336	Death of the Il-Khan Abū Saʿīd; breakup of the Il-Khanate in Iran

1348	Construction of the Gate of Justice at the Alhambra, Granada; Black Death in Egypt
1354	Ottoman-Genoese agreement. Ottomans take Gallipoli and Ankara
1369?	Ottomans take Adrianople (Edirne)
1370–1380	Tīmūr becomes ruler of Central Asia
1371	Ottomans defeat Serbs at Chirmen, on the Maritza
1380–1387	Tīmūr conquers Iran
1382	Mamlūk Sultanate in Egypt passes to Burjī (Circassian) Mamlūks
1385	Ottomans grant commercial privileges to Genoa; capture Sofia
1387	Ottomans take Salonica
1388	Ottomans grant commercial privileges to Venice
1389	First Battle of Kossovo; Ottomans defeat Serbs
1390	Death of the Persian poet Ḥāfiẓ
1392–1398	Tīmūr invades Western Iran, Mesopotamia, the Khanate of the Golden Horde, and India; occupies Moscow and Delhi
1396	Battle of Nicopolis; Ottomans defeat Crusaders
1400–1401	Tīmūr invades Georgia, Anatolia, Syria and Iraq; captures Aleppo, Damascus and Baghdād
1400	Guns used in defence of Aleppo
1402	Battle of Ankara; Tīmūr defeats Ottomans and captures Bāyezīd I
1403–	Famine and plague in Egypt
1405	Death of Tīmūr
1406	Death of the historian Ibn Khaldūn
1422	Ottomans use guns in unsuccessful attempt to capture Constantinople
1422–1438	Reign of Mamlūk Sultan Bārsbāy; attempt to control currency and monopolize sugar, pepper, and other commodities.
c.1433+	Hajji Giray Khan founds independent Khanate in the Crimea
1444	Battle of Varna; Ottomans defeat Christian powers
1448	Second battle of Kossovo; Ottomans defeat Serbs and their allies; first recorded use by Ottomans of field guns
1453	Ottomans capture Constantinople

Bibliography of Sources

'Abd al-Ḥamīd al-Kātib. *Risāla ila'l-kuttāb,* in *Jamharat Rasā'il al-'Arab,* ed. Aḥmad Zakī Ṣafwat, ii, Cairo (Muṣṭafā al-Bābī al-Ḥalabī), 1356/1937 (variant versions in Qalqashandī, *Ṣubḥ,* i, pp. 85–89; Jahshiyārī, pp. 74–79; Ibn Khaldūn, *Muqaddima,* pp. 248–251).

'Abdallāh (Sultan of Granada). *Kitāb al-Tibyān,* ed. E. Lévi-Provençal, Les "Mémoires" du roi Zīride "Abd Allah," in *al-Andalus,* iii, 1935.

Al-Abshīhī, Shihāb al-Dīn Aḥmad. *Kitāb al-Mustaṭraf fī kull Shay' Mustaẓraf,* Cairo, 1352/1933.

Abū Da'ūd, Sulaymān ibn al-Ash'ath. *Sunan.* Cairo (Al-Tāzī), n.d.

Abu'l-Faraj, Gregorius ibn al-'Ibrī. *Ta'rīkh Mukhtaṣar al-duwal,* ed. Anṭūn Ṣālḥānī, Beirut (Catholic Press), 1890.

Abu'l Faraj al-Iṣfahānī. *Kitāb al-Aghānī,* 20 vols., Būlāq, 1285. New edition (incomplete), Cairo (Dār al-Kutub), 1345/1927–.

Abū Shāma, Shihāb al-Dīn 'Abd al-Raḥmān ibn Ismā'īl. *Kitāb al-Rawḍatayn fī akhbār al-dawlatayn,* i, ed. M. Ḥilmī M. Aḥmad, Cairo (Lajnat al-ta'līf), 1962.

Abū 'Ubayd al-Qāsim ibn Sallām. *Kitāb al-Amwāl,* ed. Muḥammad Ḥāmid al-Fiqī, Cairo ('Amira), 1353/1934.

Abū Yūsuf, Ya'qūb ibn Ibrāhīm. *Kitāb al-Kharāj,* 3rd edition, Cairo (Salafiyya), 1382/1962–1963.

Akhbār al-Ṣīn wa'l-Hind (*Relation de la Chine et de l'Inde*), ed. J. Sauvaget, Paris (Les Belles Lettres), 1948.

Anonymous Ottoman Chronicle. Tevārīh-i Āl-i Osmān (*Die altosmanischen anonymen Chroniken*), ed. F. Giese, Breslau, 1922.

Ashikpāshāzāde. *Tevārīh-i Āl-i Osmān,* ed. 'Alī (old script), Istanbul ('Āmire), 1332/1914; ed. Nihal Atsız (new script) in *Osmanlı Tarihleri,* Istanbul (Türkiye Yayinevi), 1949.

Al-Balādhurī, Aḥmad ibn Yaḥyā. *Ansāb al-ashrāf,* ivA, ed. Max Schloessinger, revised and annotated by M. J. Kister, Jerusalem (Magnes Press), 1971.

——— *Ansāb al-ashrāf,* v, ed. S. D. F. Goitein, Jerusalem (University Press), 1936.

——— *Futūḥ al-Buldān*, ed. M. J. de Goeje, Leiden (Brill), 1866.

Bayhaqī, Abu'l-Fażl. *Tārīkh-i Bayhaqī*, ed. Ghanī and Fayyaż, Tehran (Bank Melli), 1324 (Persian solar)/1945.

Al-Bukhārī, Abū 'Abdallāh Muḥammad ibn Ismā'īl, *Al-Ṣaḥīḥ*, ed. L. Krehl, Leiden (Brill), 1868.

Buzurg ibn Shahriyār. *Kitāb 'Ajā'ib al-Hind*, ed. P. A. Van der Lith, Leiden (Brill), 1883–1886.

Al-Dīnawarī, Abū Ḥanīfa Aḥmad ibn Da'ūd, *Al-Akhbār al-ṭiwāl*, ed. 'Abd al-Mun'im 'Amir, Cairo (Ministry of Culture), 1960.

Geniza. Documents from S. D. Goitein, 'Te'ūda min hannamel ha'afriqani 'Aydhāb', in *Tarbitz*, xxi, 1950; idem, 'Pidyon shevuya be-Nabulus . . . ' in *Tarbitz*, xxxi, 1961–1962.

Al-Ghazālī, Abū Ḥāmid Muḥammad ibn Muḥammad, *Fayṣal al-tafriqa bayn al-Islām wa'l-zandaqa*, ed. Sulaymān Dunyā, Cairo (Iḥyā al-Kutub al-'Arabiyya), 1381/1961.

Al-Hamadānī, Badī' al-Zamān, *Maqāmāt*, ed. Shaykh Muḥammad 'Abduh, 4th edition, Beirut (Catholic Press), 1957.

Hilāl Al-Sābi', *Kitāb al-Wuzarā'*, ed. H. F. Amedroz, Leiden (Brill), 1904.

Al-Ḥusaynī, Ṣadr al-Dīn Abu'l-Ḥasan 'Alī ibn Nāṣir ibn 'Alī, *Akhbār al-Dawla al-Saljūqiyya*, ed. Muḥammad Iqbal, Lahore (Univ. of the Panjab), 1933.

Ibn 'Abd al-Ḥakam, *Futūḥ Miṣr wa-akhbāruhā* (*The History of the Conquest of Egypt, North Africa and Spain*), ed. C. C. Torrey, New Haven (Yale University Press), 1922.

Ibn 'Abd Rabbihi, Aḥmad ibn Muḥammad. *Al-'Iqd al-Farīd*, 8 vols., ed. Muḥammad Sa'īd al-'Iryān, Cairo (Al-Maktaba al-Tijāriyya al-Kubrā), 1372/1953.

Ibn 'Abdūn, Muḥammad ibn Aḥmad. *Risāla fi'l-Qaḍā' wa'l-ḥisba*, ed. E. Lévi-Provençal, in *Documents arabes inédits sur la vie sociale et économique en occident musulman au moyen age*, Cairo (Institut Français d'Archéologie Orientale), 1955.

Ibn Abī Uṣaybi'a. *'Uyūn al-anbā' fī ṭabaqāt al-aṭibbā'*, Cairo (Wahbiyya), 1299/1882.

Ibn al-'Adīm, Kamāl al-Dīn. *Bughyat al-Ṭalab fī ta'rīkh Ḥalab*, excerpts ed. B. Lewis, "Three biographies from Kamāl ad-Dīn," in *Mélanges Fuad Köprülü*, Istanbul (Yalçin), 1953, pp. 322–326.

Ibn al-Athīr, 'Izz al-Dīn Abu'l-Ḥasan 'Alī ibn Abi'l-Karm Muḥammad. *Al-Kāmil fi'l-ta'rīkh*, ed. C. J. Thornberg, Leiden (Brill), 1851–1876.

——— *Usd al-ghāba*, Cairo, 1285–1287/1869–1871.

Ibn Baṣṣāl, Muḥammad ibn Ibrāhīm. *Kitāb-al-Filāḥa*, edd. J. M. Millás

Vallicrosa and Muḥammad 'Azīmān, Tetuan (Institute Muley el-Hasan), 1955.

Ibn Baṭṭa, Abū 'Abdallāh 'Ubaydallāh ibn Muḥammad. *Kitāb al-Sharḥ wa'l-ibāna 'alā uṣūl al-sunna wa'l-diyāna* (*La profession de foi d'Ibn Baṭṭa*), ed. M. Laoust, Damascus (Institut Français de Damas), 1958.

Ibn Baṭṭūṭa. *Riḥla* (Voyages), ed. C. Defremery and B. R. Sanguinetti, 4 vols, Paris, 1854. Reprinted Paris (Anthropos), 1969.

Ibn Buṭlān, Abu'l-Ḥasan al-Mukhtār ibn al-Ḥasan. *Risāla fī Shirā al-raqīq*, ed. 'Abd al-Salām Hārūn, Cairo (Lajnat al-Ta'līf), 1373/1954.

Ibn al-Faqīh, Abū Bakr Aḥmad ibn Ibrāhīm al-Hamadhānī. *Mukhtaṣar Kitāb al-Buldān*, ed. M. J. de Goeje, Leiden (Brill), 1885.

Ibn al-Furāt, Nāṣir al-Dīn Muḥammad ibn 'Abd al-Raḥmān. *Al-Ta'rīkh al-Wāḍiḥ*, excerpt edited by G. Levi Della Vida, "L'Invasione dei Tartari in Siria nel 1260 nei ricordi di un testimone oculare," *Orientalia*, iv, 1935.

Ibn Ḥawqal, Abu'l-Qāsim. *Ṣūrat al-Arḍ* (*Opus geographicum*), ed. J. H. Kramers, Leiden (Brill), 1939.

Ibn Hishām, Abū Muḥammad 'Abd al-Malik. *Al-Sīra al-Nabawiyya*, edd. Muṣṭafā al-Saqqā, Ibrāhīm al-Abyārī and 'Abd al-Ḥafīẓ Shalabī, 2nd impression, Cairo (Muṣṭafā al-Bābī al-Ḥalabī), 1375/1955.

Ibn 'Idhārī al-Marrukushī. *Kitāb al-Bayān al-Mughrib*, ed. G. S. Colin and E. Lévi-Provençal, i, Leiden (Brill), 1948.

Ibn Jamā'a, Badr al-Dīn Muḥammad ibn Ibrāhīm. *Taḥrīr al-aḥkām fī tadbīr ahl al-Islām*, ed. Hans Kofler in *Islamica*, vi, 1934.

Ibn Kathīr, 'Imād al-Dīn ibn Abi'l-Fidā'. *Al-Bidāya wa'l-nihāya*, Cairo (Sa'āda), 1351/1932–1358/1939.

Ibn Khaldūn, 'Abd al-Raḥman ibn Muḥammad. *Al-Muqaddima*, Beirut, 1900.

——— *Kitāb al-'Ibar wa-dīwān al-mubtada' wa'l-khabar*, Būlāq, 1284/1867.

Ibn al-Khaṭīb, Muḥammad Lisān al-Dīn. *Al-Iḥāṭa fī ta'rīkh Gharnāṭa*, Cairo (Al-Mawsū'āt), 1319/1901–1902.

Ibn Māja, Muḥammad ibn Yazīd. *Sunan*, 2 vols., ed. Muḥammad Fu'ād 'Abd al-Bāqī, Cairo (Ḥalabī), 1372/1952.

Ibn al-Qiftī, Jamāl al-Dīn Abu'l-Ḥasan 'Alī ibn Yūsuf. *Ta'rīkh al-ḥukamā'*, ed. J. Lippert, Leipzig (Dietrich'sche Verlagsbuchhandlung), 1903.

Ibn Qutayba, Abū Muḥammad ʻAbdallāh ibn Muslim. *Kitāb al-Maʻārif*, ed. Tharwat ʻUkāsha, 2nd edition, Cairo (Maʻārif), 1388/1969.

——— *Kitāb al-Shiʻr waʼl-shuʻarāʼ*, ed. M. J. de Goeje, Leiden (Brill), 1904.

——— *ʻUyūn al-akhbār*, 4 vols., ed. Aḥmad Zaki al-ʻAdawī, Cairo (*Dār al-Kutub*), 1343–8/1925–1930.

Ibn al-Qūṭiyya, Abū Bakr ibn ʻUmar. *Taʼrīkh iftitāḥ al-Andalus* (*Historia de la conquista de España*), ed. J. Ribera, Madrid (Real Academia de la Historia), 1868–1926.

Ibn Rusteh, Abū ʻAlī Aḥmad ibn ʻUmar. *Kitāb al-Aʻlāq al-Nafīsa*, ed. M. J. de Goeje, 2nd edition, Leiden (Brill), 1892.

Ibn Tashköprüzāde, Aḥmad ibn Muṣliḥ al-Dīn. *Al-Shaqāʼiq al-nuʻmāniyya fī ʻulamāʼ al-dawla al-ʻUthmāniyya*, printed in the margin of Ibn Khallikān, *Wafayāt al-aʻyān*, Būlāq, 1299/1882.

Ibn Taymiyya, Taqī al-Dīn Aḥmad. *Al-Siyāsa al-sharʻiyya*, ed. Muḥammad ʻAbdallah al-Sammān, Cairo (Anṣār al-Sunna), 1381/1961.

Ibn al-ʻUmarī, Shihāb al-Dīn. *Al-Taʻrīf biʼl-Muṣṭalaḥ al-sharīf*, Cairo (Al-Āṣima), 1312/1894–1895.

Ibn al-Zubayr, al-Qāḍī al-Rashīd ibn al-Zubayr. *Kitāb al-Dhakhāʼir waʼl-tuḥaf*, ed. Ṣalāḥ al-Dīn al-Munajjid, Kuwait (Government Press), 1959.

Al-Idrīsī, Abū ʻAbdallāh Muḥammad ibn Muḥammad. *Opus Geographicum*, ed. A. Bombaci, U. Rizzitano, R. Rubinacci, L. Veccia Vaglieri, part i, Naples-Rome (Istituto Universitario Orientale di Napoli, Istituto Italiano per il Medio ed estremo Oriente), 1970.

Isaac Israeli. *Sefer Musar Rōfʼīm*, ed. David Kaufmann in *Magazin für die Wissenschaft des Judenthums*, Berlin, 1884.

Ishāq ibn al-Ḥusayn. *Kitāb Akām al-Marjān fī dhikr al-madāʼin al-mashhūra fī kull makān*, ed. Angela Codazzi in *Rendiconti della Reale Accademia dei Lincei, classa di scienze morali etc.* sixth series, vol. V, Rome, 1929.

Al-Iṣṭakhrī, Abū Isḥāq Ibrāhīm ibn Muḥammad. *Al-Masālik waʼl-mamālik*, ed. M. J. de Goeje, Leiden (Brill), 1870.

Al-Jāḥiẓ, ʻAmr ibn Baḥr, *Rasāʼil*, ed. Ḥasan al-Sandūbī, Cairo (Al-Maktaba al-Tijāriyya al-Kubrā), 1352/1933.

———*Al-Bukhalāʼ*, Damascus (Al-Nashr al-ʻArabī), 1357/1938.

———*Al-Bayān waʼl-tabyīn*, ed. ʻAbd al-Salām Muḥammad Hārūn, 4 vols., Cairo (Al-Khānjī), 1380/1940.

———*Rasāʼil*, 2 vols., ed. ʻAbd al-Salām Hārūn, Cairo (Al-Khānjī) 1965.

———(attributed to). *Al-Tabaṣṣur bi'l-tijāra,* ed. Ḥasan Ḥusnī 'Abd al-Wahhāb, Cairo (Raḥmāniyya), 1354/1935.

Al-Jahshiyārī, Abū 'Abdallāh Muḥammad ibn 'Abdūs. *Kitāb al-Wuzarā' wa'l-kuttāb,* edd. Muṣṭafā al-Saqqā', Ibrāhīm al-Abyārī, and 'Abd al-Ḥafīẓ Shalabī, Cairo (Ḥalabī), 1357/1938.

Al-Kāshgharī, Maḥmūd ibn al-Ḥusayn. *Kitāb Dīwān lughāt al-Turk,* Istanbul ('Āmire), 1333/1914.

Ka'ti, Maḥmūd Ka'ti ibn al-Ḥājj al-Mutawakkil. *Ta'rīkh al-Fattāsh,* ed. O. Houdas and M. Delafosse, Paris (Ernest Leroux), 1913–1914.

Al-Khushanī, Muḥammad ibn al-Ḥārith. *Kitāb al-Quḍāt bi-Qurtuba* (*Historia de los jueces de Cordoba*), ed. J. Ribera, Madrid (Maestre), 1914.

Kračkovsky, I. Y. *Izbranniye Sočineniya,* i, Moscow-Leningrad (Akad. Nauk), 1955.

Al-Maqdisī, Muṭahhar ibn Ṭāhir. *Kitāb al-Bad' wa'l-ta'rīkh,* ed. Clement Huart, 3 vols., Paris (Ernest Leroux), 1899–1903.

Al-Maqrīzī, Taqī al-Dīn Aḥmad ibn 'Alī. *Kitāb al-Sulūk li-ma'rifat duwal al-mulūk,* ed. M. M. Ziyāda and others, in course of publication, Cairo (Lajnat al-ta'līf), 1934–.

———*Kitāb al-Mawā'iz wa'l-i'tibār fī dhikr al-Khiṭaṭ wa'l-āthār,* 2 vols., Būlāq, 1270/1853.

Al-Mas'ūdī, Abu'l-Ḥasan 'Alī ibn al-Ḥusayn. *Murūj al-dhahab,* ed. C. Barbier de Meynard and Pavet de Courteille, Paris (Société Asiatique), 1861–1877; new edition by C. Pellat, in progress, Beirut (Université Libanaise), 1966–.

———*Kitāb al-Tanbīh wa'l-ishrāf,* ed. 'Abdallāh Ismā'īl al-Ṣāwī, Cairo (Ṣāwī), 1357/1938.

Al-Māwardī, Abu'l-Ḥasan 'Alī ibn Muḥammad. *Al-Aḥkām al-Sulṭāniyya* Cairo (Maḥmūdiyya), n.d.

Mihyār al-Daylamī. *Dīwān,* Cairo (Dār al-Kutub), 1344/1925.

Moses Ben Maimon (Maimonides). *Qōveṣ teshūvōt ha-Rambam ve-igrōtav,* ed. A. Lichtenberg, iii, Leipzig, 1858.

Al-Mubarrad, Muḥammad ibn Yazīd. *Al-Kāmil,* ed. W. Wright, Leipzig (Brockhaus), 1874.

Al-Muqaddasī, Shams al-Dīn Abū 'Abdallāh Muḥammad ibn Aḥmad. *Aḥsan al-taqāsīm fī ma'rifat al-aqālīm* (*Descriptio Imperii Moslemici*), ed. M. J. de Goeje, 2nd edition, Leiden (Brill), 1906.

Al-Muttaqī, 'Alā al-Dīn 'Alī ibn Ḥusām al-Dīn. *Kanz al-'ummāl,* 8 parts, Hyderabad (Dā'irat al-Ma'ārif), 1312/1894–1895.

Nāṣir-i Khusraw. *Safar-nāma,* Berlin (Kaviani), 1340/1921.

Al-Nawawī, Yaḥyā ibn Sharaf. *Manthūrāt,* excerpt ed. I. Goldziher, *Revue des Etudes juives,* xxviii, 1894.

Niẓām al-Dīn Shāmī. *Ẓafar-nāma,* ed. F. Tauer, Prague (Oriental Institute), 1937.

Niẓām al-Mulk. *Siyāsat-nāma,* ed. C. Schefer, Paris (Ernest Leroux), 1891.

Qāḍī Nu'mān ibn Muḥammad. *Sharḥ al-akhbār* in W. Ivanow, *Ismaili tradition concerning the rise of the Fatimids,* London (Oxford University Press), 1942.

Al-Nuwayrī, Shihāb al-Dīn Aḥmad ibn 'Abd al-Wahhāb. *Nihāyat al-arab,* iv, Cairo (Dār al-Kutub), 1343/1925. Unpublished volume Ms. Bibliothèque Nationale, Paris, Fonds arabe, 1576.

Papyri, Documents from

C. H. Becker. *Papyri Schott-Reinhardt,* I, Heidelberg (Carl Winter), 1906.

———'Arabische Papyri . . .', in *Zeitschrift für Assyriologie,* xx, 1906. A. Grohmann, 'Arabische Papyri. .', in *Archiv Orientální,* x, 1938; xi, 1939; xii, 1941; xiv, 1943.

———'Arabische Papyri . . .', in *Der Islam,* xxii, 1935.

Qāḍī Khān, al-Ḥasan ibn Manṣūr. *Fatāwī,* Cairo, 1865.

Al-Qalqashandī, Abu'l-'Abbās Aḥmad. *Ṣubḥ al-a'shā,* 14 vols., Cairo (Dār al-Kutub), 1331/1913–1337/1918.

Al-Qazwīnī, Zakariyyā ibn Muḥammad, *Āthār al-bilād wa-akhbār al-'ibād,* Beirut (Ṣādir), 1380/1960.

Al-Qudūrī, Aḥmad ibn Muḥammad. *Al-Mukhtaṣar; Le Statut personnel en droit musulman hanefite,* ed. G. H. Bousquet and L. Bercher, Paris-Tunis (Sirey), 1952.

Qur'ān. Cited by chapter (*Sūra*) and verse, according to two systems of numbering.

Rashīd al-Dīn. *Jāmi' al-tawārīkh,* iii, ed. Abdul-Kerim Ali-oglu Ali-zade, Baku (Azerbaijan Academy of Sciences), 1937.

Al-Rāwandī, Muḥammad ibn 'Alī. *Rāḥat al-ṣudūr,* ed. Muḥammad Iqbal, London (Luzac), 1921.

RCEA. Répertoire chronologique d'épigraphie arabe, 15 vols., Cairo (Institut Français d'Archéologie Orientale), 1931–1956.

Safara siyāsiyya min Gharnāṭa ila'l-Qāhira fi'l-qarn al-tāsi' al-hijrī (844), ed. 'Abd al-'Azīz al-Ahwānī in *Majallat Kulliyyat al-Adab,* Cairo, xv, 1954.

Al-Shāfi'ī, al-Imām Abū 'Abdallāh Muḥammad ibn Idrīs. *Kitāb al-Umm,* Bulaq (Amīriyya), 1321–2/1903–1904.

Al-Shaybānī, Muḥammad ibn al-Ḥasan. *Kitāb al-Siyar,* in Sarakhsī,

Sharḥ al-Siyar al-Kabīr, 2 vols., Hyderabad (Dā'irat al-Ma'ārif), 1335/1917.

Al-Ṣūlī, Abū Bakr Muḥammad ibn Yaḥyā. *Akhbār al-Rāḍī wa'l-Muttaqī,* ed. J. Heyworth Dunne, London (Luzac), 1935.

Sûret-i Defter-i Sancak-i Arvanid, ed. Halil Inalcik; Ankara (Türk Tarih Kurumu), 1954.

Al-Suyūṭī, Jalāl al-Dīn. *Ḥusn al-Muḥāḍara fī akhbār Miṣr wa'l-Qāhira,* Cairo, 1321/1902.

Al-Ṭabarī, Abū Ja'far Muḥammad ibn Jarīr. *Ta'rīkh al-Rusul wa'l-mulūk,* ed. M. J. de Goeje and others, Leiden (Brill), 1879–1901.

Al-Tanūkhī, Abū 'Alī, *Al-Faraj ba'd al-Shidda,* Cairo (Al-Khānjī), 1375/1955.

Al-Ṭarsūsī, Marḍī ibn 'Alī. *Tabṣirat arbāb al-albāb fī kayfiyyat al-najāt fi'l-ḥurūb,* ed. C. Cahen, 'Un traité d'armurerie composé pour Saladin', in *Bulletin d'Etudes Orientales,* xii, 1947–1948.

Al-Turṭūshī, Muḥammad ibn Walīd, called Ibn Abī Randaqa. *Sirāj al-mulūk,* Cairo, 1289/1872.

'Ubayd-i Zākānī. *Kulliyyāt,* ed. 'Abbās Iqbāl, Tehran (Zuvvar), 1343 Persian solar/1964.

Yaḥyā al-Antākī. *Annales,* ed. L. Cheikho, B. Carra de Vaux, and H. Zayyat, in *Corpus Scriptorum Christianorum Orientalium, Scriptores Arabici,* 3rd series, vol. vii, Paris (Poussielgue), 1909.

Al-Ya'qūbī, Aḥmad ibn Abī Ya'qūb. *Kitāb al-Buldān,* ed. M. J. de Goeje, 2nd edition, Leiden (Brill), 1892.

Yāqūt. *Irshād al-Arīb, or Dictionary of learned men,* ed. D. S. Margoliouth, London (Luzac), 1923.

1 Events

1
The Patriarchal and Umayyad Caliphate

When Muḥammad died in 632, his spiritual and prophetic mission was completed. His religious task remained, however: to maintain and defend the faith and the law of Islam and to bring them to the rest of mankind. The effective discharge of this religious task required the exercise of political and military power—in a word, of sovereignty.

The Prophet was dead, and there would be no more. The leader of the community was dead and had to be replaced, for without such a leader the community would break up, and the faith, without authority, would be lost. Some of the Medinan tribesmen were already attempting to elect new chiefs. In this emergency, the most active and able among the inner group of Muḥammad's followers chose one of their number, Abū Bakr, and hailed him as leader. The term they used was khalīfa *(whence "caliph"), an Arabic word which, by a fortunate ambiguity, combined the notions of successor and deputy, that is, of the Prophet. Later the ambiguity was compounded, and authority reinforced, by the suggestion that the Caliph was the deputy, not of God's Prophet, but of God Himself.*

From this act of improvisation arose the great historic institution of the Caliphate and, in time, the religious and juridical doctrine of the universal caliphal office.

The first four Caliphs were chosen by their peers, and the memory of an elective Caliphate remains enshrined in the Sunnī juridical theory of sovereignty. But of the four venerated patriarchs, three were mur-

dered, and the elective Caliphate foundered in civil war. Thereafter the caliphal office was in fact, though never in theory, dynastic and was held by two successive dynasties. The first, the Umayyads, were based in Syria and ruled for about a century. They were overthrown by a religiously expressed opposition movement, which after a long period of preparation, launched a successful revolution and established another dynasty, the 'Abbasids, in their place.

1. The Founding of the Caliphate (632)

An account of what happened between the Emigrants and the Helpers concerning the leadership, in the porch of the Banū Sā'ida.[1]

Hishām ibn Muḥammad told me on the authority of Abū Mikhnaf, who said: 'Abdallāh ibn 'Abd al-Raḥmān ibn Abī 'Umra, the Helper, told me:

When the Prophet of God, may God bless and save him, died, the Helpers assembled in the porch of the Banū Sā'ida and said, "Let us confer this authority, after Muḥammad, upon him be peace, on Sa'd ibn 'Ubāda." Sa'd, who was ill, was brought to them, and when they assembled Sa'd said to his son or to one of his nephews, "I cannot, because of my sickness, speak so that all the people can hear my words. Therefore, hear what I say and then repeat it to them so that they may hear it." Then he spoke and the man memorized his words and raised his voice so that the others could hear.

He said, after praising God and lauding Him, "O company of the Helpers! You have precedence in religion and merit in Islam which no other Arab tribe has. Muḥammad, upon him be peace, stayed for more than ten years amid his people, summoning them to worship the Merciful One and to abandon false gods and idols. But among his own people only a few men believed in him, and they were not able to protect the Prophet of God or to glorify his

[1] The Emigrants (*Muhājirūn*) were the Qurayshī Muslims from Mecca who accompanied the Prophet on his migration to Medina; the Helpers (*Anṣār*) were the Medinans who joined them. The Banū Sā'ida were a clan of Khazraj, one of the two main Arab tribes of Medina; the other was Aws.

religion nor to defend themselves against the injustice which beset them. God therefore conferred merit on you and brought honor to you and singled you out for grace and vouchsafed to you faith in Him and in His Prophet and protection for Him and His companions and glorification to Him and His religion and holy war against His enemies. It was you who fought hardest against His enemy and weighed more heavily on His enemy than any other, until the Arabs obeyed the command of God willy-nilly and the distant ones gave obedience, humbly and meekly; until Almighty God, through you, made the world submit to His Prophet, and through your swords the Arabs drew near to him. And when God caused him to die, he was content with you and delighted with you. Therefore, keep this authority for yourselves alone, for it is yours against all others."

They all replied to him, "Your judgment is sound and your words are true. We shall not depart from what you say and we shall confer this authority on you. You satisfy us and you will satisfy the right believer."

Then they discussed it among themselves and some of them said, "What if the Emigrants of Quraysh refuse, and say: 'We are the Emigrants and the first Companions of the Prophet of God; we are his clan and his friends. Why therefore do you dispute the succession to his authority with us?' " Some of them said, "If so, we would reply to them, 'An amir from us and an amir from you! And we shall never be content with less than that.' " Sa'd ibn 'Ubāda, when he heard this, said, "This is the beginning of weakness."

News of this reached 'Umar, and he went to the house of the Prophet, may God bless and save him. He sent to Abū Bakr, who was in the Prophet's house with 'Alī ibn Abī Tālib, upon him be peace, preparing the body of the Prophet, may God bless and save him, for burial. He sent asking Abū Bakr to come to him, and Abū Bakr sent a message in reply saying that he was busy. Then 'Umar sent saying that something had happened which made his presence necessary, and he went to him and said, "Have you not heard that the Helpers have gathered in the porch of the Banū Sā'ida? They wish to confer this authority on Sa'd ibn 'Ubāda, and the best they say is, 'an amir from among us and an amir from among Quraysh.'" They made haste toward them, and they met Abū 'Ubayda ibn al-Jarrāḥ. The three of them went on together, and they met 'Āṣim ibn 'Adī and 'Uwaym ibn Sā'ida, who both said to them: "Go back, for what you want will not happen." They said, "We shall not go back," and they came to the meeting.

'Umar ibn al-Khaṭṭāb said: We came to the meeting, and I had prepared a speech which I wished to make to them. We reached them, and I was about to begin my speech when Abū Bakr said to me, "Gently! Let me speak first, and then afterwards say whatever you wish." He spoke. 'Umar said, "He said all I wanted to say, and more."

'Abdallāh ibn 'Abd al-Raḥmān said: Abū Bakr began. He praised and lauded God and then he said, "God sent Muḥammad as a Prophet to His creatures and as a witness to His community that they might worship God and God alone, at a time when they were worshipping various gods beside Him and believed that they were intercessors for them with God and could be of help to them, though they were only of hewn stone and carved wood. Then he recited to them, 'And they worship apart from God those who could neither harm them nor help them, and they say these are our intercessors with God' [Qur'ān x, 19/18]. And they said, 'We worship them only so that they may bring us very near to God' [Qur'ān xxxix, 4/3]. It was a tremendous thing for the Arabs to abandon the religion of their fathers. God distinguished the first Emigrants of his people by allowing them to recognize the truth and believe in him and console him and suffer with him from the harsh persecution of his people when they gave them the lie and all were against them and reviled them. Yet they were not affrighted because their numbers were few and the people stared at them and their tribe was joined against them. They were the first in the land who worshipped God and who believed in God and the Prophet. They are his friends and his clan and the best entitled of all men to this authority after him. Only a wrongdoer would dispute this with them. And as for you, O company of the Helpers, no one can deny your merit in the faith or your great precedence in Islam. God was pleased to make you Helpers to His religion and His Prophet and caused him to migrate to you, and the honor of sheltering his wives and his Companions is still yours, and after the first Emigrants there is no one we hold of equal standing with you. We are the amirs and you are the viziers. We shall not act contrary to your advice and we shall not decide things without you."

. . . .

Abū Bakr said, "Here is 'Umar and here is Abū 'Ubayda. Swear allegiance to whichever of them you choose." The two of them said, "No, by God, we shall not accept this authority above you, for you are the worthiest of the Emigrants and the second of the two who were in the cave[2] and the deputy [*khalīfa*] of the Prophet of God in prayer,[3] and prayer is the noblest part of the religion of the Muslims. Who then would be fit to take precedence of you or to accept this authority above you? Stretch out your hand so that we may swear allegiance to you."

And when they went forward to swear allegiance to him, Bashīr ibn Sa'd went ahead of them and swore allegiance to him . . . and when the tribe of Aws saw what Bashīr ibn Sa'd had done . . . they came to him and swore allegiance to him. . . .

Hishām said on the authority of Abū Mikhnaf: 'Abdallāh ibn 'Abd al-Raḥmān said: People came from every side to swear allegiance to Abū Bakr.

Al-Ṭabarī, i, pp. 1837–1844.

2. The Accession Speech of Abū Bakr (632)

Then Abū Bakr spoke and praised and lauded God as is fitting, and then he said: O people, I have been appointed to rule over you, though I am not the best among you. If I do well, help me, and if I do ill, correct me. Truth is loyalty and falsehood is treachery; the weak among you is strong in my eyes until I get justice for him, please God, and the strong among you is weak in my eyes until I exact justice from him, please God. If any people holds back from fighting the holy war for God, God strikes them with degradation. If weakness spreads among a people, God

[2] A reference to Qur'ān, ix, 40.

[3] An allusion to the fact that during his last illness the Prophet appointed Abū Bakr to lead the people in prayer.

brings disaster upon all of them. Obey me as long as I obey God and His Prophet. And if I disobey God and His Prophet, you do not owe me obedience. Come to prayer, and may God have mercy on you.

Ibn Hishām, *Sīra*, ii, p. 661.

3. The Death of ʿUmar ibn al-Khaṭṭāb (644)

And in this year was his death.

The telling of the news of his murder.

I heard from Salama ibn Junāda, who heard from Sulaymān ibn ʿAbd al-ʿAziz ibn Abī Thābit ibn ʿAbd al-ʿAziz ibn ʿUmar ibn ʿAbd al-Raḥmān ibn ʿAwf, who said: I heard from my father, on the authority of ʿAbdallāh ibn Jaʿfar, on the authority of his father, on the authority of Miswar ibn Makhrama (his mother was ʿĀtika bint ʿAwf), who said, " ʿUmar ibn al-Khaṭṭāb went out one day to stroll in the marketplace, and he met Abū Lu'lu'a, a slave of Al-Mughīra ibn Shuʿba, and he was a Christian. Abū Lu'lu'a said, "O Commander of the Faithful, help me against Al-Mughīra ibn Shuʿba, for a great tax has been imposed on me." "How much is your tax?" asked ʿUmar. "Two dirhams every day," he replied. "And what is your trade?" "A carpenter, a painter, a blacksmith." "I do not consider your tax great," said ʿUmar, "for the crafts which you practice. I have heard that you say that if you wished, you could build a mill that would grind by the wind." "Yes," he answered. "Make me a mill," said ʿUmar. "If I am spared," said Abū Lu'lu'a, "I shall make you such a mill that men shall talk of it in the east and the west."

Then he left him, and ʿUmar, may God be pleased with him, said, "Indeed, this slave has just dared to threaten me!"

Then ʿUmar departed to his house, and on the next day Kaʿb al-Aḥbār[1] came and said to him, "O Commander of the Faithful, make your will, for in three days you will be dead."

[1] A Yemenite Jewish convert to Islam, and a respected figure under the early Caliphs. *Aḥbār* is the broken plural of *ḥabr*, from Hebrew *ḥabher*, which was used as a title of scholarship. See *EI*², s.v.

"What tells you this?" asked 'Umar.

"I find it in the book of Almighty God, in the Torah."

"What, do you find 'Umar ibn al-Khaṭṭāb in the Torah?"

"By God, no, but I find your description and features, and behold, your span is ended."

And 'Umar felt no pain or illness. On the morrow Ka'b came to him and said, "O Commander of the Faithful, a day has gone and two days remain." And on the following day he came again and said, "Two days have gone, a day and a night remain; it is yours until dawn."

And when dawn came 'Umar went forth to prayer, and he used to appoint men to dress the people in ranks. And when they were straight, he went forward and recited "*Allahu ákbar.*"[2] And Abū Lu'lu'a entered among the people, and in his hand was a dagger with two blades and the grip in the middle, and he smote 'Umar six blows, one of them under the navel, and it was this one that killed him. Kulayb ibn Abi'l-Bukayr al-Laythī, who was behind him, was killed with him. When Umar felt the heat of the weapon he fell and said, "Is 'Abd al-Raḥmān ibn 'Awf among the people?" and they answered, "Yes, O Commander of the Faithful, there he is." And 'Umar said, "Come forward and lead the people in prayer." And 'Abd al-Raḥmān ibn 'Awf led the people in prayer while 'Umar lay prostrate. Then he was carried out and brought to his house, and he summoned 'Abd al-Raḥmān ibn 'Awf and said to him, "I wish to make you my successor."

And he answered, "O Commander of the Faithful, yes—if you advise me to, I shall accept it from you."

And he said, "What do you want?"

"I adjure you, by God, do you advise me to do this?"

"By God, no," said 'Umar.

"Then by God I will never enter upon it," said 'Abd al-Raḥmān ibn 'Awf.

Then 'Umar said, "Be silent until I appoint my successor from among the group of those whom the Prophet, God bless and save

[2] God is (very) great. A formula frequently used in Muslim worship, in the call to prayer, and as a war cry. See *EI*[1], "Takbīr."

him, loved when he died. Bring me 'Alī and 'Uthmān and Zubayr and Sa'd."

When they came, he said, "Wait for your brother Ṭalḥa three days, and if he comes, proceed; if not, settle your business without him. O, 'Alī, I adjure you by God, if you are given any authority over the people, do not load the Banū Hāshim[3] on the neck of the people. O 'Uthmān, I adjure you by God, if you are given any authority over the people, do not load the sons of Abū 'Mu'ayṭ on the neck of the people. O Sa'd, I adjure you by God, if you are given any authority over the people, do not load your relations on the neck of the people. Arise and take counsel, then settle your affair, and let Ṣuhayb lead the people in prayer."

Then he called Abū Ṭalḥa al-Anṣārī and said, "Stand by their door and let no man go in to them. I recommend to the Caliph my successor the Helpers of Medina who 'entered the House and the Faith,' that he should treat well those of them who do good and overlook the evildoers among them, and I recommend to the Caliph my successor the Arab tribes, for indeed they are the backbone of Islam, that he should take from their religious taxes [*zakāt*] what is right and apportion it among their poor. And I recommend to the Caliph my successor those who have a covenant [*dhimma*] with the Prophet of God, may God bless and save him, that he should render them what is due to them by the pact. Oh God, have I done my duty? I have left the Caliph my successor cleaner than the palm of a hand. O'Abdallāh ibn 'Umar, go forth and see who killed me."

And he answered, "O Commander of the Faithful, Abū Lu'lu'a the slave of Al-Mughīra ibn Shu'ba killed you."

And 'Umar said, "Praise be to God that He did not cause my death by the hand of a man who bowed down before Him even once. O 'Abdallāh ibn 'Umar, go to 'Āyisha[4] and ask her if she will permit me to be buried with the Prophet, may God bless and save him, and Abū Bakr. O 'Abdallāh ibn 'Umar, if the company differ, be with the majority, and if there are three on each side, be on the same side as 'Abd al-Raḥmān. O 'Abdallāh, let the people enter!"

[3] The family to which both Muḥammad and 'Alī belonged.
[4] The daughter of Abū Bakr, the favorite wife of the Prophet.

"And the Emigrants and the Helpers began to come in and greet him, and he said to them, "Is this the result of any conspiracy of yours?" And they answered, "God is our refuge."

Then Ka'b entered among the people, and when 'Umar saw him he spoke this verse:

Ka'b promised me three days. I counted them,
And there is no doubt but that Ka'b spoke the truth.
I have no fear of death, for indeed I am dead.
But I fear the evil that follows evil.

And they said to him, "O Commander of the Faithful, you should call a physician." And a physician of the tribe of the Banu'l-Ḥārith ibn Ka'b was summoned. And he gave 'Umar mead, and the mead came forth of doubtful color. And he gave him milk, and the milk came forth white. Then 'Umar was told, "O Commander of the Faithful, make your will." And he said, "I have already done so."

And 'Umar died on Tuesday night, when three days remained of the month of Dhu'l-ḥijja in the year 23 [November 3, 644].

And they went out with him on Wednesday morning, and he was buried in the house of 'Āyisha with the Prophet, may God bless and save him, and Abū Bakr.

And Ṣuhayb came forward and prayed over him. But before this two of the disciples of the Prophet, may God bless and save him, came forward, 'Alī and 'Uthmān, and one stood by his head and the other by his feet. And 'Abd al-Raḥmān said, "There is no God but God! Why do you crave authority? Do you not know that the Commander of the Faithful said 'Let Ṣuhayb lead the people in prayer?' " And Ṣuhayb came forward and prayed and the five of them entered the tomb.

Abū Ja'far said,[5] "It is said that his death was on the first day of Muḥarram of the year 24 [November 7, 644]."

The mention of who said this

I heard from Al-Ḥārith, who heard from Muḥammad ibn Sa'd who heard from Muḥammad ibn 'Umar, who said: Abū Bakr ibn Ismā īl ibn Muḥammad ibn Sa'd told me, on the authority of his father, who said: 'Umar, may God be pleased

[5] That is, Ṭabarī himself, who introduces his own observations in this way.

with him, was stabbed on Wednesday, when four days remained of Dhu'l-ḥijja, in the year 23, and buried on Sunday morning Muḥarram 1, 24, and his reign lasted ten years, five months, and twenty-one days, from the death of Abū Bakr, exactly twenty-two years, nine months, thirteen days from the Hijra. And homage was sworn to 'Uthmān ibn Affān on Monday, Muḥarram 3. (I mentioned this to 'Uthmān Al-Akhnāsī, and he said, "You must be mistaken. 'Umar died when four nights remained of Dhu'l-ḥijja, and homage was sworn to 'Uthmān ibn 'Affān on the last day of Dhu'l-ḥijja. Thus his Caliphate just preceded Muḥarram of the year 24.")

I heard from Aḥmad ibn Thābit al-Rāzī who heard from someone, on the authority of Isḥāq ibn 'Isā, on the authority of Abū Ma'shar, who said: 'Umar was killed on Wednesday, when four days remained of Dhu'l-ḥijja at the end of the year 23, and his caliphate lasted ten years, six months, four days, and then homage was sworn to 'Uthmān ben Affān.

Abū Ja'far said: Al-Madā'inī said, as 'Umar [ibn Shabba] told me on his authority, on the authority of Sharīk, on the authority of al-A'mash or of Jābir al-Ju'fī, on the authority of 'Awf ibn Mālik al-Ashja'ī and 'Āmir ibn Abī Muḥammad, on the authority of some elders of his tribe, and 'Uthmān ibn 'Abd al-Raḥmān on the authority of Ibn Shihāb al-Zuhrī. They said: 'Umar was stabbed on Wednesday, a week before the end of Dhu'l-ḥijja. And others said, Six days before the end of Dhu'l-ḥijja.

Sayf said, according to what al-Sarī wrote to me, mentioning that Shu'ayb had told him on his authority, on the authority of Khulayd ibn Dhafara and Mujālid, who both said, 'Uthmān was made Caliph on Muḥarram 3, 24, and he went forth and prayed the afternoon prayer with the people and gave increments and sent envoys. And this became a custom.

Al-Sarī wrote to me, on the authority of Shu'ayb, on the authority of Sayf, on the authority of 'Amr, on the authority of al-Sha'bī, who said: The conclave agreed on 'Uthmān on Muḥarram 3, when the time for the afternoon prayer had already come. The muezzin of Ṣuhayb had already given the call to prayer, and they reached agreement between the call and the performance. Then 'Uthmān went forward and led the people in prayer and gave the people an increment of 100 [dirhams] and sent back the envoys from the provinces and treated them kindly. And he was the first to do this.

I was told, on the authority of Hishām ibn Muḥammad, who said: 'Umar was killed when three nights remained of Dhu'l-ḥijja, 23, and his Caliphate lasted ten years, six months, and four days.

The Mention of the Pedigree of 'Umar, May God Be Pleased with Him

I heard from Ibn Ḥumayd, who heard from Salama, on the authority of Muḥammad ibn Isḥāq. And I heard from al-Ḥārith, who heard from Ibn Sa'd, on the authority of Muḥammad ibn 'Umar and Hishām ibn Muḥammad. And I heard from 'Umar, who heard from 'Alī ibn Muḥammad. They all agreed concerning 'Umar's genealogy. He was 'Umar ibn al-Khaṭṭāb ibn Nufayl ibn 'Abd al-'Uzzā ibn Riyāḥ ibn 'Abdallāh ibn Qurṭ ibn Razāḥ ibn 'Adiyy ibn Ka'b ibn Lu'ayy. His *kunya* was Abū Ḥafṣ, and his mother was Ḥantama bint Hāshim ibn al-Mughīra ibn 'Abdallāh ibn 'Umar ibn Makhzūm.

Abū Ja'far said: He used to be called al-Fārūq, and even the early Muslims differ as to who named him thus. Some say that the Prophet of God, may God save and bless him, named him thus.

The mention of those who said this

I heard from al-Ḥārith, who heard from Ibn Sa'd, who heard from Muḥammad ibn 'Umar, who heard from Abū Ḥazra Ya'qūb ibn Mujāhid, on the authority of Muḥammad ibn Ibrāhīm, on the authority of Abū Amr Dhakwān, who said: I asked 'Āyisha who named 'Umar al-Fārūq and she said, "The Prophet, may God bless and save him." And some say that the first to give him this name were the people of the Book.[6]

The mention of who said this

I heard from al-Ḥārith, who heard from Ibn Sa'd, who heard from Ya'qūb ibn Ibrāhīm ibn Sa'd, on the authority of his father, on the authority of Ṣāliḥ ibn Kaysān, who said: Ibn Shihāb

[6] Those possessing scriptures, a term usually applied to the Jews. See *EI*², "Ahl al-Kitāb."

said, "We have heard that the People of the Book were the first to call 'Umar al-Fārūq and that the Muslims took it over from them; we have not heard that the Prophet of God, may God bless and save him, mentioned this at all."

Description of 'Umar.

I heard from Hannād ibn al-Sarī, who heard from Wakī on the authority of Sufyān, on the authority of 'Āṣim ibn Abi'l-Najūd, on the authority of Zirr ibn Ḥubaysh, who said: 'Umar went forth on a festival day or to the funeral of Zaynab, and he was ruddy, tall, bald, and ambidextrous, and walked as if he were riding.

I heard from al-Ḥārith, who heard from Ibn Sa'd, who heard of 'Āṣim, on the authority of Zirr, who said: I saw 'Umar arrive at the festival, walking barefoot, ambidextrous, tucking up his sewn garment, over-topping the people as though he were mounted, and he said, "O people, make the *hijra* and do not just pretend to have made it."

I heard from al-Ḥārith, who heard from Ibn Sa'd, who heard from Muḥammad ibn 'Umar, who heard from 'Umar ibn 'Imrān ibn 'Abdallāh ibn 'Abd al-Raḥmān ibn Abī Bakr, on the authority of 'Āṣim ibn 'Ubaydallāh, on the authority of 'Abdallāh ibn 'Āmir ibn Rabī'a, who said: I saw 'Umar, a fair, pale man, with a touch of redness, tall and bald.

I heard from al-Ḥārith, who heard from Ibn Sa'd, who heard from Muḥammad ibn 'Umar, who heard from Shu'ayb ibn Ṭalḥa, on the authority of his father, on the authority of al-Qāsim ibn Muḥammad, who said: I heard the son of 'Umar describe 'Umar, saying, 'A pale man, with a touch of redness, tall, grey, and bald."

I heard from al-Ḥārith, who heard from Muḥammad ibn Sa'd who heard from Muḥammad ibn 'Umar, who heard from Khālid ibn Abī Bakr, who said: 'Umar used to dye his beard yellow and dress his head with henna.

The Birth and Length of Life of 'Umar

I heard from al-Ḥārith, who heard from Ibn Sa'd, who heard from Muḥammad ibn 'Umar, who heard from Usāma ibn Zayd ibn Aslam, on the authority of his father, on the authority of his grandfather, who said: I heard 'Umar ibn al-Khaṭṭāb say, "I was born four years before the last and greatest of the Fijār[7] wars."

Abū Ja'far said: The early Muslims differed as to the length of 'Umar's years. Some of them said that on the day he was killed he was fifty-five years old.

Some who said this

I heard from Zayd ibn Akhzam al-Ṭā'ī, who heard from Abū Qutayba, on the authority of Jarīr ibn Ḥāzim, on the authority of Ayyūb, on the authority of Nāfi' on the authority of Ibn 'Umar, who said: 'Umar ibn al-Khaṭṭāb was killed when he was fifty-five years old.

And I heard from 'Abd al-Raḥmān ibn 'Abdallāh ibn 'Abd al-Ḥakam, who heard from Nu'aym ibn Ḥammād, who heard from al-Darāwardī on the authority of 'Ubaydallāh ibn 'Umar, on the authority of Nāfi', on the authority of Ibn 'Umar, who said: 'Umar died when he was fifty-five.

And I was told, on the authority of 'Abd al-Razzāq, on the authority of Ibn Jurayj, on the authority of Ibn Shihāb, that 'Umar died when he was just fifty-five. Others said: The day he died he was fifty-three years old and some months.

Those who said this

I was told this on the authority of Hishām ibn Muḥammad ibn al-Kalbī. And others said: He died when he was sixty-three.

Those who said this

I heard from Ibn al-Muthannā, who heard from Ibn Abī 'Adī, on the authority of Dā'ūd, on the authority of 'Āmir, who said: 'Umar died when he was sixty-three. And others said he died when he was sixty-one.

[7] Sacrilege, the name of a war fought in Arabia at the end of the sixth century, so called because it occurred in violation of the sacred months. See *EI*², "Fidjār."

THOSE WHO SAID THIS

I was told this on the authority of Abū Salama al-Tabūdhakī, on the authority of Abū Hilāl, on the authority of Qatāda.

Others said that he died when he was sixty.

THOSE WHO SAID THIS

I heard from al-Ḥārith, who heard from Ibn Sa'd, who heard from Muḥammad ibn 'Umar, who heard from Hishām ibn Sa'd, on the authority of Zayd ibn Aslam, on the authority of his father, who said: 'Umar died when he was sixty.

Muḥammad ibn 'Umar said: This is in our opinion the most reliable report.

It is related, on the authority of al-Madā'inī that he said: 'Umar died when he was fifty-seven.

The Names of His Children and His Wives

I heard from Abū Zayd 'Umar ibn Shabba, on the authority of 'Alī ibn Muḥammad, and from al-Ḥārith, on the authority of Muḥammad ibn Sa'd, on the authority of Muḥammad ibn 'Umar, and I was told on the authority of Hishām ibn Muḥammad: the meanings of what they say agree, though their words differ. They said: 'Umar married Zaynab bint Maẓ'ūn ibn Ḥabīb ibn Wahb ibn Ḥudāfa ibn Jumaḥ during the time of Ignorance (*al-Jāhiliyya*), and she bore him 'Abdallāh and 'Abd al-Raḥmān the elder, and Ḥafṣa.

'Alī ibn Muḥammad said: Then he married Mulayka bint Jarwal al-Khuzā'ī during the time of ignorance and she bore him 'Ubaydallāh ibn 'Umar, and he divorced her during the Truce,[8] and Abu'l-Jahm ibn Ḥudhayfa married her after 'Umar.

Muḥammad ibn 'Umar said: Zayd the younger and 'Ubaydallāh, who was killed at the battle of Ṣiffīn with Mu'āwiya, both had as mother Umm Kulthūm bint Jarwal ibn Mālik ibn al-Musayyab ibn Rabī'a ibn Aṣram ibn Ḍabīs ibn Ḥarām ibn Ḥabashiyya ibn

[8] The truce agreed between the Prophet and the Meccans at Ḥudaybiyya, in 6/628.

Salūl ibn Ka'b ibn 'Amr ibn Khuzā'a, and Islam separated her from 'Umar.

'Alī ibn Muḥammad said: 'Umar married Qurayba bint Abī Umayya al-Makhzūmī during the time of Ignorance and divorced her, too, during the Truce, and after him 'Abd al-Raḥmān ibn Abī Bakr al-Ṣiddīq married her.

They said: And he married Umm Ḥakīm bint Al-Ḥarith ibn Hishām ibn al-Mughīra ibn 'Abdallāh ibn 'Umar ibn Makhzūm during Islam, and she bore him Fāṭima, and then he divorced her.

Al-Madā'inī said: It has also been said that he did not divorce her. And 'Umar married Jamīla, sister of 'Āṣim ibn Thābit ibn Abi'l-Aqlaḥ, and his name is Qays ibn 'Iṣma ibn Mālik ibn Ḍubay'a ibn Zayd ibn al-Aws, of the Helpers, during Islam, and she bore him 'Aṣim, and he divorced her. And he married Umm Kulthūm bint 'Alī Ṭālib (and her mother was Fāṭima, daughter of the Prophet of God, may God bless and save him,) and he gave her as marriage portion, so it is said, 40,000 [dirhams]. And she bore him Zayd and Ruqayya. And 'Umar married Luhayya, a woman from the Yemen, and she bore him 'Abd al-Raḥmān. Al-Madā'inī said that she bore him 'Abd al-Raḥmān the younger. And it is said that she was an *Umm walad.*[9]

Al-Wāqidī said: This Luhayya was an *Umm walad.* He also said: Luhayya bore him the middle 'Abd al-Raḥmān. And he said: The younger 'Abd al-Raḥmān was the son of an *Umm Walad,* who, according to him, was Fukayha. (She was, according to their statements, an *Umm Walad,* and she bore him Zaynab). Al-Wāqidī said she was the youngest of 'Umar's children. And 'Umar married 'Ātika bint Zayd ibn 'Amr ibn Nufayl; her previous husband was 'Abdallāh ibn Abī Bakr, and when 'Umar died, Zubayr ibn al-'Awwām married her.

Al-Madā'inī said: 'Umar asked for Umm Kulthūm, the daughter of Abū Bakr, in marriage, and she was very young. He sent about her to 'Āyisha, and she said to her, 'It is for you to decide.' And Umm Kulthūm said, "I don't care for him." And 'Āyisha said to her, "Do you dislike the Commander of the Faithful?" And

[9] See glossary, and vol. II, p. 238.

she said, "Yes. He leads a rough life and is violent with women." And 'Āyisha sent for 'Amr ibn al-'Āṣ and told him about it, and he said, "I will manage it for you." And he went to 'Umar and said, "O Commander of the Faithful, I have heard news about you, such that God forbid it be true." "What is it?" asked 'Umar. And he answered, "You have asked for Umm Kulthūm, the daughter of Abū Bakr in marriage!" "Yes," said 'Umar, "Do you consider me not good enough for her or her not good enough for me?" "Neither," he replied, "But she is a young girl, brought up under the wing of the Mother of the Believers, in gentleness and kindness. And you are rough, even we fear you, and cannot turn you from one of your impulses, and how would it be with her? If she crossed you in anything and you treated her harshly, you would be replacing her father Abū Bakr with his child in a way unworthy of you." And 'Umar said, "What of 'Āyisha, I have arranged it with her." And he answered, "I shall see to that for you, and moreover, I shall show you a better one than she, namely Umm Kulthūm daughter of 'Alī ibn Abī Ṭālib, and by her you will be linked with the family of the Prophet of God, may God bless and save him."

Al-Madā'inī said: And 'Umar asked for Umm Abān bint 'Utba ibn Rabī'a, and she hated him and said, "He locks his door and hoards his wealth and comes in scowling and goes out scowling."

The Time of 'Umar's Conversion

Abū Ja'far said: It is told that 'Umar accepted Islam after forty-five men and twenty-one women.

THOSE WHO SAID THIS

I heard from al-Ḥārith, who heard from Ibn Sa'd, who heard from Muḥammad ibn 'Umar, who heard from Muḥammad ibn 'Abdallāh, on the authority of his father, who said: I mentioned to him the story of 'Umar and he said, " 'Abdallāh ibn Tha'laba ibn Su'ayr told me that 'Umar accepted Islam after forty-five men and twenty-one women."

. . . .

The Naming of 'Umar, May God Be Pleased with Him, As Commander of the Faithful

Abu Ja'far said: The first to be called Commander of the Faithful was 'Umar ibn al-Khaṭṭāb. Then it became customary and was applied to all the Caliphs till today.

THE REPORT ON THIS

I heard from Aḥmad ibn 'Abd al-Ṣamad al-Anṣārī, who heard from Umm 'Amr bint Ḥassān, the Kufan woman, on the authority of her father, who said: When 'Umar was appointed Caliph, they said to him, "O deputy of the deputy of the Prophet of God!" And 'Umar, may God be pleased with him, said, "This is a thing that will grow longer. When another Caliph comes, they will say, 'O deputy of the deputy of the deputy of the Prophet of God.' You are the Faithful and I am your Commander," so he was called Commander of the Faithful.

Aḥmad ibn 'Abd al-Ṣamad said: I asked her how old she was. She said 133 years.

I heard from Ibn Ḥumayd, who heard from Yaḥyā ibn Wāḍiḥ, who heard from Abū Ḥamza, on the authority of Jābir, who said: A man said to 'Umar ibn al-Khaṭṭāb, "O deputy of God!" 'Umar said, "May God turn you away from such a thing!" The man said, "God make me your ransom (I meant nothing wrong)." 'Umar said, "Then God will humiliate you."[10]

His fixing the date

Abū Ja'far said: 'Umar was the first to fix and write the date, according to what al-Ḥārith told me, having heard it from Ibn Sa'd, on the authority of Muḥammad ibn 'Umar in the year 16, in the month of Rabī' I. And I have already mentioned the reason of his writing this and how the affair was. 'Umar, may God be pleased with him, was the first to date letters and seal them with clay. And he was the first to gather the people before

[10] The purpose of the anecdote is to condemn the use of the title *Khalīfat Allāh* (deputy of God), which was adopted by some Caliphs but never approved by the jurists. In their view the head of the community was the deputy of the Prophet, not of God.

an Imām to pray the *Tarāwīḥ*[11] with them, in the month of Ramaḍān, and he wrote concerning this to the provinces and commanded them to do likewise.

And this is what al-Ḥarīth told me he had heard from Ibn Sa'd on the authority of Muḥammad ibn 'Umar. In the year 14, he appointed two prayer leaders for the people, one to pray with the men and one to pray with the women.

On His Carrying the Whip and His Drawing Up the Registers [Dīwān]

And he was the first to carry a whip and strike with it, and he was the first in Islam to draw up registers for the people and write them down according to their tribes and to fix their stipends.

I heard from al-Ḥārith, who heard from Ibn Sa'd, who heard from Muḥammad ibn 'Umar, who heard from 'Ā'idh ibn Yaḥyā, on the authority of Abu'l-Ḥuwayrith, on the authority of Jubayr ibn al-Ḥuwayrith ibn Nuqayd, that 'Umar ibn al-Khaṭṭāb, may God be pleased with him, consulted the Muslims concerning the drawing up of the registers, and 'Alī ibn Abī Ṭālib said to him, "Share out every year whatever property has accumulated with you and do not retain anything." 'Uthmān ibn 'Affān said, "I see much property, which suffices for all the people and which cannot be counted until you can distinguish between those who have taken and those who have not. I do not like things to be in disorder." Al-Walīd ibn Hishām ibn al-Mughīra said to him, "O Commander of the Faithful, I have been to Syria and seen their kings, and they drew up a register and formed a legion [*jund*]. You should draw up a register and form a legion." 'Umar adopted his advice and called 'Aqīl ibn Abī Ṭālib and Makhrama ibn Nawfal and Jubayr ibn Muṭ'im, who were genealogists of the tribe of Quraysh, and he said to them, "Write [a list of] the people according to their ranks!" And they wrote, beginning with the Banū Hāshim, then following them with Abū Bakr and his kind and then 'Umar and his kind, that is, following the order of the Caliphate. When 'Umar looked into it he said, "I wish to God it were as you have

[11] Special prayers at night during the month of Ramaḍān. See *EI*[1], s.v.

written, but begin with the kin of the Prophet of God, may God bless and save him, then continue in order of nearness until you put ʿUmar where God has put him."

I heard from al-Ḥārith, who heard from Ibn Saʿd, who heard from Muḥammad ibn ʿUmar, who heard from Usāma ibn Zayd ibn Aslam, on the authority of his father, on the authority of his grandfather, who said: I saw ʿUmar ibn al-Khaṭṭāb, may God be pleased with him, when the writing was shown to him, with the Banū Taym after the Banū Hāshim and the Banū ʿAdī after the Banū Taym. And I heard him say, "Put ʿUmar in his proper place. Begin with the kin of the Prophet of God in order of nearness." And the Banū ʿAdī came to ʿUmar and said, "You are the deputy of the Prophet of God." And he answered, "Surely the deputy of Abū Bakr, and Abū Bakr was the deputy of the Prophet of God." And they said, "Why do you not put yourself where these people have put you?" And ʿUmar said, "Well done, O Banū ʿAdī! Do you want to eat off my back? Do you want me to sacrifice my honor to you? No, by God, not until your turn comes, even though the register close on you and you be written last among the people. I have two masters [Muḥammad and Abū Bakr] who followed a certain path, and if I forsake them, I shall be forsaken. Whatever of plenty we have attained in this world, whatever reward for our deeds we hope from God in the next world, is from Muḥammad alone. He is our nobility, and his kin are the noblest of the Arabs, and then the rest, in order of nearness to him. Indeed, the Arabs are ennobled with the Prophet of God, and perhaps some of them have many ancestors in common with him. As for us, it is clear that our stems coincide, and right back to Adam there are but few ancestors that we do not have in common. But despite that, by God, if the non-Arabs come with deeds and we come without them, they shall be nearer to Muḥammad than we on the Day of Judgment. Let no man look to his ancestry but let him do God's work, and if any man's deeds fall short, his pedigree will not help him."

I heard from al-Ḥārith, who heard from Ibn Saʿd, who heard from Muḥammad ibn ʿUmar, who heard from Ḥizām ibn Hishām al-Kaʿbī, on the authority of his father, who said: I saw ʿUmar ibn al-Khaṭṭāb, may God be pleased with him, and he carried the *dīwān* of Khuzā'a as far as Qudayd. And there is Qudayd, the Khuzā'a came to him, and no woman, either virgin or married, was absent from him. And he gave them their money into their hands. Then he left the town at evening and halted at 'Usfān, where he did likewise. And so he continued until he died.

Al-Ṭabarī, i, pp. 2726–2735, 2748–2752.

4. Conversations with Mu'āwiya (661–668)

Abu'l-Ṭufayl 'Āmir ibn Wāthila called on Mu'āwiya who said to him, "O Abu'l-Ṭufayl, you are one of those who killed 'Uthmān."

"No," he replied, "but I am one of those who was present and did not help him."

"And what prevented you from helping him?" asked Mu'āwiya.

"What prevented me," he replied, "was that the Emigrants and the Helpers did not help him, and I did not see anyone who did help him."

"And was not my demand for the blood-wit a help to him?" asked Mu'āwiya.

Abu'l-Ṭufayl laughed and said, "O Mu'āwiya, you and 'Uthmān are as the poet said:

I shall find you after death and you will lament for me.
But in my life you did not give me sustenance.

Mu'āwiya said: "O Abu'l-Ṭufayl, what remains of your love for 'Alī?"

"It is the devotion of a childless old woman," he replied, "or of a bereaved old man."

"And how did you love him then?" asked Mu'āwiya. "As the mother of Moses loved Moses," he replied, "and I complain to God that my love falls short."

. . . .

'Amr ibn al-'Āṣ said to 'Abdallāh ibn 'Abbās, "O sons of Hāshim! By God, you have girded yourselves with the blood of 'Uthmān like the blood-stained rags of menstruating slave-girls. You have dishonored it by following the miscreants of Iraq; you have stained it with the rebels of Egypt; and you have harbored his murderers. While the people look only to Quraysh, Quraysh look to the Banū ʿAbd Manāf, and the Banū ʿAbd Manāf look to the Banū Hāshim."

Ibn ʿAbbās said to Muʿāwiya, "ʿAmr only expressed your view, but the ones with the least right to talk of the murder of ʿUthmān are you two. You, Muʿāwiya, encouraged him in what he was doing, but when he was besieged and asked for your help, you lingered and delayed and were pleased with his murder, and you seized your chance to get what you got. As for you, ʿAmr, you set Medina on fire against him, and then you fled to Palestine and did all you could to incite all comers against him. When news of his murder reached you, your hatred of ʿAlī made you join Muʿāwiya, and you sold him your religion in exchange for Egypt."

Muʿāwiya said, "Enough, may God have mercy on you! ʿAmr has exposed himself and me to you and gained nothing."

ʿAmr ibn al-ʿĀṣ came to Muʿāwiya with the proposal that he should grant him Egypt, and he would offer him allegiance as Caliph [*bayʿa*]. Muʿāwiya said, "I do not wish people to say that you only gave me your allegiance in return for a governorship and a bribe."

Then Marwān ibn al-Ḥakam said to ʿAmr, "O ʿAmr, this is not a day for requests, for things have come right thanks to you. Therefore, do not retreat but continue to advance them."

"O Marwān!" replied ʿAmr, "I came to Muʿāwiya when his cause was on a slippery slope and was in danger of bursting open like a packsaddle. I brought him new strength again and again, until I left him like the heavenly sphere. By God, if I were to leave him now, doubts and difficulties would drain his strength until what he now approaches would turn away from him."

Marwān said, "If God has used you to achieve a purpose, He has also used him, like you, to remove obstacles and help to reach a good result. Therefore, approach him, for he is favorable to you."

Then he said to Muʿāwiya, "Man! The one involves the other: therefore, act quickly and write him what he asks. ʿAmr is not a man with whom to stint the bounty for which he asks."

He therefore wrote it for him, and Mu'āwiya said to the secretary, "Write: The conditions of appointment cannot nullify the obedience due." "No," said 'Amr, "Write: The obedience due cannot nullify the conditions of appointment."

When Muḥammad ibn Abī Bakr, may God be pleased with them both, was killed in Egypt, 'Amr seized control of it and Mu'āwiya's cause prevailed. But 'Amr sent nothing from Egypt to Mu'āwiya. Mu'āwiya's people used to ask him to write to 'Amr about the gifts of Egypt, and he used to answer, " 'Amr is a willful, greedy, grasping man; therefore excuse me from writing to him. You can write to him"—and they used to write to him, and he did not send them anything. Then they said to Mu'āwiya, "Dismiss him," and he said, "As for dismissing him, no. But I will frighten him into coming here, and that will be like dismissal in his eyes." He therefore wrote to him, and he came.

"O 'Amr," said Mu'āwiya, "It has reached me that you stand in the pulpit in Egypt and you recite your prowess at the battle of Ṣiffīn. If this was for God, then He owes you a reward, and if for this world, we have already rewarded you generously. Do you know that you have defaulted on your conditions by rejecting my letters?"

"I have rejected no letters of yours," said 'Amr, "which I knew to be from you, though letters did reach me purporting to speak for you. As for my standing in the pulpit, I did not intend by this to reproach you. As for what you say about having rewarded me greatly in Egypt, that was why I swore allegiance to you."

Mu'āwiya said, "Go to your quarters," and he went. Then he returned to him on the next day, and said: "O Commander of the Faithful! I have not ceased to enjoy the best of everything in Egypt until I returned to you, and I thought that I should come to you with what I have brought you so that you may do as you think fit."

Mu'āwiya said, "Hold on to what you have. You should know that if people invite you to a banquet (or he may have said table) they expect you to eat. If you wish, eat. If you wish, go hungry. I only gave you Egypt to be of service to you; therefore, go back to your work."

Al-Balādhurī, *Ansāb al-ashrāf*, iva, pp. 76, 78–80.

5. The Arrival of al-Ḥajjāj in Kūfa (694–695)

Al-Ḥajjāj set out for Iraq as governor, with 1,200 men mounted on thoroughbred camels. He arrived in Kūfa unannounced, early in the day. Bishr ibn Marwān had sent Muhallab against the Kharijites. Al-Ḥajjāj went straight to the mosque, and with his face hidden by a red silk turban, he mounted the pulpit and said, "Here, people!" They thought that he and his companions were Kharijites and were concerned about them. When the people were assembled in the mosque he rose, bared his face, and said:

"*I am the son of splendor, the scaler of high places.*
When I take off my turban you know who I am.

By God, I shall make evil bear its own burden; I shall shoe it with its own sandal and recompense it with its own like. I see heads before me that are ripe and ready for plucking, and I am the one to pluck them, and I see blood glistening between the turbans and the beards.

. . . .

"By God, O people of Iraq, people of discord and dissembling and evil character! I cannot be squeezed like a fig or scared like a camel with old water skins. My powers have been tested and my experience proved, and I pursue my aim to the end. The Commander of the Faithful emptied his quiver and bit his arrows and found me the bitterest and hardest of them all. Therefore he aimed me at you. For a long time now you have been swift to sedition; you have lain in the lairs of error and have made a rule of transgression. By God, I shall strip you like bark, I shall truss you like a bundle of twigs, I shall beat you like stray camels. Indeed, you are like the people of "a village which was safe and calm, its sustenance coming in plenty from every side, and they denied the grace of God, and God let them taste the garment of hunger and of fear for what they had done" [Qur'ān, xvi, 112]. By God, what I promise, I fulfill; what I purpose, I accomplish; what I measure, I cut off. Enough of these gatherings and this gossip and "he said" and "it is said!" What do you say? You are far away from that! I swear by God that you will keep strictly to the true path, or I shall punish every man of you in his body. If after three days I find any member of Muhallab's[1] expedition, I shall shed his blood and seize his possessions." Then he went to his house.

Al-Jāḥiẓ, *Al-Bayān wa'l-Tabyīn,* ii, pp. 307–310.
(cf. al- Ṭabarī, ii, pp. 863–5; Ibn Qutayba,
'Uyūn, ii, p. 243; al-Qalqashandī, *Ṣubḥ,* i, p. 218).

6. Revolution from the East (c.716)

Muḥammad ibn 'Alī ibn 'Abdallāh[1] said to his emissaries [*dā'ī*] when he was dispatching them to the various provinces, "In Kūfa and its region they are partisans [*Shī'a*] of 'Alī and his descendants. In Basra and its region they are 'Uthmāniyya[2] who believe in abstention and who say, 'It is better to be 'Abdallāh the murdered than 'Abdallāh the murderer.' In Mesopotamia they are fractious Kharijites and Bedouin-like infidel barbarians and Muslims who behave like Christians. In Syria they know of nothing but obedience to the Umayyads, fierce hatred to others, and massive ignorance. In Mecca and Medina they are obsessed with Abū Bakr and 'Umar. Give your attention to the people of Khurāsān, for they are numerous and steadfast, with strong breasts and uncommitted hearts, not divided by passions and not corrupted by discord. They are an army with terrifying bodies, shoulders, backs, heads, beards, whiskers, and voices, uttering fearsome sounds that issue from dreadful depths. I take good omen from the East, where the light of the world and the lamp of mankind rises."

Ibn al-Faqīh, *Kitāb al-Buldān,* p. 315.

[1] An Arab general commanding an expeditionary force in the East. The reference is to absentees and deserters.

[1] An ancestor of the 'Abbasids who is credited with having initiated their claims to the Caliphate in about 716. See *EI*², "Hāshimiyya."

[2] A term applied to those who defended the claims of the first three Caliphs against the arguments of the *Shī'a.* They would neither defend nor attack the Umayyads.

7. The Fall of the Umayyads (Mid-Eighth Century)

One day a group of people gathered in the presence of al-Manṣūr,[1] and they spoke of the Umayyad Caliphs, their way of life, their conduct of affairs, and the cause which led to their loss of power. Al-Manṣūr said, "'Abd al-Malik was a tyrant who took no thought of what he did. Sulaymān cared only for his belly and his private parts. 'Umar ibn 'Abd al-'Azīz was a one-eyed man among the blind. The best man of that family was Hishām. The Umayyads kept a firm grip on the authority that had been prepared for them, containing it, defending it, and preserving what God had given them, while keeping to the highest and rejecting the lowest of things. This continued until their authority passed to their pampered sons, whose only care was the pursuit of passion and the quest for pleasure in those things which are forbidden by Almighty God, unaware of God's stealthy retribution[2] and lulled by His cunning. So they discarded the preservation of the Caliphate, made light of the rights of Almighty God and the duties of sovereignty, and became too feeble to govern. Then God deprived them of power, covered them with shame, and withdrew His grace from them."

Ṣāliḥ ibn 'Alī said, "O Commander of the Faithful, when 'Abdallāh ibn Marwān[3] came fleeing to the land of the Nubians with his followers, the king of the Nubians enquired about their position and condition, about what had befallen them and how they behaved. When he had learned all this, he rode to meet 'Abdallāh and asked him various questions about the affairs of his family and the cause of their downfall. He then said to him words which I do not remember, after which he expelled them from his country. If the Commander of the Faithful cares to summon 'Abdallāh, he could tell the story himself."

Al-Manṣūr therefore had him brought out of prison, and when

[1] The Caliph al-Manṣūr; reigned 754–775.
[2] Cf. Qur'ān, vii, p. 181 and lxviii, p. 44.
[3] The son of the last Umayyad Caliph.

he was in his presence he said to him, "'Abdallāh, tell me the story of your encounter with the king of the Nubians."

'Abdallāh replied, "O Commander of the Faithful, I got to Nubia and I had been there for three days when the king came to me. He sat on the ground, although a valuable carpet had been spread for him, and when I asked him what prevented him from sitting on my carpet he replied, 'Because I am a king, and it is a king's duty to humble himself before the might of God Who set him up.' Then he asked me, 'Why do you drink wine, when it is forbidden you in your Book? I answered, 'Our slaves and followers have made bold to do this.' He asked me, 'Why do you trample the crops with your horses when such wrongdoing is forbidden to you in your Book?' I replied, 'Our slaves and followers did this out of their ignorance.' He asked, 'Why do you wear brocade and silk and gold when these are forbidden to you in your Book and in your religion?' I replied, 'We have lost our kingdom, and we have sought the help of foreigners who entered our religion and wear those clothes in spite of us.' The king bowed his head, sometimes turning his hand and sometimes rapping the ground and saying, 'Our slaves and our followers and foreigners who have entered our religion.' Then he raised his head and said, 'It is not as you have said, but you are people who have made licit what God has proscribed and have done what you were forbidden to do and oppressed where you have reigned. Therefore, Almighty God deprived you of power and clothed you in shame for your sins. God's vengeance against you has not reached its end, and I fear lest His punishment descend on you while you are in my country and it touch me together with you. The claim of hospitality is three days. Therefore provision yourself with whatever you need and leave my country.' And so I did."

Al-Manṣūr was astonished and sat for a while in silence. Then he took pity on him and thought of setting him free, but 'Isā ibn 'Alī reminded him that this man had received the oath of allegiance as heir apparent, so he sent him back to prison.

Al-Mas'ūdī, *Murūj al-Dhahab*, vi, pp. 161–165.

2

The Abbasids

The ʿAbbasids shifted the center of the Empire to Iraq when they established a new capital at Baghdad. They reigned until 1258, when they were overthrown by the Mongols, but their period of effective rule was much shorter than that. The following excerpts illustrate some aspects of the politics of the Caliphate abroad and at home and the decline of the caliphal power to the advantage of their ministers and generals.

8. Between Baghdad and Constantinople (797–806)

A woman[1] came to rule over the Romans[2] because at the time she was the only one of their royal house who remained. She wrote to the Caliphs al-Mahdī and al-Hādī and to al-Rashīd[3] at the beginning of his Caliphate with respect and deference and showered him with gifts. When her son [Constantine VI] grew up and came to the throne in her place, he brought trouble and disorder and provoked al-Rashīd. The empress, who knew al-Rashīd and feared his power, was afraid lest the kingdom of the Romans pass away and their country be ruined. She therefore overcame her son by cunning and put out his eyes so that the kingdom was taken from him and returned to her. But the people of their kingdom disapproved of this and hated her for it. Therefore Nikephoros,[4] who was her secretary, rose against her, and they helped

[1] The Byzantine Empress Irene; reigned 797–802.
[2] Arabic Rūm—the common term in Islamic usage for Byzantines and, more generally, for Greek Christians.
[3] Al-Mahdī (775–785); al-Hādī (785–786); Hārūn al-Rashīd (786–809).
[4] Reigned 802–811.

and supported him so that he seized power and became the ruler of the Romans.

When he was in full control of his kingdom, he wrote to al-Rashīd, "From Nikephoros, the king of Romans, to al-Rashīd, the king of the Arabs, as follows: That woman put you and your father and your brother in the place of kings and put herself in the place of a commoner. I put you in a different place and am preparing to invade your lands and attack your cities, unless you repay me what that woman paid you. Farewell!"

When his letter reached al-Rashīd, he replied, "In the name of God, the Merciful and the Compassionate, from the servant of God, Hārūn, Commander of the Faithful, to Nikephoros, the dog of the Romans, as follows: I have understood your letter, and I have your answer. You will see it with your own eye, not hear it." Then he at once sent an army against the land of the Romans of a size the like of which was never heard before and with commanders unrivaled in courage and skill. When news of this reached Nikephoros, the earth became narrow before him and he took counsel. Al-Rashīd advanced relentlessly into the land of the Romans, killing, plundering, taking captives, destroying castles, and obliterating traces, until they came to the narrow roads before Constantinople, and when they reached there, they found that Nikephoros had already had trees cut down, thrown across these roads, and set on fire. The first who put on the garments of the naphtha-throwers was Muḥammad ibn Yazīd ibn Mazyad. He plunged boldly through, and then the others followed him.

Nikephoros sent gifts to al-Rashīd and submitted to him very humbly and paid him the poll tax for himself as well as for his companions.

On this Abu'l-'Atāhiya[5] said:

O Imam of God's guidance, you have become the guardian of religion, quenching the thirst of all who pray for rain.
You have two names drawn from righteousness [rashād] *and guidance* [hudā], *for you are the one called Rashīd and Mahdī,*
Whatever displeases you becomes loathsome; if anything pleases you, the people are well pleased with it.

[5] A famous Arabic poet, who died in 825 or 826.

You have stretched out the hand of nobility to us, east and west, and bestowed bounty on both easterner and westerner.
You have adorned the face of the earth with generosity and munificence, and the face of the earth is adorned with generosity.
O, Commander of the Faithful, brave and pious, you have opened that part of benevolence which was closed!
God has destined that the kingdom should remain to Hārūn, and God's destiny is binding on mankind.
The world submits to Hārūn, the favored of God, and Nikephoros has become the dhimmī *of Hārūn.*

Then al-Rashīd went back, because of what Nikephoros had given him, and got as far as Raqqa. When the snow fell and Nikephoros felt safe from attack, he took advantage of the respite and broke the agreement between himself and al-Rashīd and returned to his previous posture. Yaḥyā ibn Khālid [the vizier], let alone any other, did not dare to inform al-Rashīd of the treachery of Nikephoros. Instead, he and his sons offered money to the poets to recite poetry and thereby inform al-Rashīd of this. But they all held back and refrained, except for one poet from Jedda, called Abū Muḥammad, who was very proficient, strong of heart and strong of poetry, distinguished in the days of al-Ma'mūn and of very high standing. He accepted the sum of 100,000 dirhams from Yaḥyā and his sons and then went before al-Rashīd and recited the following verses:

Nikephoros has broken the promise he gave you, and now death hovers above him.
I bring good tidings to the Commander of the Faithful, for Almighty God is bringing you a great victory.
Your subjects hail the messenger who brings the good news of his treachery
Your right hand craves to hasten to that battle which will assuage our souls and bring a memorable punishment.
He paid you his poll tax and bent his cheek in fear of sharp swords and in dread of destruction.
You protected him from the blow of swords which we brandished like blazing torches.
You brought all your armies back from him and he to whom you gave your protection was secure and happy.

Nikephoros! If you played false because the Imam was far from you, how ignorant and deluded you were!
Did you think you could play false and escape? May your mother mourn you! What you thought is delusion.
Your destiny will throw you into its brimming depths; seas will envelop you from the Imam.
The Imam has power to overwhelm you, whether your dwelling be near or far away.
Though we may be neglectful the Imam does not neglect that which he rules and governs with his strong will.
A king who goes in person to the holy war! His enemy is always conquered by him.
O you who seek God's approval by your striving, nothing in your inmost heart is hidden from God.
No counsel can avail him who deceives his Imam, but counsel from loyal counsellers deserves thanks.
Warning the Imam is a religious duty, an expiation and a cleansing for those who do it.

When he recited this, al-Rashīd asked, "Has he done that?" and he learned that the viziers had used this device to inform him of it. He then made war against Nikephoros while the snow still remained and conquered Heraclea at that time.

Abu'l-Faraj al-Iṣfahānī, *Al-Aghānī*, xvii, pp. 44–46.

9. The Death of al-Mutawakkil (847–861)

It is said that on the feast of 'Id al-Fiṭr [247/861], al-Mutawakkil rode on horseback between two lines of soldiers four miles long. Everybody walked on foot in front of him. He conducted the public prayer and then returned to his palace, where he took a handful of earth and put it on his head. They asked him why and he replied, "I have seen the immensity of this gathering, I have seen them subject to me, and it pleased me to humble myself before Almighty God." The day after the feast he did not send for any of his boon companions. The third day, Tuesday, 3 Shawwāl [December 10] he was lively, merry, and happy. . . .

The singer Ibn al-Ḥafṣī, who was present at the party, said:

The Commander of the Faithful was never merrier than on that day. He began his party and summoned his boon companions and singers, who came. Qabīḥa, the mother of al-Muʿtazz, presented him with a square cape of green silk, so splendid that no one had ever seen its like. Al-Mutawakkil looked at it for a long time, praised it and admired it greatly and then ordered that it be cut in two and taken back to her, saying to her messenger, "She can remember me by it." Then he added, "My heart tells me that I shall not wear it, and I do not want anyone else to wear it after me; that is why I had it torn." We said to him, "Master, today is a day of joy. God preserve you, O Commander of the Faithful, from such words." He began to drink and make merry, but he repeated, "By God, I shall soon leave you." However, he continued to amuse and enjoy himself until nightfall.

Some said that al-Mutawakkil had decided, together with al-Fatḥ [ibn Khāqān], to call next day, Thursday 5th Shawwāl [December 12], on ʿAbdallāh ibn ʿUmar al-Bāziyār to ask him to murder al-Muntaṣir and to kill Waṣīf, Bughā, and other commanders and leaders of the Turks.

On the previous day, Tuesday, according to Ibn al-Ḥafsī, the Caliph subjected his son al-Muntaṣir to heavy horseplay, sometimes abusing him, sometimes forcing him to drink more than he could hold, sometimes having him slapped, and sometimes threatening him with death.

It is reported, on the authority of Hārūn ibn Muḥammad ibn Sulaymān al-Hāshimī, who said that he had heard it from one of the women behind the curtain, that al-Mutawakkil turned toward al-Fatḥ and said to him, "I shall renounce God and my kinship with the Prophet of God (may God bless and save him) if you don't slap him (that is, al-Muntaṣir)." Al-Fatḥ rose and slapped the back of his neck twice. Then al-Mutawakkil said to those present, "Be witnesses, all of you, that I declare al-Mustaʿjil—al-Muntaṣir—deprived of his rights to my succession." Then he turned to him and said, "I gave you the name of al-Muntaṣir [the triumphant] but people called you al-Muntaẓir [the expectant] because of your foolishness. Now you have become al-Mustaʿjil [the urgent]."

"O, Commander of the Faithful," replied al-Muntaṣir, "If you were to give the orders to behead me, it would be more bearable than what you are doing to me!"

"Give him a drink!" cried al-Mutawakkil and called for supper, which was brought. It was late at night. Al-Muntaṣir went out and ordered Bunān, the page of Aḥmad ibn Yaḥyā, to follow him. When he had gone the table was placed before al-Mutawakkil who began to eat and gobble. He was drunk.

It is related on the authority of Ibn al-Ḥafsī that when al-Muntaṣir left to return to his own quarters, he took the hand of Zurāfa and asked him to accompany him. "But my Lord," said Zurāfa, "the Commander of the Faithful has not yet risen." "The Commander of the Faithful," said al-Muntaṣir, "is overcome by drink, and Bughā and the boon companions will soon leave. I would like to talk to you about your son. Utamish has asked me to marry his son to your daughter and your son to his daughter."

"We are your slaves, my lord," replied Zurāfa, "and at your orders." Al-Muntaṣir then took him by the hand and led him away. Zurāfa had earlier said to me, "Be calm, for the Commander of the Faithful is drunk and will soon recover. Tamra called me and asked me to ask you to go to him. Let us therefore go together to his quarters." "I shall go there ahead of you," I said, and Zurāfa left with al-Muntaṣir for his quarters.

Bunān, the page of Aḥmād ibn Yaḥya, related that al-Muntaṣir said to him, "I have united Zurāfa's son to Utamish's daughter and Utamish's son to Zurāfa's daughter."

"My lord," asked Bunān, "where are the confetti, for in that lies the beauty of such a union."

"Tomorrow, please God!" he said, "for today has already passed."

Zurāfa had gone to Tamra's quarters. He entered and called for food, which was brought to him, but he had hardly begun to eat when we heard a noise and shouting. We stood up. "It is only Zurāfa leaving Tamra's quarters," said Bunān. Suddenly Bughā appeared before al-Muntaṣir, who asked, "What is this noise?"

"Good tidings, O, Commander of the Faithful," said Bughā. "What are you saying, wretch?" said al-Muntaṣir.

"May God give you a great reward in return for our master the

Commander of the Faithful. He was God's slave. God called him, and he went."

Al-Muntaṣir held an audience and gave orders to close the door of the room in which al-Mutawakkil had been murdered, as well as that of the audience chamber. All the doors were closed. He then sent for Waṣīf and ordered him to summon al-Muʿtazz and al-Mu'ayyad, in the name of al-Mutawakkil.

It is reported, on the authority of ʿAthʿath, that when al-Muntaṣir had risen and gone, taking Zurāfa with him, al-Mutawakkil had sent for his table. Bughā the younger, known as al-Sharābī, was standing by the curtain. On that day it was the turn of Bughā the elder to be on duty in the palace, but as he was in Ṣumayṣāt at the time he had himself replaced by his son Mūsā, whose mother was al-Mutawakkil's maternal aunt. Bughā the younger entered the gathering and ordered the boon companions of the Caliph to return to their quarters.

"It is not yet time for them to go," al-Fatḥ said to him, "the Commander of the Faithful has not yet risen."

"The Commander of the Faithful," said Bughā, "has ordered me to leave no one in the room after he has drunk seven pints [raṭl], and he has already drunk fourteen." Al-Fatḥ objected to their going, but Bughā said, "The Commander of the Faithful is drunk, and his women are behind this curtain. Get up and go!" They all went out, leaving only al-Fatḥ, ʿAthʿath, and four of the Caliph's servants, Shafīʿ, Faraj the younger, Mu'nis, and Abū ʿIsā Mārid al-Muḥrizī. ʿAthʿath said: The cook placed the table in front of al-Mutawakkil, who began to eat and gobble, and invited Mārid to eat with him. He was drunk, and after eating, he drank again.

ʿAthʿath said that Abū Aḥmad, the son of al-Mutawakkil and uterine brother of al-Mu'ayyad, who was present in the hall, came out to go to the lavatory. Bughā al-Sharābī had closed all the doors except that which opened to the river bank. It was by this door that those who had been appointed to murder the Caliph entered. Abū Aḥmad saw them enter, and cried out, "What is this, villains?" Then suddenly they drew their swords. Leading the murderers were Baghlūn the Turk, Bāghir, Mūsā ibn Bughā, Hārūn ibn Suwārtagīn, and Bughā al-Sharābī.

When al-Mutawakkil heard Abū Aḥmad shout, he raised his

head and saw them and asked, "What is it, Bughā?" And Bughā answered, "These are the men of the night watch, who will guard the gate of my lord, the Commander of the Faithful." When they heard al-Mutawakkil speak to Bughā, they turned back. Neither Wājìn and his men nor the sons of Waṣīf were with them. 'Ath'ath said: I heard Bughā say to them, "Villains! You are all dead men without escape; at least die with honor." They then came back into the hall, and Baghlūn attacked first, giving the Caliph a blow which cut off his ear and struck his shoulder. "Ho!" cried al-Mutawakkil. Hārūn ran him through with his sword, and he throw himself at his attacker, who, however, fended him off with his arm, and Bāghir joined them.

"Wretches!" cried al-Fatḥ, "this is the Commander of the Faithful!"

"Be quiet!" said Bughā, and al-Fatḥ threw himself over al-Mutawakkil. Hārūn ran him through with his sword, and he screamed "Death!" Hārūn and Bughā ibn Mūsā, striking him in turn with their swords, killed him, and cut him to pieces. 'Ath'ath was wounded in the head. A young eunuch who was with al-Mutawakkil hid behind the curtain and was saved. The others fled.

Al-Ṭabarī, iii, pp. 1454–1460.

10. The Story of a Spy (892–902)

When al-Qāsim ibn 'Ubaydallāh became sole vizier after the death of his father, he was a lover of wine and pleasure. He was afraid that the Caliph, al-Mu'taḍid [892–902], might come to know this and find him wanting and think him a shameless sensualist neglecting work for pleasure. He therefore only drank in the strictest secrecy and concealment.

One day when he was alone with his singing slave-girls, he put on one of their dyed garments, called for great quantities of fruit and sweetmeats, and drank and frolicked from midday to midnight, after which he slept the rest of that night. Early next morning he appeared for duty as usual before al-Mu'taḍid, who made no comment. The next day he appeared again, and when al-Mu-

ʿtaḍid's eye fell on him he said, "Well, Qāsim, what if you had invited us to your secret feast and dressed us up with you in your dyed garments?"

The vizier kissed the ground, disclosed something of the truth, expressed his gratitude for the Caliph's pleasure, and went out consumed with worry because al-Muʿtaḍid was so fully informed about him and wondering why his affairs had not remained secret from him.

He returned home dejected. Now he had in his house an informer called Khālid, who reported to him on the affairs of his household. He sent for him, told him what had happened between himself and al-Muʿtaḍid, and said, "If you can find out for me who took this report to the Caliph I shall increase your pay and also give you a reward. If you fail, I shall exile you to ʿUmān!" and he swore an oath to both the offer and the threat. The informer left his presence perplexed and dejected, not knowing what to do. He thought and schemed and tried very hard but could not think of any idea on which to act.

The informer said: Early next day I went to al-Qāsim's house, earlier than my usual hour, because of my extreme sleeplessness and anxiety during the night and because of my keeness to investigate. When I got there the door of al-Qāsim's house was not yet open. I sat down, and suddenly a man appeared, dragging his foot, dressed like a beggar and with the sort of bag that beggars carry. When he reached the door he sat and waited until it was opened, and he went in ahead of me. The porters welcomed him with affection, asked him what news he had, and slapped him on the back. He joked with them, bantered them, and exchanged good-humored abuse. Then he sat in the hall and asked, "Is the vizier riding today?"

"Yes," they said, "he is going out now."

"And what time did he go to sleep last night?"

"At such and such an hour."

When I saw him ask these questions, I guessed that he was the informer. I paid close attention to him and did not see them take much notice of him. There was not a single porter, whether of those with access to the vizier or of those without access, whom he did not question about him. And the porter would answer his questions and volunteer other stories for good measure. Then the beggar went limping into the servants' quarters and dealt with them, and they with him, in the same way. Then he went limping into the general hall, and I asked the servants who he was. "A poor sick fellow," they replied, "simple-minded, but good-hearted. He comes into the house, jokes with everybody and asks for alms. The servants and other staff give him something."

I followed him. He went into the kitchen, and asked what the vizier had eaten, who had been with him at table, and what they had discussed. The cook and his scullions and the master of the table's assistants all had something to tell him. He left the kitchen and dragged himself along until he came to the drinking room, never ceasing to inquire about everything and to converse. Then he went to the wardrobe, still acting and looking the same way. Then he came to the office of the secretaries in the *dīwān*, and began to listen intently to what was happening, questioning one boy after another and one youth after another on and about their business, extracting information at every place and occasion and following it up, mixing jest and earnest and banter in his words. Information flowed to him and was showered on him, and small things were given him with which he filled his bag.

When he had finished all this, he started to make his way to the door. When he reached it, I seized him, brought him indoors, locked him up, and sat by the door. When the vizier was alone, I informed him, and he said, "Bring me the man."

Another version runs as follows: When he reached the door I followed him until he came to a house in the Khuld quarter, which he entered. I stood outside waiting for him, and after a while he came out again, dressed in fine clothes and walking without deformity. I followed him as far as a house near the gatehouse of the Ibn Ṭāhir palace, where he entered. I made enquiries and was told that this was the house of so-and-so the Hāshimite, a man of good character. I lay in wait for him until sunset, when a servant came out of Ibn Ṭāhir's house. He knocked at the door and spoke to my man through a small window. My man called him and threw him a small paper. The servant picked it up and went away.

I returned to the vizier, asked him for a certain number of servants, which he gave me, and went with them at dawn to the house in al-Khuld, and there was the man, dressed as when he went into his own house near the Ibn Ṭāhir palace. I surprised him in the room and found that he had already taken off these clothes and had put on the beggar's garments in which I had first seen him. I carried him away, covering his face and keeping the matter secret, and brought him to al-Qāsim's house, where I went to see al-Qāsim and told him the whole story. Al-Qāsim turned over the business on which he was engaged to someone else, and when we were alone, he summoned the man and said to him, "Tell me the truth about yourself or you will never see the light of day again, nor, by God, will you ever walk out of this room."

"Do you promise me safety?" the man asked.

"Yes," said the vizier, "you are safe."

Then he stood up, without deformity. Al-Qāsim was astonished, and the man said, "I inform you that I am so-and-so, the son of so-and-so the Hashimite, a man of good character, and I have been spying on you for al-Muʿtaḍid since such-and-such a date. I live in the street of Yaʿqūb, near the Ibn Ṭāhir palace, and al-Muʿtaḍid pays me fifty dinars a month. I go out every day, dressed so as not to attract attention of the neighbors, and I go into a house in al-Khuld where I have rented a room. The people there think me one of their own kind and pay no attention to my clothes. I go out of there in these clothes, wearing a false beard of a different color over my own, so that if by chance I meet an acquaintance in the street, he would not recognize me. Then I go limping from al-Khuld to your house, where I do what you already know, collecting information about you from your servants. They do not know my purpose, and they let themselves go in casual conversation, telling me things which they would never reveal if they were offered money for it. Then I go back to my room in al-Khuld, change my clothes, give to the poor the things which I have collected in my beggar's bag, put on the clothes in which my neighbors know me, return to my own house, and eat, drink, and enjoy myself for the rest of the day.

At sunset a servant from the Ibn Ṭāhir palace entrusted with this duty comes, and I throw him from the window a paper with my report for the day, without opening the door to him. Every twenty-nine days when the servant comes, I go down to him, give him my report for that day, and he gives me my pay for that month. If I had seen your informer and realized what he was, this would not have happened to me. Even if I had only caught a single glimpse of him, I would have seen that he was a spy, I would have gone back from the place where I saw him, and he would have known nothing about me. But it happened as it did because my predestined time had come. O God, my God, my blood is forfeit."

The vizier asked: "Tell me the truth, what did you report to al-Muʿtaḍid about me?" and he mentioned various things he had reported, including the story of the dyed garment. Al-Qāsim kept him prisoner for several days and kept everything secret. He sent me to the man's house and told me to keep an eye on the matter and see what happened next. I went to the house which he had described in the street of Yaʿqūb and stayed there until sunset. Then the servant came and shouted for him, and a slave-girl replied, "He has not returned today. He has never done this before, and by God we are greatly disturbed." The servant went away, and so did I. The next day I returned at sunset. The servant came and the slave-girl said, "He has not come today either. By God, we are even more anxious, and we are afraid that something may have happened to him that we do not know about." The servant went away, and so did I.

Next day I returned. The servant returned, and was told, "By God we have given up hope of seeing him again. We can no longer doubt that he is dead, and the ceremonies of mourning have already been arranged in his mother's and his uncle's house."

The servant went away, and I reported this to al-Qāsim. Next day he rode to see al-Muʿtaḍid who, when he saw him, called him and said, "Ibrāhīm the Hashimite, that poor invalid! By my life, let him go and treat him well, and you have my surety that in future I shall not set any spies on you. But, by God, if you have done him any harm, I shall hold you alone guilty of his blood."

Al-Qāsim kissed the ground, left, and went home, thanking Almighty God that he had not made haste to kill him. He told us what had happened, summoned the Hashimite, presented him with a fine suit of clothing, gave him money, and dismissed him. Thereafter, his affairs were no longer reported to al-Muʿtaḍid.

Al-Tanūkhī, *Al-Faraj baʿd al-Shidda,* pp. 108–111.

11. The Confessions of a Caliph (934–940)

Al-Rāḍī[1] said to us one day, "By God, I suppose people ask, Is this Caliph content [*rāḍī*] that a Turkish slave should run his affairs and even control finance and exercise sole power? They do not know that this authority [of the Caliphate] was already ruined before my time and that certain people put me in it without my desiring it. I was handed over to the life guards and palace guards, who acted insolently toward me, demanded audiences several times a day, and even came to seek me during the night. Every one of them wanted me to favor him above his fellows and to have his own treasury. To save my life I played no tricks on them, until at last God rid me of them. Then Ibn Rā'iq[2] seized power and acted even more insolently than they in the treasury. He had no peer in drinking and pleasure. If he or his predecessors were told that one parasang away there were horsemen looting property and killing people and if they were told to travel one parasang to fight against them, they would first ask for money and demand arrears of pay—and even so, they might well have taken the money and then not moved. Any one among them or among their companions might commit an offense against my subjects or even my intimates, and if I ordered action against him, my order was not obeyed or carried out or put into effect. What usually happened was that one of these dogs asked me for something, and I had no power to refuse. For if I refused they grew angry, gathered together, and talked.

[1] Reigned 934–940.

[2] The first to hold the title Amīr al-Umarā'—chief amir. He was killed in 942. See *EI*[2], "Ibn Rā'ik."

When this slave [Bajkam][3] came to power, I had in him someone who did not say to me: "I made you, or I enthroned you," as the others used to say. On the contrary, I had the advantage of having made him. I found that if one of his followers committed a wrong, he was not satisfied with less than his execution or severe punishment. If he heard that an enemy had invaded a province, he set out against him without exercising constraint on me by asking for money or exacting arrears of pay. Of course, I was satisfied with him. He served me better than those who went before him and is dearer to me. The best would have been for me to hold all power myself, as did the Caliphs, my predecessors, but fate did not decree this for me."

Al-Rāḍī invited Bajkam several times, never without spending at least 20,000 dinars on robes of honor and other gifts, which he gave him to carry away, and in addition, trays of gold, silver, ambergris, incense, musk, camphor, and crystal. He learned that it was Bajkam's custom, at home and in his circle, never to drink the water that was brought to him until the bringer had tasted it in his presence, pouring some of it into a cup which he had, tasting it, and then serving it to him. Al-Rāḍī himself followed this practice with him. When a dish was served, it was first placed before al-Rāḍī, who ate some of it, and then it was placed before Bajkam. It was the same with the mead and everything else that was served to him. Bajkam begged him to desist from this, but he insisted.

At the last festivity to which al-Rāḍī invited him, Bajkam kissed his thigh and his hand. The Caliph embraced him, drew two rings from his finger, and placed them on Bajkam's finger. One of them resembled "The Mountain" [a famous ruby] in redness and size. Ibn Ḥamdūn looked at me and I at him, and we were distressed that "The Mountain" should be on a hand other than the Caliph's. He understood us, and when Bajkam had left he said to us, "I saw your looks when I gave him the ring, and I think that you supposed that this was 'The Mountain'! It is not, but is the stone which most closely resembles it in the whole world."

[3] A Turkish amir in the service of the Caliphs, who died in 941. See *EI*[2], "Badjkam."

After the death of al-Rāḍī, when I was in Wāsiṭ with Bajkam and he was surrounded by a group of al-Rāḍī's eunuchs, he said to me, "These people tell me that al-Rāḍī wanted to have me arrested during a party to which he had invited me. Is it true?" "The amir knows," I answered, "that at this time there is nothing more to fear nor to hope from al-Rāḍī. By God, we have never observed any such intention in him, whether drunk or sober, in earnest or in jest. He never felt anything but love for the amir and he was delighted with him. On the other hand, he used to dissimulate when he praised Ibn Rā'iq at the time when he was under his control. He lauded him and commended him, but we were not unaware of his inner feelings toward him, even before he had revealed them to us." "You speak the truth, by God," said Bajkam, "and these people lied. What do they know of it? For my part, it was as you say."

I told him of al-Rāḍī's remarks, which I have quoted above, about what people say. He laughed and said, "Al-Rāḍī was intelligent, wily, and a flatterer to the highest degree (that was Bajkam's purport, though perhaps not his actual words) but I held it against him that he was very cowardly. He put his pleasure and desire before his judgment."

I admired the intelligence of Bajkam, who had indeed found al-Rāḍī's only two defects. I then told him that we were aware that the Caliph had written to the amir secretly to authorize him to march on Baghdad and to complain of how Ibn Rā'iq was treating him. "You must," he wrote, "be faithful to the one who has appointed you and dealt kindly with you." "God preserve me," replied the amir, "from the thought that my Master could have wished my death as Ibn Rā'iq wished it, for he gave me an army with a fixed rate of pay and then did not pay me the sums which were due to these troops. In addition, he tried to have me murdered." Then when the Caliph received the amir's letter to this effect, he wrote to him, "By God, I would not wish the least of your soldiers or followers to suffer harm, because of my regard for you and of what your courage and devotion deserve. How then could I desire that which you mention? But since matters have reached this point and since my injunction to you to be loyal and keep faith has resulted in your losing power, and since this is not what I desire, do, therefore, that which would be to your own advantage."

When the amir had read this letter he advanced on Baghdad. "That," he told me, "was how it was, and by God I did not set out until after this letter had reached me."

Al-Ṣūlī, *Akhbār*, pp. 41–44.

3

Syria, Egypt, North Africa

From the ninth century onward, the 'Abbasids gradually lost control of the provinces, which, while remaining nominally under their suzerainty, were in fact governed by virtually independent rulers. One such was the Nubian eunuch Kāfūr, who rose to power in Egypt. He was an exception. More commonly, these rulers were of Arab, local, or Turkish origin. Many of them founded dynasties.

The Fatimids, who ruled first in Tunisia and then in Egypt, were moved by more than personal or dynastic ambition. They were the heads of a great religious movement, the Ismā'īlīs, which aimed at nothing less than the transformation of all Islam. As such, they refused to give even token recognition to the 'Abbasid Caliphs; on the contrary, they claimed that they alone were the true and rightful heirs to the Caliphate, which they would wrest from the 'Abbasid usurpers. The Fatimid Caliphate, which lasted for nearly three centuries, for a while offered a major challenge to the 'Abbasids. They failed, however, to supplant them, and in time declined and disappeared. The Zirid rulers of North Africa transferred their allegiance from the Fatimids to the 'Abbasids, with consequences described in one of the following excerpts. The struggle in Syria between Western and Eastern invaders threw up new forces and leaders. One such was the Kurdish general Saladin, who in time founded his own dynasty. He is remembered chiefly for two achievements: the defeat of the Crusaders and the restoration of Sunnī orthodoxy and 'Abbasid suzerainty in Egypt.

12. Kāfūr (946–968)

Kāfūr al-Ikhshīdī was a black slave eunuch with a pierced lip, a fat belly, ugly feet, and a heavy body. He was taken to

Egypt for sale when he was more than ten years old, in the year 310 [922]. From the moment he entered Egypt, he hoped to become its ruler. The slaver who brought him sold him to Muḥammad ibn Hāshim, one of the tax farmers of the estates, and he sold him to Ibn ʿAbbās the scribe. One day in Egypt he called on an astrologer, who cast his horoscope and said to him, "You will enter the service of a great man and with him you will attain great fortune." Kāfūr gave the astrologer two dirhams, which were all that he had. The astrologer threw them back at him saying, "I give you such good tidings, and you give me only two dirhams! I will add to it! You will become master of this country and more. Remember me."

It happened that Ibn ʿAbbās, the scribe, sent him one day to take a present to the amir Abū Bakr Muḥammad ibn Tughj, called the Ikhshīd,[1] who was then one of the commanders of Tekin, the governor of Egypt. The Ikhshīd sent back the present and kept Kāfūr. Kāfūr rose in his service until he became one of his closest servants. When the Ikhshīd died in Damascus, Kāfūr took over the conduct of affairs. He won people over with coaxing and promises, calming the populace and ending the turmoil that had occurred. He arranged his master's funeral and took his body to Jerusalem and then went to Egypt, which he entered. Abu'l-Qāsim Onujur, the son of the Ikhshīd, was recognized as his successor. Suddenly news was received that Sayf al-Dawla ʿAlī ibn Ḥamdān had captured Damascus and had advanced as far as Ramla. Kāfūr left at once with the army. The great drums were beaten at the entrance to his tent at each of the hours of prayer. He advanced, won a victory, took great booty, and returned to Egypt, having gained great authority. He governed in the name of Onujur, and the commanders addressed him as *Ustādh* [master]. The commanders gathered at his house, and he gave them robes of honor, horses, and other gifts. On one day he gave to Janak, one of the Ikhshīd's commanders, 14,000 dinars, making him his slave until he died.

Kāfūr's power in the state grew. He appointed and dismissed,

[1] The Ikhshīd and his successors ruled in Egypt from 935 to 968.

bestowed and withheld; he was named in the Friday bidding-prayer in all the pulpits except those of Fusṭāṭ, Ramla, and Tiberias, and he was named even in these in the year 340 [951–952]. Every Saturday he held a court for the redress of grievances [*maẓālim*], at which were present the qāḍīs, the viziers, the legal witnesses, and the notables of the city. A dispute arose between him and the amir Onujur, and each was on his guard against the other. Their estrangement grew worse, and the army was divided, a party supporting either one of them. Then it happened that Onujur died in the month of Dhu'l-Qa'da 349 [January–February 961], and it is said that Kāfūr poisoned him. Kāfūr appointed his brother Abu'l-Ḥasan 'Alī ibn al-Ikhshīd in his place, but retained all power himself to the exclusion of the amir, to whom he assigned 400,000 dinars a year. Kāfūr was thus in undivided control of the government of Egypt and Syria.

Dissension soon appeared between the amir Abu'l-Ḥasan 'Alī and Kāfūr, who restricted him and prevented anyone from going to see him. Then Abu'l-Ḥasan fell sick of the same disease as his brother Onujur and died after a long illness in the month of Muḥarram 355 [December 965–January 966]. Egypt then remained without an amir for some days, only the Caliph al-Muṭī' being named in the Friday bidding-prayer, while Kāfūr held sway in Egypt and Syria over both taxes and men. Four days before the end of Muḥarram of that year [January 23, 966] Kāfūr procured a diploma from the Caliph al-Muṭī' investing him as successor of 'Alī the son of Ikhshīd, but he took no title other than that of *ustādh*. He was now named in the bidding prayer in the pulpits after the Caliph.

Great events took place in his time. The army of al-Mu'izz li-Dīn Allāh Abū Tamīm Ma'add[2] arrived from North Africa at the oases. Kāfūr sent an army against the troops of al-Mu'izz which drove them out and killed many of them. The drums were beaten at his door five times by day and night; there were 100 great copper drums. The missionaries [*dā'īs*] of al-Mu'izz came from North Africa to summon Kāfūr to recognize his authority. Kāfūr treated them well. Most of the followers of

[2] The fourth Fatimid Caliph and the first to rule in Egypt.

the Ikhshīd and of Kāfūr, all the pious men and the scribes, had pledged allegiance [*bay'a*] to al-Mu'izz.

In Kāfūr's time the flood of the Nile was deficient. In that year it only reached twelve cubits and some fingers. Foodstuffs became dear, and death was rampant so that they could not shroud and bury the dead. It was rumored that the Carmathians[3] were advancing on Syria and Kāfūr's slaves, consisting of 1070 Turks, apart from Greeks and local blacks [*muwallad*], turned against him. He died when ten days remained of Jumādā I, 357 [April 13, 968], at the age of 60. They found in his possession 700,000 gold dinars, and coined silver, jewels, precious stones, ambergris, scents, stuffs, utensils, furnishings, tents, slaves, slave-girls, and animals, to the value of 600 million dinars. He ruled Egypt and Syria and the two Holy Cities for twenty-one years, two months and twenty days, of which two years, four months and nine days he ruled alone, after the deaths of his master's children. When he died, he had made no will, endowed no charity, and left no monument by which he would be remembered. He was named in the bidding-prayer in the pulpits for fourteen Fridays by the *kunya* which the Caliph had given him, that is, Abu'l-Misk [Father of Musk].[4] After him, Egypt was in upheaval and on the verge of destruction until the coming of the armies of al-Mu'izz, under the commander Jawhar, when Egypt became the seat of the Caliphate.

Al-Maqrīzī, *Khiṭaṭ,* ii, pp. 26–27.

13. The History of the Caliph al-Ḥākim bi-amr Allāh (996–1021)

Al-Ḥākim bi-amr Allāh Abū 'Alī Manṣūr, the son of al-'Azīz billāh Nizār and grandson of al-Mu'izz li-dīn Allāh Abū Tamīm Ma'add, was born in the palace in Cairo on the night of Thursday, 23 Rabī' I of the year 375 of the Hijra [August 14, 985], at the ninth hour of the day, at the moment when the 27th degree of the sign of Cancer was ascending. He was hailed as Caliph

[3] A group of sectarian rebels. See *EI*[2], s.v.
[4] A reference to his blackness.

in the town of Bilbays after the hour of noon on Tuesday, 20 Ramadan 386 [October 7, 996]. On the Wednesday he went to Cairo with the whole court. The body of his father al-ʿAzīz, in a covered litter, was carried before him on a she-camel. Al-Ḥākim wore a plain cloak and a jeweled turban. He had a lance in his hand and a sword hung on a baldric. No unit of the army was missing. He entered the palace before the hour of the sunset prayer and arranged the funeral and burial of his father al-ʿAzīz billāh. The following day, Thursday, the whole court attended in the early morning at the palace. A golden throne had been set up for al-Ḥākim in the main hall, with a gilded mattress. He came out of his palace on horseback, wearing a jeweled turban. Those present were standing on the floor of the hall. They kissed the ground before him and walked in front of him until he seated himself on the throne. Then those whose rule it was to stand, stood, and those whom usage allowed to sit, sat, and all of them hailed him as Imam. The regnal title chosen for him was Al-Ḥākim bi-amr Allāh [he who governs by the order of God]. He was then eleven years, five months, and six days old. As *wāsiṭa* [first minister] he appointed Abū Muḥammad al-Ḥasan b. ʿAmmār al-Kitāmī, with the honorific title "Amīn al-Dawla." He abolished certain taxes which were levied on the coast. To the qāʾid al-Ḥusayn b. Jawhar he gave the postal service [*barīd*] and also the chancery. Al-Ḥusayn's assistant was Ibn Sūrīn. Al-Ḥākim confirmed ʿIsā b. Nasṭūrus as intendant of the administration of domains. He appointed Sulaymān b. Jaʿfar b. Falāḥ governor of Syria. Manjutekin then revolted in Damascus, and having made a sortie to repel Sulaymān b. Jaʿfar b. Falāḥ, he advanced as far as Ramla, where he was joined by Ibn al-Jarrāḥ al-Ṭāʾī and a large number of Bedouin and attacked Ibn Falāḥ. But he was defeated and took flight. He was then arrested and taken to Cairo, where he was honorably received.

A party was formed at court against Ibn ʿAmmār. A struggle took place, which ended in his dismissal from the office of *wāsiṭa*. He had held it for eleven months less five days. He was placed under house arrest and was allowed his salary and rations. The eunuch Barjawān al-Siqillī was appointed as *wāsiṭa* in his place, three days before the end of Ramaḍān 387 [the beginning of October 997]. He appointed his scribe Fahd ibn Ibrahīm to act as secretary in his name and gave him the honorific title of *ra'īs* [chief].

Al-Ḥākim dismissed Sulaymān b. Falāḥ from the governorship of Syria and appointed Jaysh b. al-Ṣamṣāma. He appointed Faḥl ibn Ismā'īl al-Kitāmī governor of Tyre, the eunuch Yānis governor of Barqa, the eunuch Maysūr governor of Tripoli, and the eunuch Yaman governor of Gaza and Askalon. Jaysh attacked the Greeks near Afāmiya, killed 5000 men, and advanced as far as Mar'ash, which he seized. Abū 'Abdallāh al-Ḥusayn b. 'Alī b. al-Nu'mān was appointed chief qāḍī in Ṣafar 389 [January–February 999], after the death of the chief qāḍī Muḥammad b. al-Nu'mān.

Barjawān was put to death four days before the end of the month of Rabī' II 389 [April 999]. He had held his office for two years and eight months less one day. The Caliph transferred the whole care of public affairs, the administration of the realm, and the functions of the secretariat to al-Ḥusayn ibn Jawhar, who was given the honorific title of chief qā'id, with the *ra'īs* Ibn Fahd acting as his deputy.

Al-Ḥākim began to hold his audiences at night, with many of the principle persons of the court attending. Then he stopped this.

Jaysh b. al-Ṣamṣāma died in Rabī' II 390 [March–April 1000], and his son went to Cairo with his estate, taking with him a document written by the hand of his father which contained his will, a detailed inventory of his estate, and a declaration that all this in its entirety belonged to the Commander of the Faithful al-Ḥākim bi-amr Allāh and that none of his children had any right to a single dirham of it. The value of this estate amounted to about 200,000 dinars in specie and in goods and animals. Ibn Jaysh placed all of it under the walls of the palace. Al-Ḥākim took the document, read it, and then returned it to the children of Jaysh; he gave them robes of honor and said to them in the presence of the lords of his court, "I have read your father's will, may God have mercy on him, and the statement of the money and goods of which he disposed. Take it and enjoy it with God's blessing." They then withdrew, taking the whole estate.

Al-Ḥākim then appointed Faḥl ibn Tamīm governor of Damascus and, when he died after a few months, appointed 'Alī ibn Falāḥ. He appointed 'Abd al-'Azīz ibn Muḥammad ibn al-Nu'mān inspector of grievances. He forebade people to address anyone, in speech or writing, as Lord or Master, save only the Commander of the Faithful. He gave license to dispatch summarily anyone who disobeyed this order. In the month of Shawwāl he put Ibn 'Ammār to death.

In the year 391 [1000–1001], al-Ḥākim went riding every night through the streets and alleys, and people outdid themselves with torches and decorations. They spent much money on food, drink, music, and entertainment and enjoyed themselves in this way beyond all limits. Al-Ḥākim therefore forbade women to go out at night, and then he also forbade men to sit in shops.

In Ramaḍān 392 [July–August 1002] he appointed Tamwasalt b. Bakkār governor of Damascus, in place of Ibn Falāḥ.

In the year 393 [1002–1003] he began to rebuild the Rāshida mosque. On 8 Jumādā II of the same year [April 14, 1003] he put Fahd b. Ibrāhīm to death. He had held office as *ra'īs* for five years nine months and twelve days. 'Alī ibn 'Umar al-'Addās was appointed in his place. The amir Marūḥ went to Tiberias as amir of this town. In the same year they began the rebuilding of the mosque situated outside the Bāb al-Futūḥ [Gate of Victories] to complete this building. Al-Ḥākim stopped riding about at night. Tamwasalt died, and the eunuch Mufliḥ al-Liḥyānī was appointed in his place. Al-Ḥākim put to death 'Alī ibn 'Umar al-'Addās, the eunuch Raydān al-Ṣiḳillī, and many other persons.

In Muḥarram 394 [October–November 1003] he appointed Sandal the negro amir of Barqa. In Ramaḍān of the same year [June–July 1004] he dismissed al-Ḥusayn b. al-Nu'mān from the post of chief qāḍī, which he had held for five years, six months, and twenty-three days. He had also held the position of chief *dā'ī* and was entitled qāḍī of qāḍīs and dā'ī of dā'īs. Al-Ḥākim appointed 'Abd al-'Azīz b. Muḥammad b. al-Nu'mān to both offices, in addition to the position which he already held as inspector of grievances.

In the year 395 [1004–1005] al-Ḥākim ordered the Jews and Christians to wear sashes [*zunnār*] round their waists and distinguishing badges on their clothes. He also forbade people to eat mulūkhiyya, roquette, mutawakkiliyya, or tellina,[1] or to slaughter a cow free from defect except for the feast of sacrifices. He forbade outright the sale and making of beer. He gave orders that no one should enter the public baths without wearing a loincloth, that women should not uncover their faces in the street or in a funeral procession and should not bedeck themselves, and that no fish without scales should be sold or caught by any fisherman. He enforced all these rules with the utmost rigor, and many persons were flogged for disobeying his orders and prohibitions.

In the same year the troops went on campaign to fight against the Banū Qurra living in the province of Buḥayra. Al-Ḥākim also caused notices to be placed on the doors of the mosques, on the doors of shops, barracks, and cemeteries, abusing and cursing the early Muslims.[2] He forced his subjects to write and inscribe these curses in different colors in all these places. Then people came from every side to enter the *daʿwa*. He appointed two days in the week for them, and the crowd was so great that a number died.

Al-Ḥākim forbade people to go out into the street after sunset or appear there to buy or to sell. Thus the streets became empty of passersby. Everywhere the wine jars were broken and the wine was spilt. People were seized with terror, horror increased, and alarm became general. A number of secretaries and other persons assembled under the palace walls, shouting and begging for mercy, and many letters of safe-conduct were written for all the personnel of the court as well as for shopkeepers and other people.

[1] Mulūkhiyya (Jew's mallow, *Corchorus olitorius*) is a pot herb much used in Egypt. Tellina is a small shellfish. Mutawakkiliyya appears to have been a pot herb, named for some reason after the Caliph al-Mutawakkil.

[2] It was Shiʿite practice to pronounce curses on Abū Bakr, ʿUmar, ʿUthmān, and others considered to have deprived ʿAlī of his rights.

Al-Ḥākim also gave orders that dogs should be killed, and innumerable dogs were killed so that none were to be seen. A House of Wisdom was opened in Cairo. Books were brought there and the public entered. Al-Ḥākim was particularly severe against the stirrup-holders who were employed at the stirrup. He put many of them to death, then pardoned the survivors and gave them safe-conduct. He gave orders that no person whatsoever was to enter the gates of Cairo mounted. He did not allow anyone to pass by his palace, even on foot. The chief Qāḍī Ḥusayn b. al-Nuʿmān was put to death and thrown into a fire, and a large number of people were killed and decapitated.

In the year 396 [1005–1006], Abū Rakwa rebelled. He made propaganda on his own behalf and claimed to be descended from the house of Umayya. The Banū Qurra, because of all that al-Ḥākim had done to them, rallied to him and pledged allegiance to him. Luwāta, Mezāta, and Zenāta also joined him. He seized Barqa, several times defeated al-Ḥākim's armies, and took what they had as booty. The qāʾid Faḍl b. Ṣāliḥ went out to fight him in Rabīʿ I [December 1005] and encountered him but he, too, was defeated. There was great alarm in Cairo, and prices went up. Preparations were intensified to fight Abū Rakwa. The army made camp at Jīza. Abū Rakwa having advanced, the qāʾid Faḍl attacked him but lost many of his men. This was a shock, and there was great fear. People left the city and slept on the roads, fearing an attack by Abū Rakwa's troops. Fighting continued until Abū Rakwa was defeated near Fayyūm and retreated on 3 Dhu'l-Ḥijja [August 31, 1006]. The qāʾid Faḍl, after having sent 6000 heads and 100 prisoners to Cairo, pursued Abū Rakwa until he captured him in the land of the Nubians and brought him to Cairo, where he was put to death. The qāʾid Faḍl was given a robe of honor, and news of his victory and of Abū Rakwa's death was sent to all the provinces.

In the year 397 [1006–1007], al-Ḥākim gave orders to erase the curses against the early Muslims, and all these writings were duly erased. Prices rose because of the low Nile, which only reached sixteen cubits and sixteen fingers of the seventeenth cubit and then dropped. Manjutekin died in the month of Dhu'l-Ḥijja [August–September 1007].

Prices rose high in 398 [1007–1008]. ʿAlī ibn Falāḥ was appointed governor of Damascus. Al-Ḥākim confiscated all goods belonging to churches and placed them under sequestration. He burned many crosses by the gate of the Fusṭāṭ Mosque and sent orders to all the provinces to do the same thing.

On the 16th Rajab [March 27, 1008] he appointed Malik b. Saʿīd al-Fāriqī to the office of chief qāḍī. He also took charge of the books of the *daʿwa,* which were read in the palace of the initiates. ʿAbd al-ʿAzīz ibn al-Nuʿmān, who had previously held this position, was dismissed. Al-Ḥākim likewise dismissed the Chief Qāʾid al-Ḥusayn b. Jawhar from his office on 7 Shaʿbān [April 17, 1008], and appointed Ṣāliḥ b. ʿAlī al-Rūdhbārī in his place. The bureau of Syria, previously held by Rūdhbārī, was given to the scribe Abū ʿAbdallāh al-Mawṣilī. Ḥusayn b. Jawhar and ʿAbd al-ʿAzīz were placed under house arrest, and they and all their children were forbidden to take part in processions. A few days later, however, al-Ḥākim pardoned them and ordered them to take part. The Nile flood having ceased, public prayers for water were held twice, and the Caliph abolished several taxes. Bread became so dear and so scarce that it was difficult to find. The canal was opened on 4 Tot, the flood being fifteen cubits, and prices rose higher. On 9 Muḥarram 399 [September 13, 1008][3] corresponding to the middle of the [Coptic] month of Tot, the water fell and the flood did not quite reach sixteen cubits. Al-Ḥākim forbade people to hold public musical performances or to indulge in trips on the river. He prohibited the sale of intoxicating drinks and forbade anyone whatsoever to go out into the streets before daybreak or after nightfall. Times were very hard for everybody, because of the great fear which came upon them, in addition to the high prices and the spread of disease and death among people.

In the month of Rajab [March 1009] food prices fell. An order was published, that those who begin and end the fast according to their calculations should do so, but that those who begin and end the fast by the sight [of the moon] would not

[3] In a few places the year is not stated in the text. It has been restored from the parallel passages in al-Maqrīzī's History of the Fatimid Caliphs (*Ittiʿāẓ al-ḥunafā,* ii, Cairo, 1971).

be obstructed.[4] Likewise, those who, in accordance with what has come down to them, perform the *khamsīn* prayers,[5] the morning prayer, or the *tarāwīḥ* prayers should not be prevented or obstructed. At funerals the *takbīr* would be pronounced either five times or four times, in accordance with the various customs and without obstruction; the muezzin would include the formula "Come to good works," but those who omitted it would not be molested; no curses would be pronounced against any of the first Muslims and no action taken against anyone for applying any formula to them or swearing by their name; every Muslim would act in accordance with his own judgment in matters of religion.

Ṣāliḥ ibn 'Alḥ al-Rūdhbārī was given the title of Chief Trustee [*Thiqqa*] of the Sword and the Pen.[6] The qāḍī 'Abd al-'Azīz ibn al-Nu'mān was reappointed inspector of grievances [*maẓālim*]. Sicknesses spread, deaths increased, and medicines became scarce. Taxes which had been abolished were reimposed, the churches which were on the Makas road were destroyed, as was also a church which was in the street of the Greeks in Cairo, and its contents were pillaged. Many eunuchs, scribes, and Slavs were put to death, after some of the scribes had had their hands cut off from the mid-arm with a chopper on a block. The qā'id Faḍl ibn Ṣāliḥ was put to death in the month of Dhu'l-Qa'da of the same year [June–July 1009].

On 11 Ṣafar [400; October 4, 1009], Ṣāliḥ ibn 'Alī al-Rūdhbāri was dismissed, and Ibn 'Abdūn the Christian scribe was appointed to replace him. He acted as secretary to al-Ḥākim and as intendant. He [Al-Ḥākim] wrote, ordering the destruction of the church of the Resurrection. He also established a new *dīwān*, called the Special *Dīwān*, to register property seized from executed persons and others. Sickness increased, and medicines grew

[4] In Sunnī practice, the beginning and end of the fast are determined by observation of the sky. The Ismā'īlīs, like other Shi'ites, fixed the times by computation. The resulting discrepancies, with other differences of usage, sometimes gave rise to recriminations between the two.

[5] Prayers recited during the period of the *khamsīn*, the hot southerly wind that affects Egypt for a period of about fifty days in the spring and early summer.

[6] That is, of both the military and bureaucratic arms of the government.

scarce. Several people found in possession of beer, mulūkhiyya and tellina were publicly reviled and flogged. He destroyed [the monastery known as] Dayr al-Qaṣr and strictly enforced the rule against Christians and Jews, requiring them to wear the special mark. He wrote abolishing the levy of a fifth, the *najwā*, and the *fiṭra*.[7] Ḥusayn ibn Jawhar and his children took flight, as did also ʿAbd al-ʿAzīz ibn al-Nuʿmān and Abu'l-Qāsim al-Ḥusayn ibn al-Maghrabī. He wrote a number of safe-conducts for a number of people, because of their great fear. The readings in the House of Wisdom in the palace were interrupted. The ban on intoxicants was more strictly enforced, and many scribes, eunuchs, and servants were put to death. In Shawwāl [May–June 1010] Ṣāliḥ ibn ʿAlī al-Rūdhbārī was put to death.

On 4 Muḥarram 401 [August 18, 1010], al-Kāfī ibn ʿAbdūn was dismissed both as intendant and as secretary and was replaced in both positions by the scribe Aḥmad ibn Muḥammad al-Qashūrī. Ḥusayn ibn Jawhar and ʿAbd al-ʿAzīz ibn al-Nuʿmān returned to Cairo and were well received. Al-Qashūrī, after holding his posts for only ten days, was dismissed and decapitated. He was replaced by the Christian scribe Zarʿa ibn ʿĪsā ibn Nasṭūrus, with the honorific title al-Shāfī.

Al-Ḥākim forbade people to sail on the canal on boats and had the doors and windows of houses overlooking the canal blocked up. He made the chief qāḍī Malik b. Saʿīd inspector of grievances. The lectures [in the House] of Wisdom and the collection of the *najwā* were restored. Ibn ʿAbdūn was put to death and his property confiscated. Many people were flogged and publicly reviled for selling mulūkhiyya, scaleless fish, and wine. On 12 Jumādā II 401 [January 21, 1011], Ḥusayn ibn Jawhar and ʿAbd al-ʿAzīz ibn al-Nuʿmān were put to death and their property confiscated. Several taxes were abolished, music and games were forbidden, as also were the sale of singing-girls and pleasure parties in the desert.

In the same year Ḥassān ibn Mufarrij ibn Daghfal ibn al-Jarrāḥ

[7] The names of taxes. The *najwā* appears to have been a "voluntary" levy paid by adherents of the Ismāʿīlī sect; the *fiṭra*, a contribution given at the end of the fast Ramaḍān (*ʿId al-Fiṭr*). For another use of the term *fiṭra* see vol. II, p. 63.

threw off his allegiance to al-Ḥākim. He recognized Abu'l-Futūḥ Ḥusayn ibn Ja'far al-Ḥasanī the amir of Mecca as Caliph, took an oath [*bay'a*] to him, and called on people to do the same and obey him, and fought against the armies of al-Ḥākim.

In the year 402 [1011–1012] the sale of dried grapes was forbidden, and written orders were sent out to prevent their import. A large quantity of these dried grapes was thrown into the Nile or burned. Women were forbidden to visit graves and not a single woman was henceforth seen in the cemeteries on public holidays. It was also forbidden to foregather on the banks of the Nile for amusement. It was forbidden to sell fresh grapes except in quantities of four raṭls or less, and it was also forbidden to squeeze out the juice. Large quantities of grapes were thrown into the streets and trampled underfoot or thrown into the river. The import of grapes was forbidden, all the vines of Jīza were cut down, and orders were sent to all parts to do the same thing.

In the year 403 [1012–1013] food prices rose, and the people jostled to get bread. On 2 Rabī' [September 21, 1012] of the same year 'Isā ibn Nasṭūrus perished. The Christians were ordered to dress in black and to hang wooden crosses from their necks, one cubit long, one cubit wide, weighing five raṭls, and uncovered so that people could see them. They were forbidden to ride horses and allowed to ride only mules or donkeys, with wooden saddles and black girths without any ornament. They had to wear the *zunnār* and could not employ any Muslim or buy any slave of either sex. These orders were strictly enforced, so that many of them became Muslims.

On 29 Rabī' I of this year [October 18, 1012] Ḥusayn ibn Ṭahir al-Wazzān was confirmed as *wāsiṭa* and secretary by al-Ḥākim and given the honorific title of commissioner of commissioners. Al-Ḥākim at this time had engraved on his seal these words, "By the help of God the Almighty and Protector the Imam Abū 'Alī is victorious." Several people were flogged for playing chess. Churches were destroyed and their contents pillaged, as also were their tenement houses and the houses pertaining to them. Orders to this effect were written and sent to the provinces, and churches there were also destroyed. In this same year Abu'l-Fatḥ came to Mecca and named al-Ḥākim there in the public prayers and on the coins. Al-Ḥākim gave orders that no one was to kiss the ground in front of him, nor kiss his stirrup nor his hand when greeting him in public processions, because bowing to the ground before a mortal was an invention of the Greeks; that they should say no more than "Greeting to the Commander of the Faithful, and the mercy and blessings of God be upon him;" that in addressing him, whether in writing or in speech, they should not use the formula "May God pray for him," but that in writing to him they confine themselves to these words, "The peace of God, His favors and the abundance of His blessings upon the Commander of the Faithful;" that only the customary invocation should be used for him, and no more; that the preachers at the time of the Friday prayer should say no more than "O God, bless Muḥammad Your Chosen One, give peace to the Commander of the Faithful 'Alī your Well-beloved. O God, give peace to the Commanders of the Faithful the forebears of the Commanders of the Faithful. O God, give your most precious peace to Your servant and deputy [*khalīfa*]." He forbade them to beat drums or to sound trumpets around the palace, so that they marched around without drums or trumpets.

Al-Ḥākim, having bestowed many benefactions, the chief Commissioner Ḥusayn b. Ṭāhir al-Wazzan stopped endorsing them, whereupon al-Ḥākim wrote to him in his own hand, after appropriate blessings and praise of God, as follows: "My hope and fear are of God alone, for merit is His. My forebear is my Prophet, my father my Imam, my religion sincerity and justice. Our wealth is the wealth of God, mankind the slaves of God, and we are His trustees on earth. Pay people their stipends in full and cut nothing. Farewell."

On the 'Id al-Fiṭr, al-Ḥākim rode on horseback to the place of prayer without adornment, sumpter animals, or any pomp, save only ten led horses with saddles and bridles adorned with light white silver, with plain flags and with a white parasol without any golden adornment. He was dressed in white without embroidery or gold braid; there were no jewels on his turban and no carpets on his pulpit. He forbade people to curse the first Muslims and had those who disobeyed flogged and publicly reviled. He prayed on the Feast of Sacrifice, as he prayed on the 'Īd al-Fiṭr, without any pomp. 'Abd al-Raḥīm ibn Ilyās ibn Aḥmad ibn al-Mahdī performed the sacrifice for him. Al-Ḥākim often rode to the desert outside the city. He wore plain sandals on his feet and a cloth on his head.

In the year 404 [1013–1014] he compelled the Jews to wear bells round their necks when they entered the public baths, and the Christians to hang crosses from their necks. He forbade people to talk about the stars, and astrologers disappeared from the streets. They were pursued, hid themselves, and were banished. Al-Ḥākim gave many gifts, much charity, and freed many slaves.

He ordered the Christians and the Jews to leave Egypt and go to the land of the Greeks or elsewhere. 'Abd al-Raḥīm ibn Ilyās was declared heir apparent of al-Ḥākim, and orders were issued that he be greeted as follows: "Greeting to the cousin of the Commander of the Faithful, the heir apparent of the Muslims." A seat was assigned to him in the palace. Al-Ḥākim began to ride about in a white woollen cloak, with a piece of cloth as turban and with Arab sandals tied with cord to his feet, and 'Abd al-Raḥīm took over the whole conduct of government. Al-Ḥākim went to excess in his gifts and returned all estates and properties that had been confiscated to their owners.

In Rabī' II [October–November 1013] he had both hands of Abu'l-Qāsim al-Jarjarā'ī, who had been the secretary of the qā'id Ghayn, cut off. He had Ghayn's remaining hand cut off, so that he lost both hands. Then, after cutting off his hands, al-Ḥākim sent him a thousand pieces of gold and garments, but later he also had his tongue cut out. He abolished a number of taxes, had all the dogs killed, and rode much by night. He forbade women to walk in the streets, and no woman was seen in the streets at all. The public baths for women were closed, the shoemakers were forbidden to make women's shoes, and their shops fell into disuse.

The rumor grew that many would perish by the sword. People

therefore fled. The markets were closed, and nothing was sold. ʿAbd al-Raḥīm ibn Ilyās was named in all the pulpits, and his name was placed on the coinage as heir apparent.

In Rabīʿ II 405 [October 1014] Mālik ibn Saʿīd al-Fāriqī was put to death, after having held the post of chief qāḍī for six years, nine months, and ten days. His grant [*iqṭāʿ*] amounted to 15,000 dinars a year. Al-Ḥākim rode more and more frequently, until he went riding several times a day. He bought donkeys and rode them instead of horses. In Jumādā II [November–December 1014] he put to death al-Ḥusayn ibn Ṭāhir al-Wazzān who had been *wāsiṭa* for two years, two months, and twenty days. He gave orders that all persons employed in government offices should stay in their offices. Al-Ḥākim went riding mounted on a donkey and wearing a head cloth and no turban. Then he appointed the scribe ʿAbd al-Raḥīm b. ʿAbiʾl-Sayyid and his brother Abū ʿAbdallāh al-Ḥusayn as *wāsiṭa* and secretary, and he appointed as chief qāḍī Aḥmad ibn Muḥammad ibn Abīʾl-ʿAwwām. Al-Ḥākim went beyond all limits in gifts, giving grants to sailors, to hangmen, and to the Banū Qurra. The grants he gave included Alexandria, Buḥayra, and their dependencies. He had the two sons of Abuʾl-Sayyid put to death, after holding office for sixty-two days. He appointed Faḍl ibn Jaʿfar ibn al-Furāt as *wāsiṭa,* and then put him to death on the fifth day of his appointment. The Banū Qurra seized Alexandria and its dependencies. Al-Ḥākim rode more and more often, going out six times a day, sometimes on horseback, sometimes on a donkey, sometimes carried in a litter on men's shoulders, sometimes in a boat on the Nile, always without a turban. He gave many grants to soldiers and to [black] slaves. He gave the offices of *wāsiṭa* and secretary to Qutb al-Dawla Abuʾl-Hasan ʿAlī ibn Jaʿfar ibn Falāḥ, known as "the man with the two headships." ʿAbd al-Rahīm ibn Ilyās was appointed governor of Damascus. He went there in Jumādā II, 409 [October–November 1018], and had been there two months when suddenly he was set upon by a group of men who killed some of those who were with him, seized him, put him in a box, and carried him to Egypt. After this he was sent back to Damascus and he stayed there until the eve of the 'Īd al-Fiṭr, when he was taken out of the city.

Two days before the end of the month of Shawwāl of the year 411 [February 13, 1021], al-Ḥākim disappeared. It was said that his sister had killed him, but this is untrue. He was thirty-six years and seven months old and had reigned for twenty-five years and one month. He was generous but a shedder of blood, who killed numberless victims. His way of life was the strangest that can be. He was named in the Friday prayer in all the pulpits of Egypt, Syria, Barbary, and the Ḥijāz. He studied the sciences of the ancients and observed the stars. He made astronomical observations, and he had a house on Mount Muqaṭṭam, to which he used to retire alone for this purpose. It is said that he was afflicted with a dryness in his brain and that this was the cause of his many contradictions. It was well said of him that, "His actions were without purpose and the dreams of his imaginings without interpretation."

Al-Muṣabbiḥī says that in Muḥarram of the year 415 [March–April 1024] they arrested a man of the house of Ḥusayn, who had started a rising in the remotest part of Upper Egypt. This man confessed that it was he who had killed al-Ḥākim bi-amr Allāh. He said that there were four accomplices who had fled to different countries. He showed a piece of the skin of al-Ḥākim's head and a piece of the head-cloth which he was wearing. He was asked "Why did you kill him?" and replied, "Out of zeal for God and Islam." He was asked "How did you kill him?" and he drew a dagger, struck himself to the heart and killed himself, saying "That is how I killed him." His head was cut off and sent to the Caliph, together with the things which were found with him. This is the truth regarding the murder of al-Ḥākim and not the story the Easterners tell in their books about his sister killing him.

Al-Maqrīzī, *Khiṭaṭ,* ii, pp. 285–289 (variants from other texts).

14. The Invasion of North Africa (1052)

It was in this year [443/1051–1052] that the upheaval [*fitna*] in North Africa began.

Account of a Part of This Great Upheaval and of the Destruction of Qayrawān

Ibn Sharaf[1] said: When orders were given to curse the Banū 'Ubayd[2] from the pulpits and when al-Mu'izz ibn Bādīs[3] gave orders to kill their followers, the Banū 'Ubayd allowed the Arabs[4] to cross the Nile. Until then this was forbidden, and none of the Arabs had crossed it. Then [the Fatimid Caliph] issued orders to give a dinar to every one of them who crossed the river, so that a great number of them crossed without being given any orders, for he knew that they needed no urging. They crossed in masses and established themselves in the region of Barqa [Cyrenaica].

Some time passed after this, and then one of them, Mu'nis ibn Yaḥyā al-Riyāḥī, came to see al-Mu'izz. He had turned against his brothers, the Ṣanhāja, and wished to replace them with others; he hated them, but concealed it from them. This Mu'nis enjoyed a position of favor with him. He was a chief among his people, brave and wise. Al-Mu'izz consulted him about adopting his cousins the Riyāḥ[5] as troops, but Mu'nis advised him against it, pointing to their disunity and lack of discipline. Al-Mu'izz however insisted, and said, "You wish to remain alone [in my favor] out of jealousy of your own tribe!" Mu'nis then decided to go and join them, after having argued in his defense, and called some of the Sultan's officers as witnesses. Then he set out in their direction and made proclamation to his tribe. He mustered them, made promises to them, and excited them, depicting to them the generosity of the Sultan and his beneficence to them. After that he led a troop of horsemen who had never known comfort or seen

[1] A North African chronicler who died in 1068.

[2] The descendants of 'Ubaydallāh—i.e. the Fatimids. This form is often used by writers who do not recognize their claim to descent from Fāṭima, the daughter of the Prophet.

[3] A Zirid amir; ruled 1016–1062. By casting off the suzerainty of the Fatimids and persecuting their adherents, he provoked the vengeance of the Caliph in Cairo.

[4] From 'Abbasid times onward, the substantive "Arab" was normally used only in reference to Bedouin. It here refers to the Bedouin tribes of the Banū Hilāl and the Banū Sulaym.

[5] The most important branch of the Banū Hilāl.

inhabited places. When they came to a village, he cried, "This is Qayrawān," and they pillaged it at once.

When news of this reached Qayrawān, al-Mu'izz ibn Bādīs was greatly distressed and said, "This is something which Mu'nis has done to prove his words were true and his advice well founded." He gave orders to arrest his children and women and to seal his house, so as to see what he would do in response. When Mu'nis heard of what had been done to his women and children, he was very grieved and afflicted. "I gave good advice," he said, "and it has turned against me and the fault is ascribed to me." He then did greater damage than his tribe, for he knew the weak points of Qayrawān. The Sultan then sent jurists out to them with messages, conditions, and exhortations. They informed them that the Sultan had restored their families to them and obtained from them promises and agreements to return to their obedience. The Arabs sent some of their shaykhs for this purpose. But later they broke faith with the Sultan and wrought havoc on every side.

The Defeat of al-Mu'izz ibn Bādīs by the Arabs

On the second day of the Feast of Sacrifices [11 Dhu'l-Ḥijja 443/April 14, 1052] the great calamity, the dread disaster took place. The Sultan celebrated the second day of the feast, and on the morning of that day he left for a village known [thereafter] by the name of the Banū Hilāl. At midday news reached him that the whole tribe was approaching. He gave orders to make camp in the clefts and wadis. But the camp was not yet ready when the Arabs burst upon them as a single man. The army was beaten. Al-Mu'izz stood firm with great endurance until the Arab lances reached him and many of his black slave guards[6] had died at his side, sacrificing their lives to save his. The Banū Manād[7] and all the Ṣanhāja and other [Berber] tribes fled, and the Arabs pillaged their tents. The Arabs entered the camp of Sultan Mu'izz and took possession of it. God alone knows what it contained of gold, silver, baggage, effects, furnishing, camels, and horses. There were more than 10,000 tents and such, nearly 15,000 camels, and mules with-

[6] The Zirids maintained a palace guard of bought black slaves.
[7] The Ṣanhāja Berber clan to which the Zirids belonged.

out number. Not one of the soldiers retained as much as a headband.[8] Most of them reached the mountain known as Ḥaydarān, where they scattered. Later they came together again. The people of Qayrawān knew nothing of this, but they were expectant and watchful. On the third day of the feast, Ibn al-Bawwāb arrived with two horsemen. Overwhelmed by dejection and gloom, their condition made question unnecessary. Many asked them for news of the Sultan, and they replied that he was more or less safe. Shortly after he and his sons entered his palace; the rest straggled after him in ones and in groups. Many failed to come. The fate of some was known, but not of others. It was said that the Arabs had taken many of the Ṣanhāja, and others were prisoners."

Ibn Sharaf said: The defeated army consisted of 80,000[9] horsemen and a corresponding number of foot soldiers. The Arabs had 3,000 horsemen and a corresponding number of foot. On this 'Alī ibn Rizq composed an ode, beginning with this verse

The ghost of Umaym came visiting at midnight
when the hooves of the horses were galloping fast

and including this line

Thirty thousand of yours have been defeated
by three thousand; this is, indeed, condign punishment.

The Arabs then reached the outskirts of Qayrawān. The first of them to arrive at a quarter gave his name to the inhabitants, granted them safe-conduct, and gave them his headgear or a scrap on which he wrote a sign to inform the others that he had got there ahead of them. The people of Qayrawān spent two nights in a fear which God alone knows, unaware of what was to befall their city. For two days no one entered nor left; the Arab horsemen roamed freely everywhere, while the people watched them open-eyed.

On the seventh day of the Feast of Sacrifices, the Sultan went out with his troops, accompanied by the common people of Qayrawān, but he could not get beyond the open air prayer-place. The Arabs withdrew the safe-conduct which they had given to

[8] *'Iqāl,* the knotted cord tied around the head cloth.
[9] Probably an error for 30,000, as in the poem cited below.

the country people; they pillaged them all, and the inhabitants fled to Qayrawān. The Sultan gave orders to all to despoil the farmlands around Qayrawān and Ṣabra, that is al-Manṣūriyya. The Muslims were delighted with this and treated the farms as their perquisites. These farms, ravaged and eaten by animals, suffered the fate which God had decreed for them.

On 17 Dhu'l-Ḥijja [April 20, 1052] the Arab horsemen appeared three miles from Qayrawān. The Sultan then went through the town on foot and urged the people to defend themselves and to build, and they began to fortify their houses. Sultan Mu'izz ordered the common people and the market people of Ṣabra to move to Qayrawān and to empty all the shops in Ṣabra. He ordered all the soldiers in Qayrawān, Ṣanhāja and others, to move to Ṣabra and to occupy the shops and marketplaces. This convulsed the city; there was great concern and distress. The black slave guards and the Ṣanhāja laid hands on the woodwork of the shops and on their galleries and tore them down. Within a hour this immense edifice was ruined. The people passed the night in great fear, and in the morning they saw the Arab horsemen. The Sultan forbade the troops to go up on the city wall of Ṣabra. Ibn Sharaf said: Someone whom I trust told me this story: I came out of Qayrawān, traveling by night and hiding by day. Every village I passed had been crushed and consumed. Their inhabitants, men, women, and children, naked in front of their walls, were all weeping from hunger and cold. Food supplies ceased to reach Qayrawān and the markets were deserted. The Arabs kept all those whom they had taken prisoners, releasing none except against ransom, like European [Rūm][10] prisoners. As for the powerless and the poor, they kept them as servants.

Some Details on the Battle at the Tunis Gate, One of the Gates of Qayrawān

When the Arabs attacked this gate, the common people came out to fight them, some with a weapon, some with a stick not big enough to ward off the feeblest dog. The Arab horsemen charged them and overwhelmed them with the swords and lances. They

10 Strictly Byzantines, but sometimes used loosely for European Christians in general.

went down, one after another, on their faces or on their sides. The Arabs laid them out in the space between the end of the brick ovens and this gate. Only those whose time had not yet come escaped. They left none of them, alive or dead, with a rag to cover him. When the Arabs had gone, the families of the dead went to collect their bodies, and the lamentations of the wailing women and of the mourners rose from every side in the streets of Qayrawān. It was a sight and a sound to cleave mountains. Many bodies of strangers were left lying there. Many were wounded and their wounds were so terrible as to drive those who saw them to distraction. Livers were burned,[11] hearts and bodies melted at the sight of little girls who had blackened their faces and shaved their heads in mourning for their fathers and their brothers. It was a day of calamities and misfortunes and disasters, the like of which had never been seen in any place or at any time. The people passed the night in anguish and affliction.

Here ends the abridged account of Ibn Sharaf.

Ibn ʿIdhārī, *Bayān,* i, pp. 228–295.

15. Portrait of a Warrior (1089–1106)

Khalaf ibn Mulāʿib al-Ashhabī, surnamed Sayf al-Dawla, was generous, brave, overbearing, and oppressive. He committed banditry on the roads and terrorized the highways. Qubbat ibn Mulāʿib, a ruined fortress near Aleppo, between there and Salamiyya, is named after him.

In the year 482 [1089–1090], Ḥimṣ belonged to Sayf al-Dawla Khalaf ibn Mulāʿib al-Ashhabī. He attacked Salamiyya, seized the Sharīf Ibrāhīm al-Hāshimī, and threw him in a mangonel from the tower of Salamiyya. He also seized a number of his nephews and held them as prisoners. The rest of them left and appealed to the Caliph and Sultan Malikshāh for help against him. The Sultan's command went forth to the amirs of Syria, Tāj al-Dawla Tutush, the lord of Damascus, and Qasīm al-Dawla, the lord of

[11] The liver is conventionally the seat of the emotions.

Aleppo, and Bozān ibn Alp, the lord of al-Ruhā, and Yaghisighan, the lord of Antioch, to march against Ḥimṣ, to capture Sayf al-Dawla Khalaf ibn Mulā'ib, and to send him to him. They marched against Ḥimṣ and besieged it and sent him to the Sultan. He stayed in prison until Malikshāh died in Shawwāl 485 [November 1092], whereupon the lady, the wife of the Sultan, released him. He came to Afāmiya from Egypt in the year 489 [1096] because the people of Afāmiya had gone to Egypt to ask for a governor to be appointed over them and they suggested him. He arrived on Wednesday the 8 Dhu'l-Qa'da [October 28, 1096] and entered Afāmiya and ruled it. . . .

Some of the Afamiyans who were Ismā'īlīs plotted against its ruler and conspired against him. It happened this way. Six of them came. They had obtained a horse, a mule, and Frankish accoutrements, with a shield and armor, and took this equipment and these animals from Aleppo to Afāmiya. They said to Sayf al-Dawla Khalaf ibn Mulā'ib, who was a generous and brave man, "We were coming to enter your service, and we met a Frankish knight. We killed him and we have brought you his horse and mule and accoutrements." He received them generously and lodged them in the citadel of Afāmiya, in a house adjoining the wall. They bore a hole in the wall and they made a tryst with the Afamiyans for Sunday night, 24 Jumādā I 499 [February 3, 1106]. The Afamiyans came in through this hole, killed Khalaf ibn Mulā'ib, and took possession of the citadel of Afāmiya. . . .

The Ismā'īlīs plotted against the citadel of Afāmiya, and they killed Ibn Mulā'ib in it by treachery, and they took possession of the citadel, but the Franks overtook them and attacked them and besieged them in it until they captured it.

Ibn al-'Adīm, *Bughyat al-ṭalab*, pp. 332–336.

16. Inscription of Saladin (1191) on the Dome of Yūsuf in Jerusalem

In the name of God the Merciful and the Compassionate. His blessings upon Muḥammad His Prophet and his family. Its construction and the digging of the ditch were ordered by our master al-Malik al-Nāṣir Ṣalāḥ al-Dunyā wa'l-Dīn, the Sultan of Islam and of the Muslims, the servant of the two noble sanctuaries and of Jerusalem, Abu'l-Muẓaffar Yūsuf ibn Ayyūb, the reviver of the empire of the Commander of the Faithful, may God lengthen his days and give victory to his standards, during the days of the amir, the great Commander, Sayf al-Dīn 'Alī ibn Aḥmad, may God glorify him, in the year 587 of the Hijra of the Prophet [1191], under the supervision of the amir Nāṣir al-Dīn Alṭun-Bā al-Sayfī, may God grant him success.

RCEA, ix, no. 3447, pp. 174–175.

17. A Visit to Saladin (1192–1193)

News came that Saladin had concluded a truce with the Franks and returned to Jerusalem. Necessity impelled me to go to him. I took as many of the books of the ancients as I could with me, and I went to Jerusalem. I found a great king who inspired both respect and affection, far and near, easy-going and willing to grant requests. His companions took him as model and competed in good deeds. As God said, "We shall take all rancor from their hearts [Qur'ān, vii, 4]."

The first night that I spent in his presence I found a great gathering of scholars who were discussing various sciences. He excelled at the gathering and in his contribution to the discussions. He began to speak of the business of building walls and digging trenches and discussed it with both knowledge and elegance. He was then concerned with building walls and digging trenches round Jerusalem. He took charge of it himself and even carried stones on his own shoulders, so that all, rich and poor, strong and weak, followed his example, including even the scribe 'Imād al-Dīn and the qāḍī al-Fāḍil.

He rode to the works before sunrise and stayed till noon, when he returned to his house, took food, and rested. In the afternoon he rode out again and returned when the lamps were lit. He spent most of the night arranging what he had to do by day.

Saladin wrote me an assignment for 30 dinars a month, on the *dīwān* of the mosque of Damascus. His sons also assigned me allowances so that I had an assured income of 100 dinars a month. I therefore returned to Damacus where I applied myself to study and to giving lectures at the mosque. . . .

Saladin had come to Damascus. He went out of the city to bid farewell to the pilgrim caravan, and when he returned he was seized with a fever. An inexperienced physician bled him, his strength ebbed, and he died before the fourteenth day. Men grieved for him as they grieve for prophets. I have seen no other ruler for whose death the people mourned, for he was loved by good and bad, Muslim and unbeliever alike.

'Abd al-Laṭīf, cited in Ibn Abī Uṣaybi'a,
'Uyūn al-anbā', ii, p. 206.

4

Iran and the East

In the East a new power was rising—that of the Turks. At first these came as individuals—slaves recruited by capture or purchase and trained for military duties. Many reached high positions, becoming generals, governors, and founders of dynasties. They were followed by incursions of free Turks, still in their own tribal organization and under their own leaders. The most important of these were the Seljuqs, a family which appears to have entered the Islamic lands in the late tenth century and which established the great Sultanate during the eleventh century. The first passage is translated from an Arabic chronicle and is probably based on a Turkish family or tribal tradition. The following three are taken from Persian chronicles; one of them deals with an episode in Ghaznavid history; the others with Seljuq rulers. The final passage shows very clearly the new and reduced role assigned to the Caliphate under the aegis of the Sultanate.

18. The Ancestor of the Seljuqs (Tenth Century?)

Tuqaq, which in the Turkish language means iron bow, was a man of resource, discernment, and competence. The king of the Turks left the reins of government in his hands and was illuminated by the lamps of his judgment and resource. One day the king of the Turks, whose name was Yabgū, mustered his soldiers to invade the land of Islam. The amir Tuqaq stopped him from this. The king of the Turks saw in this opposition to himself. Tuqaq went too far and slapped the king's face. The king gave orders to seize and bind him. The amir Tuqaq, becoming angry, resorted to the mercy of God [gap in original] separated from him, and they carried the king to his house. He stayed quietly, like a hyena in its lair, and was perplexed as to his conduct and opinion. He chose to go to amir Tuqaq and conciliate him. Yabgū, the king of the Turks, kept his wiles hidden in his heart until amir Tuqaq died. When the amir Seljuq, the son of the amir Tuqaq, reached the age of puberty, the king of the Turks gave him the command of the army and conferred on him the title Subashi, which in their language means commander of the army.

The wife of the king of the Turks used to make her husband fear the amir Seljuq ibn Tuqaq and prevented him from trusting him or being at ease with him. This woman did not hide herself from him. One day she said to her husband, "Kingship is barren and cannot bear partnership. You will not savor the wine of kingship unless Seljuq is killed, and the dawn of your dominion will not shine unless you let him taste the cup of death. For soon he will trouble your realm and strive for your destruction." This was said within the sight and hearing of amir Seljuq. Thereupon the amir Seljuq went with his horses and soldiers to the land of Islam and was vouchsafed the bliss of the true religion. Choosing the neighborhood of Jand, he drove out the infidel rulers and established himself there. Amir Seljuq lived for a hundred years. One night in a dream he saw himself ejaculate a fire, the sparks of which reached to the East and to the West. He asked an interpretor of dreams, who said, "From your seed kings will be born who will rule the farthest ends of the world."

Al-Ḥusaynī, *Akhbār al-Dawla al-Saljūqiyya,* pp. 1–2.

19. The Looting of Āmul (1035)

Amir Mas'ūd, may God be pleased with him, reached Āmul on Saturday, 12 Rabī' I [426/January 25, 1035], in safety, triumph, and victory. He stopped at a place and gave orders to set up the pavilion and the big tent, and he made camp there in good fortune. Then he told the chief of the office of chancery, Abū Naṣr, that letters must be sent all over the land, by the hand of messengers, announcing the victory which had been won. The letters were written and soldiers and palace pages took them. On Friday he held an audience, with great pomp, at which the 'Alawī[1] and the notables of the city all came to pay their respects. Then the amir said to his vizier, "Sit down in the tent and seat the 'Alawī and the notables of the city, for we have a message for them." So the vizier went to the tent and he seated these people. Then the amir began to drink and make merry, and the boon companions and the revelers joined him. Meanwhile, Abū Naṣr returned, having endured much trouble in dispatching the victory letters and the messengers. I was on duty in the office of chancery when a retainer came and summoned me. I took ink and paper and went before the throne. He made me a sign to sit, and I sat. The amir said, "Write: This is what must be collected from Āmul and Ṭabaristān and what must be collected by Abū Sahl Ismā'īl. Nīshāpūrī gold, 1 million dinars; Greek and other robes, 1000 pieces; *Maḥfūrī*[2] and carpets, 1000 pieces; garments, 5000 pieces."

I wrote this down. Then I rose, and he said, "Take this copy to the vizier and give him my message. Let him tell these people that they must arrange to supply what we have demanded quickly and in full so that we shall not be obliged to send a collector or to write orders of assignment for the army to seize the money by force."

I took the copy to the vizier and presented it to him secretly and gave him the message. He laughed and said to me, "You see how they loot and burn this country and ruin our reputation. They will not get 3000 dirhams! This is a great sin! Even if they turn all Khurāsān upside down, they will not get this gold and these clothes. As for the Sultan, he is busy drinking wine. When he said this, he was thinking of his own luxuries and money and treasures." Then the vizier turned to the 'Alawī and the notables of Āmul and said, "Know that the Gurgānīs, after having unsheathed their swords against their sovereign and rebelled against him and been scattered, will certainly not see this country with their own eyes again. He will set up a strong ruler here, like the

[1] A descendant of 'Alī, and therefore a leading figure among the townspeople.
[2] A kind of textile.

one in Khārazm, to establish order in this country, and you will be free from troubles."

The Āmulīs called down blessings, and then he said, "And know that our lord, the Sultan, has spent a great deal of money to send his army here and to overcome these oppressors, and a contribution to him from these parts would therefore be proper." They said, "We shall obey and do all that is within our power, but this country is poor and its people are impoverished. Our contribution was fixed by decree some time ago as, from Āmul and Ṭabaristān, 100,000 dirhams and an equal quantity of *maḥfūrīs* and carpets. If he asks for more than this, the subjects will endure great hardship. What, therefore, does the lord vizier command now?"

"The Sultan," said the vizier, "has commanded what is in this letter and has given Abu'l-Faḍl such and such a message." Then he read the letter to them and explained the message and said, "I will make it easier for you, in such a way that what is written in the document will come from Gurgān and Ṭabaristān and Sārī and all these parts so that you should not suffer hardship."

When the Āmulīs heard this statement they stood aghast and did not know what to do, and they said, "We cannot reply to this offhand, for no one is able to pay all this money. If it is permitted, we shall return to our people and tell them all about it."

The vizier said to me, "Tell the Sultan what you have heard." So I went and told him, and he replied, "That is fine. Today they have gone to their people; tomorrow they will return ready to pay. This money must come quickly so that we do not have to stay here long."

I came and I said this, and the Āmulīs returned in the deepest distress. The vizier also returned, and the next day the Sultan held an audience. After the audience, when he was alone with the vizier, he said to him, "What should be done today about this money?"

To this the vizier replied, "May my master's life be long! I would be happier if the treasury could be filled from the country, but this amount is immense, and the Āmulīs yesterday gave a very poor response. What, therefore, does my master command?"

"What is written in the document," said the Sultan, "is required from Āmul alone. If they comply willingly, well and good; if they do not, then we must send Abū Sahl Ismāʿīl to the city to take a larger amount by force."

The vizier returned to the tent and assembled the Āmulīs, of whom far fewer had come this time, and told them what the Sultan had said.

The ʿAlawī and the qāḍī said, "Yesterday we held a meeting and went over this matter. A great lamentation arose, and, indeed, they made no response and went away. It is certain that last night many people fled from the city. But we could not flee, for we would not commit a sin, and we remain obedient. Now it is for the Sultan and the lord vizier to decide what the situation requires."

The vizier knew that what they said was the truth, but he did not dare to speak. He therefore summoned Abū Sahl Ismāʿīl, entrusted the notables to him, and sent him to the city. Abū Sahl convened a *dīwān* and assembled the people, and those who fell into his hands informed him about those who had fled, so that there was no place in the city from which wailing and lamentation did not arise. The horsemen and the foot soldiers went and seized the fugitives and brought them back, and Abū Sahl Ismāʿīl distributed written assignments to the army to collect their pay from the people. They set fire to the city and did whatever they wanted and took whomever they wanted, and it was like the end of the world. The *dīwān* did its work, and the Sultan was not aware of what was happening, and no one had the courage to inform him of it and tell him the truth. In four days the army collected 160,000 dinars, as well as twice that amount in random looting, and also various provisions. This gave rise to a great scandal, in that seven or eight months later it became known that some of the afflicted from this city went to Baghdad and appealed to the Caliph, and it was said that they even went on to Mecca, may God preserve it. The men of Āmul are weak but they are eloquent and litigious, and they were right in what they said.

All these crimes and misdeeds are the fault of Abu'l-Ḥasan ʿIrāqī and the others, but it was the duty of the amir, may God be pleased with him, to take proper care in such matters. It is very hard for me to write such words with my pen, but what else can

I do? In history there is no complaisance. If those who were with us in Āmul read these chapters and desire justice, they will say that what I have written is the truth.

Bayhaqī, *Tārīkh*, pp. 460–462.

20. Sultan Malikshāh (1072–1092)

The army which was always at the side of Malikshāh and whose names were recorded in the muster rolls of the *dīwān* consisted of 45,000 horsemen. Their fiefs [*iqṭā*ʿ] were scattered in different parts of the realm so that wherever they went they should have fodder and expenses ready at hand. The justice and statecraft of Sultan Malikshāh were such that during his time nobody suffered any injustice. And if any man appeared, claiming to have suffered an injustice, no one interposed to deny him access. He spoke with the Sultan face-to-face and demanded justice. As the proverb says, "Whose zeal is great, his value is high." Among the good deeds of Sultan Malikshāh are the water reservoirs which he had constructed on the road to the Ḥijāz, the abolition of tolls and protection tax on the pilgrim road, and the granting of an *iqṭā*ʿ and revenues to the amir of the two holy places, who previously used to take seven red dinars from every pilgrim. He showed much kindness to the desert Arabs and the sojourners [*mujāwir*] of the mighty Kaʿba, and some of these revenues still remain.

Give your religion a share of your worldliness
and yourself be censor over yourself
Give every one of your limbs reins of sense
and reason, and a bridle of piety.

Among sports and spectacles his favorite was hunting. I saw his hunt book, written by the hand of Abū Ṭāhir Khātūnī, in which it was recorded that in one day the Sultan had hit seventy gazelles with arrows. It was his rule to give a Maghribī dinar to the poor for every quarry he hit. In every hunting ground in Iraq and Khurāsān he made towers of hoofs of gazelles and wild asses. In the land of Transoxania, in the Arabian desert, in Marj, Khūzistān and the province of Iṣfahān, wherever there was plentiful hunting, he left memorials.

As his seat of government and personal residence he chose Iṣfahān from all his lands, and there he erected many buildings, inside and outside the city, including palaces and gardens, such as the garden of Kārān, the House of Water, the garden of Aḥmad Siyāh, the garden of Dasht-i Gūr, and others. He erected the citadel of the city and the citadel of Dizkūh and kept his treasury there.

Al-Rāwandī, *Rāḥat al-Ṣudūr*, pp. 131–132.

21. Sultan Tughrul ibn Arslān (1175–1194)

Sultan Tughrul was very handsome. He divided his hair into three and threw it behind his back. His beard was copious, and his moustaches were pomaded and reached to the lobes of his ears. He was of full height, with a broad chest and a long neck. No one could lift his mace or draw his bow.

His sign manual was "I seek the help of God alone."

His viziers were the vizier Jalāl al-Dīn, the vizier Kamāl al-Dīn al-Zanjānī, the vizier Sadr al-Dīn al-Marāghī, the vizier 'Azīz al-Dīn al-Mustawfī, the vizier Mu'in al-Dīn al-Kāshī, and the vizier Fakhr al-Dīn ibn Ṣafī al-Dīn al-Verāmīnī.

His chamberlains were the privy chamberlain, the chief chamberlain Karagöz al-Sulṭānī, and the chief of the amirs Jamāl al-Dīn. . . .

Sultan Tughrul was a ruler who was born in the nest of state and grew up in the house of fortune. Kingship came to him unsought; he donned its garment without effort. He was translated from the cradle to the throne and mounted from school, without the travail of study, on the horse of kingship. He was not in bondage to the promise of the days, the coquetry of the years, the influence of destiny and fate. The bird of state entered his snare without bait; the horse of fortune was curbed without bridle or bit. Without enduring the pain of strife or feeling the point of the arrow, he came to a well-laid table, a well-ordered audience, and a well-filled treasury.

All this good fortune, which befell him in his early days, was due to the glorious state, the felicitous rearing, the wisdom and discernment, the conquering sword and triumphant flag of the emperor [*Pādishāh*] of Islam, the glorious lord, the mighty Atābek, the khāqān of the Persians, the sun of the world and the faith, the help of Islam and the Muslims, Abū Ja'far Muḥammad ibn Ildegiz, may God have mercy on him. It happened that one domain was lost from his hand and a petty king set himself up near Iṣfahān in the midst of the province, and the neighboring rulers held back the reins of help and sat awaiting the outcome of the turning of the wheel of fortune. Therefore, without their help or support, Sultan Tughrul relied on the help of Almighty God and on his own strong arm. Within the space of one month he made two campaigns, one to Fārs and the other to Iṣfahān, whereby he rescued both countries and induced the two greedy kinglets to stay at home in their castles. Fortune followed his gleaming sword and success was attached to his auspicious stirrup. The world was subject to his command amid the pomp and state of his kingdom, victory at will, and the quelling and crushing of his foes. The emblem of solicitude was raised concerning the affairs of the gentry and the peasants; all were secure and calm on the banks of sweet waters and grazing in fertile fields. They prayed to Almighty God for the prolongation of his reign and the extension of his beneficence. The flow of justice and the flood of solicitude were required, for before very long all the countries of the world came under the command and were subject to the servants of the mighty Sultan. He, with the glory of Jamshīd, the heart of 'Alī, the body of Tehemten, the hand of Ḥātim,[1] gave every day a new sign of the attributes of empire and the marks of world mastery.

. . . .

The loyalty to the sovereign of the great Atābek and the other amirs who were the servants of the state was joined in his days with growing joy. In none of the sovereigns, his fathers or his grandfathers, may God illuminate their proofs, were all these qualities combined—perfection of mind, plenitude of justice, abundance of knowledge, breadth of magnanimity,

[1] Jamshīd and Tehemten are figures from ancient Iranian mythology, Ḥātim from pre-Islamic Arabian legend. 'Alī is, of course, the cousin and son-in-law of the Prophet.

vigilance, concern, love of scholars, virtue, calligraphy, eloquence, horsemanship, and skill with the javelin and all other weapons, for Almighty God had endowed him with these from the beginning of his life and from the early days of his youth.

. . . .

This auspicious Sultan was the ornament of crown and throne, his deeds were a source of increasing joy and adorned the realm. For ten years, the great lord, the mighty Atābek, the sun of the world and the faith Muḥammad ibn Ildegiz, may God have mercy on him, maintained well-being, security, and happiness in the state, attending to affairs and procuring what was needful, while the Sultan was untroubled by the business of mounts and provisions and undisturbed by the hardihood of underlings. His loyalty to the Sultanate was such that the Atābek's entire concern, in secret and in public, was devoted to one thing—the need to procure for this Sultan what Sanjar and Malikshāh had never had. He sent envoys to different parts and had his name and titles inserted in the bidding-prayer and on the coinage. At all times he proclaimed his sovereignty over Baghdad and sent a man there to require the rebuilding of the Sultan's palace. Now at that time the officers of the Caliphate were planning to use blandishments on the neighboring amirs and to create confusion in the land so as to establish their own rule and extend it over others, but they could not prevail against the Atābek Muḥammad. The Atābek said to a gathering of people, "The Caliphs should busy themselves with sermons and prayers, which serve to protect worldly monarchs and are the best of deeds and the greatest of activities. They should entrust kingship to the Sultans and leave the government of the world to this Sultan."

Al-Rāwandī, *Rāḥat al-Ṣudūr*, pp. 331–334.

5

The Mongols

The coming of the Turks was the first phase in the penetration of the Middle East by the steppe peoples; the second, and more dramatic, was the great Mongol invasion of the thirteenth century. The Turks came in stages and were converted and assimilated; their advent brought new military and political strength to the Islamic world at a time when these were sorely needed. The Mongols came as pagans and conquerors. Their destruction of the Baghdad Caliphate, though of more symbolic than practical importance, was the final blow to the old Islamic order.

The first of the following excerpts comes from a chronicle written by a Persian historian in the service of the Mongols. The remainder are translated from Arabic. The last passage, containing a personal account, is of unusual interest.

22. The Coming of the Mongols (1253–1258)

When Mengü Khan [1251–1259], in the place called Karakorum and Kelüren, which was the original home and the seat of government of Jenghiz Khan, after a meeting of the princes and the amirs, with their common consent, seated himself on the throne; when he had done justice and administered punishment, he turned his attention to ordering the affairs of the realm. He sent armies to the provinces and to the frontiers. Petitioners and men of affairs, Persians and Turks, who had gathered from far and near, were accorded their requests and their business and were then dismissed, as it is written in his history. He sent Bayju Noyon,[1] of the Yisüt nation, with a vast army to protect

[1] Noyon or Noyan is a Mongol term denoting a military chief.

the land of Iran. When he arrived here, he sent envoys to lay complaints against the Ismāʿīlīs[2] and the Caliph in Baghdad. At that time the late chief qāḍī Shams al-Dīn Qazvīnī, who was in attendance at court, appeared one day before the Khan wearing a breastplate. He admitted that for fear of the Ismāʿīlīs he always wore this breastplate under his clothes, and gave some examples of their power and encroachments.

The Khan had observed in the character of his brother Hülegü Khan the marks of a ruler and had detected in his actions the signs of a conqueror. He reflected that since the time of Jenghiz Khan, some countries had been won by conquest or surrender, while others had not yet been liberated; and since the world was of limitless extent, he would send one of his brothers to every part, to subjugate that country entirely and to keep guard over it, while he himself would sit in the center of his realm, in the ancient home of the Mongols, free from care and well-sustained, and would pass his time in tranquillity and in dispensing justice. If any nearby country opposed him, he would send the troops around its capital to liberate it.

Having completed his plan, he appointed his brother Qubilay Khan over the eastern lands, Khitay [China], Machin, Karachanak, Tangut, Tibet, Jurje, Solanga, Gaoli, and the part of India which adjoins Khitay and Machin. His brother Hülegü he appointed to the western countries, Iran, Syria, Egypt, Rūm, and Armenia. These two, with the troops placed under their command, were to form his right wing and his left wing.

After a great assembly [*Qurultay*] he despatched Qubilay Khan to the borders of Khitay and the other above-mentioned countries and assigned an army to him. He appointed Hülegü Khan, with the assent of all the princes, over Iran and the other countries which have been mentioned. He gave orders that the army that had previously been sent, under the orders of Bayju Noyon and of Jurmagun, to Iran, and the army that had been sent to Kashmir and India, under the command of Dayr Bahadur, would both belong to Hülegü Khan. The army which

[2] The allusion is to the terrorist sectarian groups operating from castles in Iran and Syria. They were known in Syria and hence in Europe, as the Assassins. See *EI*², "Ḥashīshiyya" and "Ismāʿīliyya."

Dayr Noyon commanded when he died . . . commanded it, and after him[3] . . . they gave it to Sali Noyon of the Tatar nation. He conquered the land of Kashmir, from which he brought several thousand prisoners. All these troops, which had been under Sali Noyon, wherever they were, have now become by right of inheritance the special contingent [*inju*] of the king of Islam, Ghazan Khan.[4] In addition to these, he ordered that from all the troops of Jenghiz Khan that had been divided among his sons, brothers, and nephews, two men out of every ten were to be taken and assigned to the special contingent of Hülegü Khan, to accompany him and stay with him. The princes appointed those who were to go with Hülegü Khan from among their children, their kinsmen, and their retainers. That is the reason why in this land there have always been and still are amirs of the line and kin of every one of the amirs of Jenghiz Khan, each holding some hereditary office.

Having made these appointments, Mengü Khan sent envoys to Khitay to bring a thousand Khitayan families of mangonel-operators, naphtha-throwers, and crossbowmen. They sent envoys ahead of the army from Karakorum to the banks of the Oxus, in all the extent through which the soldiers of Hülegü Khan were to pass, to forbid access to the meadows and pastures and to build strong bridges over deep streams and profound waters. Bayju Noyon and the troops, which had previously been under the orders of Jurmagun, were ordered to march toward the land of Rūm. In all the provinces provisions were prepared for the army, at the rate of one *tagar* [about 180 pounds] of flour and a skin of wine for every soldier.

When those princes and noyons who had been appointed were ready to leave with their units of 1000 and of 100 men, Kitbuga Noyon of the nation of the Naymans, who had the rank of *Baurji* [intendant], was sent on ahead as vanguard with 12,000 men. He moved swiftly, and when he reached Khurāsān,

[3] Gaps in the text.

[4] Mongol ruler of Persia; reigned 1295–1304. Brought up as a Buddhist, he was converted to Islam and made Islam the state religion in the Mongol Khanate based in Persia.

while awaiting the arrival of the imperial banners, he spent his time in conquering the land of Quhistān.

When the preparations for the expedition of Hülegü Khan were completed, in accordance with custom and to make his farewells, he gave banquets in his camp. His young brother Arīgh Böke and the other princes, having agreed at the spring camp in Karakorum, all gave banquets and offered all kinds of festivities and delights. Mengü Khan, because of brotherly love, gave advice to Hülegü Khan and said to him, "Now you are going with an immense army and innumerable soldiers from the march of Turan to the realm of Iran.

March in glory from Turan to Iran
carry your fame to the blazing sun.

"Maintain in all matters, both general and particular, the usages, customs, and laws of Jenghiz Khan. From the Oxus and to the far limit of the land of Egypt, to every man who submits and obeys your orders and your prohibitions, you should show special kindness and favor and benevolence. But if anyone is stiff-necked and fractious, leave him in the wilderness with his wife, his children, his family, and his kin, exposed to violence and humiliation. Beginning with Quhistān of Khurāsān, destroy utterly the citadels and the fortresses.

Tear down Girdkūh and the fortress of Lammasar
and turn them upside down[5]
Leave not a single fortress in the world,
let not even a piece of earth remain.

"When this is done, advance toward Iraq. Rid the roads of the Lurs and the Kurds who always infest them. If the Caliph of Baghdad hastens to offer service and obedience, do not trouble him in any way, but if he shows pride and if his heart and tongue do not accord, treat him as you treat the others. In all matters you should be guided by keen intelligence and weighty counsel, and in all affairs be vigilant and wary. Keep your subjects contented and free from improper imposts and exactions. Resettle countries which have been devastated. By the power

[5] Girdkūh and Lammasar were Ismāʿīlī castles.

of Almighty God subdue the lands of the enemies so that you may have ample summer and winter quarters. In all matters consult and take counsel with the lady Doquz Khatun."[6]

Rashīd al-Dīn, *Jāmiʿ al-tawārīkh,* iii, pp. 20–24.

23. The Last Caliph of Baghdad (1242–1258)

In the year 640 [1242] allegiance was sworn to al-Mustaʿṣim on the day when his father al-Mustanṣir died. He was devoted to entertainment and pleasure, passionately addicted to playing with birds, and dominated by women. He was a man of poor judgment, irresolute, and neglectful of what is needful for the conduct of government. When he was told what he ought to do in the matter of the Tatars, either to propitiate them, enter into their obedience and take steps to gain their goodwill, or else to muster his armies and encounter them on the borders of Khurāsān before they could prevail and conquer Iraq, he used to say, "Baghdad is enough for me, and they will not begrudge it me if I renounce all the other countries to them. Nor will they attack me when I am in it, for it is my house and my residence." Such baseless fancies and the like prevented him from taking proper action, and so he was stricken by calamities which he had never imagined.

Abu'l-Faraj, *Ta'rīkh Mukhtaṣar al-duwal,* pp. 445–446.

24. The Fall of Baghdad (1258)

Then came the year 656 [1258], in which the Tatars captured Baghdad and killed most of its people, including the Caliph, and the dominion [*dawla*] of the sons of ʿAbbās ended there.

When this year began, the Tatar armies had already attacked Baghdad, under the two amirs who commanded the troops of the Sultan of the Tatars, Hülegü Khan. To them came the auxiliaries of the lord of Mosul, to help them against the Baghdadis, with provisions and gifts and offerings from him. He

[6] Hülegü's (Christian) wife.

did all this because he feared for himself from the Tatars and wished to ingratiate himself with them, may God condemn them. Baghdad was defended, and mangonels and onagers were set up, with other instruments of defense, which, however, cannot avert any part of God's decree. As the Prophet said, "Caution does not avail against fate" and as God said, "When God's term comes it cannot be deferred" [Qur'ān, lxxi, 4] and, also: "God does not change what is in a people until they change what is in themselves; when God wishes evil for a people, they cannot avert it, and they have no other protector" [Qur'ān, xiii, 11].

The Tatars surrounded the seat of the Caliphate and rained arrows on it from every side until a slave-girl was hit while she was playing before the Caliph and amusing him. She was one of his concubines, a mulatto called 'Urfa, and an arrow came through one of the windows and killed her while she was dancing before the Caliph. The Caliph was alarmed and very frightened. The arrow which had hit her was brought to him, and on it was written, "When God wishes to accomplish His decree, he deprives men of reason of their reason." After this the Caliph ordered increased precautions, and the defenses of the seat of the Caliphate were multiplied.

The arrival of Hülegü Khan at Baghdad with all his troops, numbering nearly 200,000 fighting men, occurred on Muḥarram 12 of this year [January 19, 1258] . . . he came to Baghdad with his numerous infidel, profligate, tyrannical, brutal armies of men, who believed neither in God nor in the Last Day, and invested Baghdad on the western and eastern sides. The armies of Baghdad were very few and utterly wretched, not reaching 10,000 horsemen. They and the rest of the army had all been deprived of their fiefs [*iqṭā'*] so that many of them were begging in the markets and by the gates of the mosques. Poets were reciting elegies on them and mourning for Islam and its people. All this was due to the opinions of the vizier Ibn al-'Alqamī the Shi'ite, because in the previous year, when heavy fighting took place between the Sunnīs and the Shī'a, Karkh and the Shi'ite quarter were looted, and even the houses of the vizier's kinsmen were looted. He was filled with spite because of this, and this was what spurred him to bring down on Islam and its people the most appalling calamity that has been recorded from the building of Baghdad until this time. That is why he was the first to go out to the Tatars. He went with his family and his companions and his servants and his suite and met Sultan Hülegü Khan, may God curse him, and then returned and advised the Caliph to go out to him and be received by him in audience and to make peace on the basis of half the land tax of Iraq for them and half for the Caliph. The Caliph had to go with 700 riders, including the qāḍīs, the jurists, the Sufis, the chief amirs, and the notables. When they came near the camp of Sultan Hülegü Khan, all but seventeen of them were removed from the sight of the Caliph; they were taken off their horses and robbed and killed to the very last man. The Caliph and the others were saved. The Caliph was then brought before Hülegü, who asked him many things. It is said that the Caliph's speech was confused because of his terror at the disdain and arrogance which he experienced. Then he returned to Baghdad in the company of Khoja Naṣīr al-Dīn al-Ṭūsī, the vizier Ibn al-ʿAlqamī, and others, the Caliph being under guard and sequestration, and they brought great quantities of gold and jewels and gold and silver objects and precious stones and other valuables from the seat of the Caliphate. But this clique of Shiʿites and other hypocrites advised Hülegü not to make peace with the Caliph. The vizier said, "If peace is made on equal shares, it will not last more than a year or two, and then things will be as they were before." And they made the killing of the Caliph seem good to him so that when the Caliph returned to Sultan Hülegü he gave orders to kill him. . . .

They [the Tatars] came down upon the city and killed all they could, men, women and children, the old, the middle-aged, and the young. Many of the people went into wells, latrines, and sewers and hid there for many days without emerging. Most of the people gathered in the caravanserais and locked themselves in. The Tatars opened the gates by either breaking or burning them. When they entered, the people in them fled upstairs and the Tatars killed them on the roofs until blood poured from the gutters into the street; "We belong to God and to God we return" [Qur'ān, ii, 156]. The same happened in the mosques and cathedral mosques and dervish convents.

No one escaped them except for the Jewish and Christian *dhimmīs,* those who found shelter with them or in the house of the vizier Ibn al-ʿAlqamī the Shīʿite, and a group of merchants who had obtained safe-conduct from them, having paid great sums of money to preserve themselves and their property. And Baghdad, which had been the most civilized of all cities, became a ruin with only a few inhabitants, and they were in fear and hunger and wretchedness and insignificance.

Ibn Kathīr, xiii, pp. 200–202.

25. The Battle of ʿAyn Jālūt (1260)

In this year 658 [1260] the envoys of Hülegü arrived in Egypt with a letter, the text of which was as follows:

> From the King of Kings in the East and the West, the mighty Khan:
>
> In your name, O God, You who laid out the earth and raised up the skies.
>
> Let al-Malik al-Muẓaffar Qutuz, who is of the race of mamlūks who fled before our swords into this country, who enjoyed its comforts and then killed its rulers, let al-Malik al-Muẓaffar Qutuz know, as well as the amirs of his state and the people of his realms, in Egypt and in the adjoining countries, that we are the army of God on His earth. He created us from His wrath and urged us against those who incurred His anger. In all lands there are examples to admonish you and to deter you from challenging our resolve. Be warned by the fate of others and hand over your power to us before the veil is torn and you are sorry and your errors rebound upon you. For we do not pity those who weep, nor are we tender to those who complain. You have heard that we have conquered the lands and cleansed the earth of corruption and killed most of the people. Yours to flee; ours to pursue. And what land will shelter you, what road save you; what country protect you? You have no deliverance from our swords, no escape from the terror of our arms. Our horses are swift in pursuit, our arrows piercing, our swords like thunderbolts, our hearts like rocks, our numbers like sand. Fortresses cannot withstand us; armies are of no avail in fighting us. Your prayers against us will not be heard, for you have eaten forbidden things and your speech is foul, you betray oaths and

promises, and disobedience and fractiousness prevail among you. Be informed that your lot will be shame and humiliation. "Today you are recompensed with the punishment of humiliation, because you were so proud on earth without right and for your wrongdoing" [Qur'ān, xlvi, 20]. "Those who have done wrong will know to what end they will revert" [Qur'ān, xxvi, 227]. Those who make war against us are sorry; those who seek our protection are safe. If you submit to our orders and conditions, then your rights and your duties are the same as ours. If you resist you will be destroyed. Do not, therefore, destroy yourselves with your own hands. He who is warned should be on his guard. You are convinced that we are infidels, and we are convinced that you are evil-doers. God, who determines all, has urged us against you. Before us, your many are few and your mighty ones are lowly, and your kings have no way to us but that of shame. Do not debate long, and hasten to give us an answer before the fires of war flare up and throw their sparks upon you. Then you will find no dignity, no comfort, no protector, no sanctuary. You will suffer at our hands the most fearful calamity, and your land will be empty of you. By writing to you we have dealt equitably with you and have awakened you by warning you. Now we have no other purpose but you. Peace be with us, with you, and with all those who follow the divine guidance, who fear the consequences of evil, and who obey the Supreme King.

Say to Egypt, Hülegü has come,
with swords unsheathed and sharp.
The mightiest of her people will become humble,
he will send their children to join the aged.

Qutuz assembled the amirs, and they agreed to kill the envoys and to proceed to Ṣāliḥiyya. The envoys were arrested and imprisoned. The Sultan arranged for the amirs he had chosen to swear loyalty and then gave the order to march. The amirs set out unwillingly, because they were reluctant to encounter the Tatars. On Monday, 15 Shaʿbān [July 26, 1260], al-Malik al-Muẓaffar Qutuz, with all the troops of Egypt and those of the army of Syria, the Bedouin, the Turcomans, and others who had rallied to him, emerged from the citadel and set out for Ṣāliḥiyya.

That day he had the Tatar envoys, four in number, brought before him. One of them was cut in two in the horse market at the foot of the citadel, another outside the Zawīla Gate, the third outside the Naṣr Gate, and the fourth at Raydāniyya. Their heads were hung on the Zawīla Gate, and these were the first Tatar heads to be hung there. Qutuz spared a youth who was with the envoys and enrolled him among his own mamlūks.

In Cairo, Fusṭāṭ, and the rest of Egypt proclamations were issued to go out on the Holy War for the cause of God and to defend the religion of the Prophet of God, may God bless and save him. Qutuz sent orders to the governors to rouse the troops for the campaign. Those who hid themselves and were discovered were to be flogged.

Qutuz proceeded to Ṣāliḥiyya, where he made camp and where his forces assembled. Having summoned the amirs, he spoke with them about the expedition, but they all declined and refused to go. Qutuz said to them, "Amirs of the Muslims! For a long time you have been eating the money of the treasury and now you don't want to fight. I, myself, will set out. He who chooses the Holy War will accompany me; he who doesn't can go home. God observes him, and the guilt of those who violate the women of the Muslims will be on the heads of the laggards." He addressed the chosen amirs and had them swear agreement to the expedition. The others could not but agree, and the meeting broke up.

When night came the Sultan rode about, had his drums beaten, and said, "I shall fight the Tatars by myself." When the amirs saw the Sultan's action, they too went, however unwillingly. Qutuz ordered the amir Rukn al-Dīn Baybars al-Bunduqdārī to go ahead with some troops to seek intelligence of the Tatars. He came to Gaza in which there were some Tatars. They withdrew when he arrived, and he took possession of Gaza.

The Sultan and the main forces made camp by Gaza and stayed for one day. Then he took the coastal road to the town of Acre, which was then in the hands of the Franks. They came out to greet Qutuz and wanted to join him as auxiliaries. He thanked them and gave them robes of honor and obtained their oath that they would be neither for him nor against him. He swore to them that if any of them, on horse or on foot, followed him and tried to harass the army of the Muslims, he would return and fight them before meeting the Tatars.

He then summoned the amirs, and he urged them to fight the Tatars. He reminded them of the carnage, the enslavement, and the fire which had befallen other lands and struck fear in them with the thought that the same could happen again. He urged them to save Syria from the Tatars and to defend Islam and the Muslims, and he warned them of God's punishments. They burst into tears and swore together that they would strive to fight the Tatars and drive them out of the land. The Sultan ordered the amir Rukn al-Dīn Baybars al-Bunduqdārī to advance with a detachment, and he did so until he encountered the Tatar vanguard. He wrote to the Sultan to inform him of this and began to skirmish with the Tatars, sometimes advancing, sometimes retreating, until the Sultan joined him near ʿAyn Jālūt.

When Kitbugha and Baydarā, the two deputies of Hülegü, learned of the advance of the army, they gathered together the Tatars who were scattered through Syria and set out to fight the Muslims. The vanguard of the Muslim army met the Tatar vanguard and defeated them. On Friday, 25 Ramaḍān [September 3] the two sides met, and in the hearts of the Muslims there was great fear of the Tatars. The sun had just risen, and the valley was full of men. There was much shouting from the peasants in the villages and a continuous beating of the Sultan's and of the amirs' drums. The Tatars were disposed towards the mountain. When the two armies clashed, one of the wings of the Sultan's army was thrown into confusion and part of it destroyed. When this happened al-Malik al-Muẓaffar took off his helmet, threw it to the ground, and cried with all his might, "O Islam!" He then hurled himself, with those around him, straight at the enemy. God granted him victory. Kitbugha, the commander of the Tatars, was killed; then al-Malik al-Saʿīd Ḥasan ibn al-ʿAzīz, who was with the Tatars, was also killed. The rest were defeated, and God made them turn their backs to the Muslims, who followed them, killing and capturing them. The amir Baybars proved his courage in the presence of the Sultan.

It happened during this battle that the young man who had

been with the Tatar envoys and whom the Sultan had spared and enrolled among his own mamlūks was riding behind him when the armies met. When the battle was joined he aimed an arrow at the Sultan, but was observed by someone near him, seized, and killed on the spot. According to another version, he in fact shot the arrow at the Sultan, hit his horse, and knocked it down, leaving the Sultan standing on his feet. Fakhr al-Dīn Māmā dismounted from his horse, gave it to the Sultan, and when the led horses were brought, mounted one of them.

The army pursued the Tatars as far as the neighborhood of Baysān, where they turned and fought an even fiercer battle than the first. But God defeated them, and their chiefs and many of them were killed. The Muslims had been violently shaken. The Sultan cried out three times in a loud voice, heard by most of the army, "O Islam! O God, give your servant Qutuz victory over the Tatars." When the Tatars had been defeated for the second time, the Sultan dismounted from his horse, rubbed his face in the dust, kissed it, and recited a prayer with two prostrations, in thanksgiving to God, and then rode on. The troops advanced, their hands full of booty.

The news of the defeat of the Tatars reached Damascus on Sunday night, the 27th day of the month [September 5]. The head of Kitbugha, the Tatar commander, was carried to Cairo. Zayn al-Ḥāfiẓī and the Tatar deputies fled from Damascus, followed by their henchmen, but the country people attacked them and looted their belongings. The Tatar occupation of Damascus had lasted seven months and ten days.

The same Sunday the Sultan made camp at Tiberias. From there he wrote to Damascus to inform them of the victory which God had given to him and of his defeat of the Tatars. It was his first letter to reach Damascus. When it came, the people rejoiced greatly, and at once attacked the houses of the Christians, looting them and destroying whatever they could. They destroyed the Church of the Jacobites and the Church of Mary and set fire to them so that only a heap of ruins remained. They killed a number of Christians, and the rest hid themselves. This was because, during the Tatar occupation, the Christians had planned several times to rise against the

Muslims and had destroyed mosques and minarets which were in the neighborhood of their churches. They openly rang their bells, carried the cross in processions, drank wine in the streets, and sprinkled Muslims with it.

On the twenty-eighth day of the same month the Muslims plundered the Jews in Damascus, leaving them nothing. Their shops in the markets became rubble. However, a group of soldiers prevented the crowd from burning their synagogues and houses. On the same day, the Damascenes took vengeance on a number of Muslims who had helped the Tatars and killed them. They destroyed the houses which were near the churches and killed a number of Mongols. It was a terrifying business.

On the twenty-ninth day of the same month [September 7], in the early morning, the amir Jamāl al-Dīn al-Muḥammadī al-Ṣāliḥī arrived in Damascus, bringing a decree from al-Malik al-Muẓaffar Qutuz, and alighted at Dār al-Sa'āda [House of Felicity]. The decree granted safe-conduct to the people and their country.

On Wednesday, the last day of the month of Ramaḍān [September 8], al-Malik al-Muẓaffar and his troops arrived outside Damascus. He set up tents there and stayed until Shawwāl 2 [September 10], when he made his entry into Damascus and moved into the Citadel. He sent the amir Rukn al-Dīn Baybars on an expedition to Ḥimṣ. He killed and captured many Tatars and returned to Damascus.

Al-Maqrīzī, *Sulūk*, i, pp. 427–432.

26. A Visit to the Mongols (1260)

From the chronicle of Qirṭāy al-'Izzī al-Khaznadārī, d. 734/1333; cited by Ibn al-Furāt (d. 807/1405), and thence published from a manuscript in the Vatican library by G. Levi Della Vida in *Orientalia*, n.s. iv (1935), pp. 358–366.

Al-Ṣārim Uzbek, a mamlūk of al-Malik al-Ashraf, the Ayyubid, the ruler of Ḥimṣ said:

When Hülegü camped before Aleppo, I was out of the city, and I hid myself for three days in a cave near Aleppo, where I heard the hoofbeats over my head. When they ceased, I came out of the cave, and at the entrance I found a dead Mongol. I put on his clothes, and thus disguised in Mongol costume, I sought the camp of Hülegü. It was part of the justice of the Mongols that when they made camp in any place, they set up a pole near the king's encampment. From the top of the pole a small box was hung with string, and around the pole was a guard of the most trusted Mongols. If a man had a complaint or had suffered an injustice, he would write his grievance in a petition, seal it, and place it in this box. When Friday came, the king would have the box brought to him and would open it with a key which he kept and thus discover the injustices suffered by people.

Al-Ṣārim said: I therefore wrote a petition as follows, "The mamlūk al-Ṣārim." (I did not say Uzbek, fearing to write this in my petition, since the Mongols at that time did not call me Ṣārim but Uzbek.) I therefore wrote in the petition, "The mamlūk al-Ṣārim, mamlūk of al-Malik al-Ashraf, lord of Ḥimṣ, kisses the ground and seeks permission to appear in the presence of the Khan." When he sent for me and I appeared before him, I saw before me a king of majestic demeanor, high distinction, and great dignity, of short stature, with a very flat nose, a broad face, a loud voice, compassionate eyes. The ladies sat at his side, with the lady Doquz Khatun sitting at his left.

Al-Ṣārim said: When I stood before Hülegü, he spoke with me through the intermediary of four chamberlains and said to me, "You are a mamlūk of al-Malik al-Ashraf, the lord of Ḥims, the bahadur[1] of the Muslims, that is to say, the knight of the Muslims?" I said, "Yes." Then he began to talk to me through one chamberlain after another, the fourth chamberlain addressing me in the Turkish language. When Hülegü saw that I had an eloquent tongue, a good mind, and a quick answer, he brought me near to him and ordered that there should only be one chamberlain between him and me. Then he asked me, "Do

[1] A term occurring in Mongol and other languages of the steppe peoples, meaning brave or hero, and thence used as a title or honorific. It also appears as a loanword in Persian and Russian (*bogatîr*). Ṣārim or his editor explains the term by the Arabic word *fāris,* horseman, here rendered "knight." See EI², articles "Bahādur" and "Fāris," where the Arab-Muslim view of knightliness or chivalry is briefly discussed.

you drink wine?" I answered, "Yes." Thereupon he ordered them to bring me a basin full of wine and made a sign to the chamberlain to give it to me. Then I kissed the ground and danced and did the things which the tumblers used to do before the kings of Islam when the country still belonged to them.

Al-Ṣārim said: The ladies were astonished at this. They were amused and they smiled. As for Hülegü, he did not raise his eyes from the ground. Then Hülegü ordered me to sit, and I sat, to drink, and I drank, to eat, and I ate. When he saw that I did whatever he ordered me to do, he ordered me to sit above his courtiers in a more dignified place and of a higher rank. From that time onward I was always present when he ate and drank, and when Hülegü slept, the lady Doquz Khatun, his wife, summoned me. I remained in this situation for a first, a second, and a third night, while we were laying siege to Aleppo.

Al-Ṣārim said: Then Hülegü asked me concerning a certain matter, and I gave him an untrue answer, and I wished that the earth had swallowed me rather than I should speak to him thus. He asked me through the chamberlain how long it would take to conquer this country, that is to say, Aleppo, and I answered ten years. Then Hülegü looked down toward the ground in anger against me and said to his chamberlain, "Ask him how long it would take us to capture this Citadel (that is to say, the Citadel of Aleppo)." "Thirty years," I replied. My purpose in saying this was that when Hülegü heard what I said he would withdraw from Aleppo. But Hülegü smiled and said to his chamberlain, "If this man had not already rendered me service I would have cut off his head. Is he not ashamed to speak in this way? This would be the time which it would take their kings, that is to say, the kings of the Muslims, who are of differing opinions and busy with one another." All this was in the Mongol language, and I did not know what he was saying.

Al-Ṣārim said: I was silent and I repented of my answer because of the anger which I saw appear on his face. Hülegü had not yet finished speaking when a Mongol came in with a human head in his hands, hanging by the hair and stained with blood. He threw it down in front of Hülegü and spoke with him in the Mongol language. Then he picked up the head again and went away. The chamberlain then turned to me and said, "Ṣārim, do you know what this head is and who this man is?" "No," I said. Then he said, "This man is the greatest of the Mongol commanders. He was in one of the mines excavated under the Citadel, and he went out to relieve himself, leaving his son in his place. The Aleppines surprised them and attacked them through the mine shaft. His son fled and a number of Mongols fled with him. The father heard of this, recaptured the mine, cut off his son's head with his own hand, and brought it to the Khan."

Al-Ṣārim said: From this I understood that the Mongols would inevitably capture Aleppo, and that our sons, our daughters, and our followers would fall into their hands, and that this was the will of Almighty God which no one could gainsay.

One night I was drinking with Hülegü when a group of Mongol commanders came into his presence, bringing with them a great variety of objects, including dried grapes, cottonseed, flour, wood shavings, charcoal, and carobs. Hülegü began to look at me and smile, and I did not know what was in his mind. Then he ordered us to drink from large goblets and china cups. When I went out to attend to a need, the chamberlain accompanied me (he was very fond of me and I was very fond indeed of him), and he said to me, "Ṣārim, do you know what this is that the commanders have brought?" "No, by God," I replied. Then he said, "They have already brought their tunnel under the Citadel and reached these things which you have just seen. Then Hülegü asked the commanders, 'How wide is the tunnel?" they said, 'Wide enough to hold 6000 men.' Then Hülegü said, 'Widen it so that it can hold 10,000 men.' Tomorrow afternoon the Mongols will capture the Citadel of Aleppo, and your daughters and your wives and the daughters of the kings who are enclosed in this Citadel will become the slave-girls of this lady Doquz Khatun, and Hülegü will consider them captives of war.' Therefore, take care, Ṣārim, what you do."

Ṣārim said: By God, when I heard him say this, I grew sober from my drinking, and I went in to the company, and I sat down before Hülegü, and I said to him as if joking, "By God, the kings of the Mongols are like donkeys." Doquz Khatun looked toward me and smiled, and she said, "And how is that, Ṣārim?" And I said, "The kings of the Muslims, when they used to drink wine, ordered pistachio nuts, citrus juice, slices of lemon in china cups, ewers of rosewater, basil, violets, myrtle, cloves, narcissus, and other such fine things. You Mongols, on the other hand, drink your wine with charcoal, cottonseed, dried grapes, wood shavings, and similar ugly objects." Hülegü smiled and the ladies burst out laughing.

Al-Ṣārim said: Then I let slip a word for which I might have paid with my head. I said, "I know from where the commanders brought these objects." Then Hülegü grew angry and said, "How do you know this?" I kissed the ground and I said, "May God preserve the Khan. By the king's head, I, myself, with my own hands, collected all these supplies in the Citadel for fear of the Mongols and to prepare for a siege." Then Hülegü's anger cooled, since he had believed in his own mind that the chamberlain had betrayed something to me of what had been said, as in fact happened. I rose, kissed the ground, and said, "May God help the Khan! Great is your majesty and vast your realm, and the kings fear you, nor is any of them capable of withstanding you. By God, by God, O my Lord, the kings would be glad to stand before you as we your slaves stand before you now, but they fear your wrath." My words pleased Hülegü, who said to me, "Ṣārim." I replied, "At your command," and he said, "Could you bring me your master, al-Malik al-Ashraf, the lord of Ḥimṣ?" I answered, "Yes." Hülegü said, "Mount your horse and bring him here." I answered, "After two days." And he said, "Yes."

Al-Ṣārim said: Hülegü had them give me a horse, and he said, "Go and do not stop," and I said, "On one condition." He asked, "What condition?" I answered, "That you do not conquer this Citadel until al-Malik al-Ashraf reaches the presence of the Khan." He answered, "Yes." Then I mounted the horse and took ten packhorses with me. I tied the emblem of the courier service around my neck, and I rode until I reached Gaza. There I heard that the kings were fleeing through the desert, scattered, distraught, and stumbling. Word had reached the Muslim kings of my position with Hülegü. I rode on and I caught up with the kings at a place called Birkat Zīra. When the kings saw me, they dismounted from their horses and kissed my hands as I used to kiss theirs, and even my own master, al-Malik al-Ashraf, kissed my hand. This was too much for me, and I was ashamed of my master and of al-Malik al-Nāṣir. Then I said to al-Malik al-Ashraf, "The Khan calls you." He was frightened, and I said to him, "Whom do you fear?" He replied, "The Khan." I said, "I warrant you that you will return to being a great king in accordance with your desire and that nothing unpleasant will happen to you." Then al-Malik al-Nāṣir turned to me and said, "And I, Ṣārim al-Dīn?" I answered, "To you I have nothing to say." Then al-Malik al-Nāṣir wept [gap in text].

When I took al-Malik al-Ashraf to Hülegü and he stood in his presence, he was assigned a goatskin tent as a dwelling, with a sheep, a pot, and some firewood. By God, the tent which Hülegü had set up for al-Malik al-Ashraf was such that dogs would not wish to live there; the sheep was such that wolves would not have eaten it; and the firewood such that a scavenger would not have taken it to light his torch. This is how the Mongols always live.

He said: I left al-Malik al-Ashraf in his tent and passed to the service of Hülegü. He seated me at my usual place, ordered me to eat, and I ate, to drink, and I drank. He asked me about the condition of the kings and how they were and how I had left them, and I said, "In the filthiest condition, fleeing, scattered, stumbling, distraught in the desert, not even able to enjoy sleep for fear of the might of the Khan."

Al-Ṣārim said: Hülegü was pleased with my words and said to me, "How did you leave your master, Ṣārim?" I answered, "I have no master other than the Khan." He said, "No? Is not your master al-Malik al-Ashraf?" I said, "I know nothing of how he is." He said, "How could you leave him alone?" I said, "I shall not leave the presence of the Khan, may God help him." Then Hülegü inclined his head for a while and said, "Do not say that, Ṣārim, but go to your master and see how he is." So I went to al-Malik al-Ashraf and I found him dejected, with his cheek in his hand, while the sheep was tied with string, and the wood was scattered on the ground. I asked him, "What is the matter, Master?" And he answered, "Don't you see what a state I am in, Ṣārim al-Dīn?" and he wept. I said to him, "Do not weep, Master. By God, by God, by God, this is how the Mongols always live. This is their condition. By God, Master, they did not do this in order to slight you, but, on the contrary, this is the best way of life that the Mongols know."

Al-Ṣārim said: Then al-Malik al-Ashraf smiled and said, "That is how kings should be. With this life and with these men, kings conquer countries." Now while I was conversing with al-Malik al-Ashraf and calming his mood, an order came from Hülegü for him to appear before him. Then, by God, I saw al-Malik al-Ashraf change color. I had never seen al-Malik al-Ashraf change color before. Al-Malik al-Ashraf had defeated the Khwarazmians when they were 6,000 strong, and he had only 1,500 horsemen, and he did not change color. He had defeated the Mongols at a time when the Mongols had 2,500 horsemen, and al-Malik al-Ashraf had only 800, but he did not change color.

When al-Malik al-Ashraf stood before Hülegü, I was holding him on his left and the chamberlain was holding him on his right. By God, I saw that al-Malik al-Ashraf was trembling like a cane and was unable to stand on his two feet, and all this in fear of Hülegü. Al-Malik al-Ashraf was a young man with a handsome face, of reddish brown color, of medium height, with birthmarks scattered about his face. He was wearing a green Mongol cloak with a belt of red Atlas, Bulgar sandals with gold clasps, and a small gold-embroidered turban. Doquz Khatun looked at al-Malik al-Ashraf and then looked toward Hülegü and said, "This is a fine young man and the knight of the Muslims. That is how kings should be." Then Hülegü looked back at her, smiling, and said, "Yet we are the kings before whom these kings stand on foot, humbled and in fear of our power." While all this was happening, al-Malik al-Ashraf stood in front of Hülegü, not knowing what fate would do with him. Then Hülegü raised his head and said, "Ashraf, choose what gift you will." And al-Malik al-Ashraf kissed the ground three times.

Al-Ṣārim said: I said to him, "Ask him to give you the tower of the Citadel in which are your mother, and two sisters, your daughters, the wives of the kings, and the daughters and wives of al-Malik al-Nāṣir. If you do not ask for this tower now, on this very night the Mongols will capture the Citadel of Aleppo, and the womenfolk of the Muslim kings will become slave-girls of this lady Doquz Khatun." Al-Malik al-Ashraf asked, "Will he not kill me?" I answered, "The Mongols do not kill those who are with them as guests." Then Hülegü said a second time, "Choose what you will as a gift, Ashraf Sultan." Then al-Malik al-Ashraf said, "I ask of the Khan's grace that he give me that tower in which are my women, the women of al-Nāṣir, and those of the kings who are fleeing from the power of Khan." Al-Ṣārim said: This angered Hülegü who looked downward and said, "Ask for something else." But al-Malik al-Ashraf remained silent. Then Doquz Khatun looked at King Hülegü and said to him, "Are you not ashamed? A man like this king asks you for that tower and you refuse it to him. By God, if he had asked me for Aleppo, I would not have refused it, for he is the knight of the Muslims." Hülegü said, "But I only refused it to him for your sake, so that the daughters and the wives of the kings may be your slaves." Then she said, "I declare them free before Almighty God and for the sake of al-Malik al-Ashraf." Thereupon Hülegü granted al-Malik al-Ashraf what he asked, and al-Malik al-Ashraf kissed Hülegü's hand three times.

Al-Ṣārīm said: When al-Malik al-Ashraf had kissed Hülegü's hand and had returned to us, he stood between us and wanted to kiss the ground while I held him on his left and the chamberlain held him on his right. By God, al-Malik al-Ashraf kissed the ground, and when he wanted to stand up again he could not stand, and this through fear of Hülegü. Then I and the chamberlain pulled him up by his shoulders, and I said to him, "Be strong," and I recited, "God will strengthen those who believe with a steadfast word in this world and the next" [Qur'ān, xiv, 32].

6
After the Mongols

In time the Mongols, too, were Islamized and assimilated, and a new Islamic political order arose under their successors and imitators. Two main centers of power emerged within the Middle East. One was based in Egypt where the Mamlūk Sultanate, maintained by imported Turkish slaves, defended the heartlands of Islam against both Mongols and Crusaders; the other had its center in Iran, which was dominated by the Islamized Mongols and their heirs, noteworthy among whom was the great conqueror Tīmūr (sometimes known as Tīmūr Lang, the lame, whence Tamerlane). The first two excerpts come from Arabic works; the third and fourth, from a contemporary Persian biography of Tīmūr.

27. On the Mamlūks (Thirteenth to Fourteenth Centuries)

When the [ʿAbbasid] state was drowned in decadence and luxury and donned the garments of calamity and impotence and was overthrown by the heathen Tatars, who abolished the seat of the Caliphate and obliterated the splendor of the lands and made unbelief prevail in place of belief, because the people of the faith, sunk in self-indulgence, preoccupied with pleasure, and abandoned to luxury, had become deficient in energy and reluctant to rally in defense, and had stripped off the skin of courage and the emblem of manhood—then, it was God's benevolence that He rescued the faith by reviving its dying breath and restoring the unity of the Muslims in the Egyptian realms, preserving the order and defending the walls of Islam. He did this by sending to the Muslims, from this Turkish nation and from among its great and numerous tribes, rulers to defend them and utterly loyal helpers, who were brought from the House of War to the House of Islam under the rule of slavery, which hides in itself a divine blessing. By means of slavery they learn glory and blessing and are exposed to divine providence; cured by slavery, they enter the Muslim religion with the firm resolve of true believers and yet with nomadic virtues unsullied by debased nature, unadulterated with the filth of pleasure, undefiled by the ways of civilized living, and with their ardor unbroken by the profusion of luxury. The slave merchants bring them to Egypt in batches, like sand-grouse to the watering places, and government buyers have them displayed for inspection and bid for them, raising the price above their value. They do this not in order to subjugate them, but because it intensifies loyalty, increases power, and is conducive to ardent zeal. They choose from each group, according to what they observe of the characteristics of the race and the tribes. Then they place them in government barracks where they give them good and fair treatment, educate them, have them taught the Qur'ān and kept at their religious studies until they have a firm grasp of this. Then they train them in archery and fencing, in horsemanship, in hippodromes, and in thrusting with the lance and and striking with the sword until their arms grow strong and their skills become firmly rooted. When the masters know that they have reached the point when they are ready to defend them, even to die for them, they double their pay and increase their grants [*iqṭā'*], and impose on them the duty to improve themselves in the use of weapons and in horsemanship, and so also to increase the number of men of their own race in the service for that purpose. Often they use them in the service of the state, appoint them to high state offices, and some of them are chosen to sit on the throne of the Sultans and direct the affairs of the Muslims, in accordance with divine providence and with the mercy of God to His creatures. Thus, one intake comes after another and generation follows generation, and Islam rejoices in the benefit which it gains through them, and the branches of the kingdom flourish with the freshness of youth.

Ibn Khaldūn, *'Ibar*, v, p. 371.

28. An Envoy from the Franks (ca. 1300)

As regards the king of France, I only recall a single envoy from him to us, breathing fire and lightning and thunder. He came to demand Jerusalem and the opening to him of the coast of Caesarea or Askalon. The Muslims would keep their governors in these two places together with his governors, and the country would be shared equally. The mosques would be maintained and the needs of those serving them fully met. He would also pay 200,000 dinars a year in advance, representing half the revenue of the country he would occupy, calculated on an average of three years. To this he would add fine gifts and presents every year.

This proposal was found good by certain Coptic secretaries, who had become high officials of the state and who had white turbans and black secrets and remained fierce [literally blue][1] enemies who swallow red death. They worked to make the plot succeed. Poison seeped into the body, and an antidote was sought in vain. "This," they said, "is a large amount of ready money. What harm can they do us? They are but a drop in the sea, a few pebbles in the desert."

My father,[2] God have mercy on him, heard about this, and he resolved to speak out and do everything in his power to prevent it for fear that the Sultan be misled into following the advice of these liars. "Come with me," my father said to me, "and we will speak out even if our clothes are dyed with our blood. We approached the chief qāḍī, the Qazvīnī preacher, who responded and made good preparations. The next morning we reported for duty and attended the Sultan's audience in the Hall

[1] According to the ancient lexicographers, a fierce enemy was so called because the Greeks and the Daylamites, the traditional enemies of the Arabs, were predominantly blue-eyed.

[2] 'Umarī's father was at that time a secretary in the office concerned with dealings with other states.

of Justice. The envoys were summoned, and one of those Coptic secretaries was present and ready to speak. We also were ready on our side. They had not yet finished speaking when the Sultan[3] became furious and flew into a rage, almost consuming them in his anger. The hypocrite was silenced in his shame, and we too kept silent, content that he was frustrated by the Sultan. That devil was thwarted; God saved the Faithful a battle and turned the spearheads back against those who had cast them.

This is what the Sultan said: "Wretches! You know what disaster you suffered at Damietta[4] at the hands of the army of al-Malik al-Ṣāliḥ, and they were only an assemblage of Kurdish bands. These Turks were not yet there![5] All that kept us from you was our wars against the Tatars. But today, thanks be to God, we are at peace. We and they are one race who hold together. All we want is to begin, so now come along! And if you do not come we shall come to you, even if we have to cross the sea on horseback. Wretches! You have found tongues to mention Jerusalem! By God, all that any man among you will touch of her soil is what the winds will blow over his crucified body!"

Then he uttered a shout, which shook the strongest of them, and dismissed them ignominiously. He read no letter to them and gave them no answer beyond this.

Ibn al-ʿUmarī, *Al-Taʿrīf bi'l-muṣtalaḥ al-sharīf,* Cairo, 1312, pp. 63–64. (Cf. Al-Qalqashandī, *Subḥ,* viii, pp. 36–38.)

29. Tīmūr and His Historian (1401–1402)

Sultans and rulers, in accordance with the need of every time, belong to one of three groups. They may be completely given to kindness and mercy, completely given to force and vengeance, or may combine both of these. That being is nearest to perfection,

[3] The Sultan at this time was al-Malik al-Nāṣir (reigned 1293–1294, 1299–1309, and 1310–1341).

[4] A reference to the defeat of Louis IX in 1249.

[5] This sentence, missing in ʿUmarī, is restored from Qalqashandī. The allusion is to the Turkish Mamlūks who took over from the late Ayyubids.

that person more perfect, who combines the manifestations of majesty and grace. The signs of his kindness or his force are manifested according to the occasion and in relation to the person with whom he is dealing. Righteous and wicked, worthy and worthless, good and bad, believer and unbeliever, pious and evildoer, each is treated by him as befits his quality. Such a person, combining in himself these two attributes, appears only once in centuries. His works, his practices, and the results of his words and deeds remain in the world for years, perhaps for centuries, and after him his children and descendants and followers and successors follow his rules and conform to his actions and orders.

The witness of this case and exponent of this meaning is the noble existence and lofty presence of the most mighty, just, and noble amir, the elect of the court of God, the Shadow of the presence of the Almighty, the master of empire, the lord of the auspicious conjunction, the pole of the truth, the world, and the faith, the Amir Tīmūr Göregen,[1] may God make his kingdom and sultanate eternal on the surface of the earth and extend his mercy and generosity to all the world. For his justice is conjoined with statecraft, and his force is mixed with kindness; his sting is together with his honey, his magnanimity with his anger. At the point of the revelation of beauty, he strives to honor the commandments of the holy law of Muḥammad. With meticulous solicitude in honoring the Sayyids, who are the branches of the tree of prophecy, the seeds of the sheaves of saintship, the children of the Prophet of God, and the light of the eyes of Fāṭima the Resplendent, he gives orders to respect them and at audiences gives them precedence above all others. He neglects no particular in deference to the dignity of the *ulema,* who are the legatees of the apostolate and the deputies of the court of prophecy. Distinguishing the better from the worse, he appoints each to his proper rank, assigns every person to the place appropriate to his quality and knowledge, and strives to the utmost in honoring shaykhs and righteous men. He is

[1] A Mongol title meaning son-in-law. Tīmūr married a Mongol princess of the line of Jenghiz Khan.

always desirous to meet and talk with them. He cares for the weak, the peasants, the merchants, and the gentry and treats them with justice. To Iran and Turan, which two countries for centuries no suitor had claimed as bride, he has brought such perfect order and all-embracing justice that wise men are astonished. From the furthest point of Transoxania, perhaps from the borders of China and Khotan, to the regions of Delhi and Cambay, and from Darband to the borders of Egypt and Rome, in the days of his justice and law, not only merchants but even children and widows can come and go with cloth, gold, silver, and costly merchandise, and nobody expects a grain of anything from them, nor do they suffer a dirham's worth of damage. This endless beneficence and infinite generosity are the result of the statecraft and justice of the Auspicious Amir.

His blessed person is adorned with the honor of both merit and descent. Merit is that which men attain by their own efforts and endeavors, descent is that which they inherit from their fathers. Concerning the first, this book from beginning to end will give information about the perfections and distinctions attained by his own great efforts, which need not therefore be elaborated here. For whoever is honored hereafter by reading this blessed history will know about his great endeavors in the business of government and the country and his efforts in the important affairs of religion and the state, in what degree and whence and whither.

As regards his illustrious descent, at the time when the august sovereign Jenghiz Khan was bringing up his children, he gave special favor to his second son, Chagatay, who was distinguished above his other children in Mongol law and custom. He set aside a special group of the best men of his army, whose commander was Qarachar, of the tribe of Barlas. He had complete confidence in his judgment, competence, discipline, and courage. He entrusted the conduct of state affairs and the maintenance of authority and custom to his wisdom and direction. He was the illustrious grandfather of the Auspicious Amir. Of necessity, what the august sovereign in his farsighted prescience had seen, came to pass after some time in this day. The Auspicious Amir brought the land from sedition and tumult to control and order. He made the blessed line of Chagatay rulers of Iran and Turan and, indeed, of most of the inhabited quarter of the earth and installed their royal authority. He brought the necks of the rebellious under the yoke of humiliation and hurled the heads of the refractory into the dust of destruction. Those who were granted quarter from the stroke of his lustrous sword realized that to lay hands on the flag, to clutch at the mountain, to seek the upper hand over the sea, or to wrestle with an elephant is the summit of stupidity and the extremity of error; they saw no recourse but to obey his command, and they joined the ranks of his servants and henchmen. After their sins and crimes, by agreeing to pay taxes and tolls, they saved themselves from the sea of calamity and reached the shore of salvation. In fine, bending their heads on the threshold of submission, they became obedient. . . .

The reason for the writing of this book was that in the year 804 [1401–1402] the Auspicious Amir (may God make his kingdom eternal amid the passage of time) gave orders to summon me, his humble servant Niẓām Shāmī. When I had the honor of kissing his carpet, after I had paid my respects, he showed kindness and generosity and beneficence to this devoted slave and then deigned to indicate that the history of his own deeds and of the deeds of the rulers who had held sway from the foundation of this eternal kingdom until today have been written but have not been fittingly presented and, therefore, I should make it my task to correct, arrange, order, and subdivide it, on condition that this book should be safe and immune from verbal conceits and florid magniloquence and remain free and exempt from the style of eloquence and imagery, for in books which are embellished in this way and adorned with the language of simile and metaphor, the meaning may be lost and disappear. Only a person who has a knowledge of words can understand these meanings, while ten others, perhaps a hundred, may be unable to perceive their purport. For this reason the use of such a book is not general, nor its usefulness complete.

Thereupon I kissed the carpet before him and said, "However

many the gradations of words may be and however innumerable their degrees in the time of this eternal kingdom, your slave has some power in this art and some reputation among its practitioners. Nevertheless, the wise have finely said about words, 'that which the many understand and the few do not reject,' which means that good words are those of which the common people seize the meaning and in which the educated find no fault. They also say

None but your slave knows how to speak
words which the many know and the few approve.

To which he deigned to reply, "These are the kind of words I want."

Niẓām al-Dīn Shāmī, *Zafarnāma,* pp. 8–11.

30. The Capture of Aleppo by Tīmūr (1400)

When the imperial standards reached Behisni, fear and terror invaded the hearts of the people of Aleppo. Timurtash, who was the chief amir in Aleppo, informed the seat of government in Egypt of the situation. Thereupon the ruler of Egypt gave orders that the amirs of the adjoining provinces, such as Damascus, Tripoli, Ḥimṣ, Ḥamā, Ba'albekk, Ṣafad, Qal'at al-Rūm, and others, assemble in Aleppo so as to help him. Accordingly, they all assembled and formed an immense multitude. Sudun, the chief amir of Damascus, came with a huge army. As all these places were near to one another, within a short time a vast army was assembled.

When they met together, Timurtash, who was cleverer than the others, did not wish to make a precipitate choice and said, "We must consider this business; we must take counsel with the wise and reach agreement on a course, because if people do not achieve unity in a great matter, they give strength to their enemies. These people who are coming against us follow the advice of their sovereign, Jenghiz Khan, and by unity they have conquered the world.

Yes, indeed, by unity the world may be won.

"In this matter, let each say what he has in mind so that a decision may be reached on what the situation requires."

A group of experienced wise men, with practical experience of affairs, said, "This man is supported by God. Wherever he goes, he conquers; whoever opposes him, suffers. The sultans of the inhabited quarter of the world have bent their necks before him. To oppose such a man would accomplish nothing and would end in regret. Do not delude yourselves, but consider what they have already done to cities and fortresses, especially in Khurāsān, Sīstān, Khārazm, and Transoxania. Do not strive for your own destruction. The course of wisdom would be for us to take the path of compliance and appeasement. Let us send him suitable gifts and offerings so that he may extend the garment of mercy over us and turn away from us, and the country may remain in safety."

But certain arrogant persons, with little experience of the world, puffed up with their own strength and power, like Sudun and others, did not want to follow this advice but were misled by the multitude of their soldiers, the ramparts of their city, and the thickness of their citadel. In answer they said, "Whoever fears does harm. This country is not like other countries. In those countries fortifications are mostly of clay and earth, whereas our fortresses and cities are made of stone and even steel. If they wish to take any of our cities by siege and assault, it will require months or even years. If you are afraid of their warriors and are perturbed at the multitude of their arms, and armor, then praise be to God, there is a great difference between them and us. Our bows are Damascene, our swords Egyptian, our spears Arabian, our shields of Aleppo. If you are thinking of the size of the army, in this country 60,000 villages and country towns are registered. If only one soldier comes from each place, we shall outnumber them. What is more, they will be in the open while we shall be behind fortifications. The walls of their dwellings are of hide and cord, whereas our fortresses are of stone and iron."

A group of the wise men said, "Only one who has not seen the vicissitudes of fortune wishes to go to war. To try and settle by war a question which you can settle by gentler means is far from the path of sense. To give up one's person, property, and children to destruction for vain fancies is far from wisdom. It would be safer to make peace."

Another group, not thinking of the consequences, said, "What words are these? In such an affair there can be no protection but courage, no help but firmness of resolve. If a wise man in the time of need shows weakness and uncertainty, he works for his own destruction and will not be forgiven either by men or by God. Have no fear, and prepare for war!"

Among them there was a group of Persians, famous for having lived very well among the Mongols for a time. When they saw that their opinions differed, they supposed that their words would be heard dispassionately and warned them. "We are better informed about these people," they said, "and we know them well, and we know where this will end. Do not hasten to battle. Do not regard this as a small matter."

But the others ascribed these words to self-interest. They began to revile them and said, "These men are spies. They came here by a trick, and they intend to make this country Mongol one day."

The wise ones laughed at this, but fate wept for them. Since the advice of well-wishers was unavailing, they decided not to go outside the city but to shelter behind their walls, ramparts, and fortifications and to respond to the enemy with arrows.

Indeed, if they had kept to this idea, the struggle would have been long and the army would have encountered difficulties. When the Auspicious Amir [Tīmūr] was informed of this situation, he took his own clear mind and farsighted wisdom as minister and counselor and put his trust in the help of God. He made no haste in his advance, but took a week to cover two days' march. Each day he marched one parasang or more. When they reached the city and made camp, they dug trenches round the army and set up oxhide shields and screens so that the enemy should suppose that they had no intention of advancing and lacked the strength to advance very soon. Emboldened by this, they gave up their rather more sensible previous plan, and putting great trust in their force and power, they went outside the city, made camp, and set up tents and pavilions. . . .

On that day Prince Sulṭān Ḥusayn Bahadur, one of the dear sons of the Auspicious Amir, reached the enemy outposts with a few of his personal retainers [*nöker*]. Although they were very numerous, he showed great courage and advanced against them and did brave deeds. Seizing three of them, he bound their hands and feet and carried them off. The other soldiers, seeing his strength, took flight.

Also on the same day his grandson, Prince Abū Bakr Bahadur, advancing with sixty men, encountered an innumerable enemy force and joined in fierce battle. In the end, remaining on equal terms, each of the two sides returned to its own place.

The following day the warriors again encountered the enemy and fought bravely. On the third day when the true dawn appeared, the Auspicious Amir arranged his victorious soldiers, placed his right wing and his left wing to the best advantage, appointed his great amirs and famous soldiers, each in his proper place, and his own blessed person, glorious with victory and triumph, remained on the flank of the army. He formed a line of elephants carrying veteran warriors with arms and armor. So fearsome and dreadful was this sight that the hearts of the enemy champions began to tremble in their breasts, and in awe and terror their minds were dazzled and their judgment confused.

He left a brigade of chosen warriors from the right flank on top of the hill and ordered them to keep their positions even if the enemy was defeated and fled.

At this time Prince Abū Bakr Bahadur and his personal retainers advanced against the enemy from the right flank and assailed the enemy with spears, arrows, maces, and swords. Prince Sulṭān Ḥusayn Bahadur attacked from the left flank, and Amīr Jihānshāh came after him and with God's help put the enemy to flight.

But then they had the idea of gathering together and attacking. The Auspicious Amir began to wage royal war and marched in person against the enemy. When the men of Aleppo saw the size of this army, they were bewildered and helpless and found no other resort but to flee. Perforce, they turned and fled.

The victorious army pursued and attacked at full gallop. They killed so many of their horsemen and footmen that heaps of dead arose, and the gates and streets of Aleppo were so crammed with corpses that the horsemen had to ride over the dead, and the horses and mules could only pass with difficulty. The soldiers who had come from other parts fled toward Damascus. The victorious army, following them, killed many with arrows and swords. They threw those who remained alive from their horses. They captured so much equipment and so many animals that skilled accountants were unable to count them. The rest of the army captured the city, plundered it, and took the people captive. They carried off more gold, money, and cloth than can be imagined or reckoned.

Sudun and Timurtash went into the citadel, trusting in its strength and height. This was one of the most famous citadels. The width of the moat was estimated at 30 ells, wide enough to sail boats on it if they wished. The height of the earthworks was estimated at 100 ells, surmounted by ramparts and turrets made of stone. The earthworks were so steep that foot soldiers could not walk on them.

When they took refuge in the citadel, the army was brought to order. When the enemy saw how numerous the soldiers were, their evil thoughts increased. They sounded the kettledrums and began to shoot their ordnance [*raʿdandāz*].[1] The Auspicious Amir, seated on a royal carpet facing the citadel, occupied his luminous mind with plans for the capture of that place. He ordered the soldiers to take up positions around the moat, and by shooting arrows, they did not allow anyone to put his head out of the tower. He gave orders to laborers and sappers, who in one night made holes round the trench like a sieve and, crossing the water, ran up the earthworks like partridges and undermined the foundations of the citadel, which were made of solid stone.

At that time I had come to Aleppo with the intention of proceeding to the Ḥijāz and had fallen prisoner in the hands of a group of them. I saw strange things which it is fitting to record here. It happened that I was on a roof facing the citadel, and thus observed God's work and the intrepidity of these men.

[1] Literally thunder-thrower. This is one of the earlier references to the use of firearms in Syria. See *EI*[2], "Bārūd."

I saw five armed men come out of an opening in the citadel and attack the sappers. When the sappers became aware of this, they came out of the holes which they had dug, went up from below, and pinned the five men to the ground with arrows. Thereupon a great noise broke out in the citadel. Ropes were tied around the waists of these men and the other ends of the ropes were in the hands of men in the citadel. These men pulled the ropes and drew them up, but whether alive or dead I do not know. Nobody else dared to put his head out of the opening in the tower, let alone come out of the citadel. The people in the citadel began to quake with fear and understood that to contend against the decree of God, to try to fend off the hand of fate, is not the work of men of sense nor within the power of wise men.

While they were reflecting thus, a messenger brought a letter from the Auspicious Amir. Its admonition to these heedless ones was as follows: "Almighty God has subjugated the world to our domination, and the will of the Creator has entrusted the countries of the earth to our power. Fortresses cannot withstand our soldiers, fortifications cannot hold off our wrath. If you wish to save your lives, it will go well with you. Otherwise you will be sacrificing yourselves, your wives, and your children."

When they realized that they had no other recourse, Sudun and Timurtash, with the qāḍīs, the Imams, and other notables, took the keys of the citadel and the treasury, opened the gates, came to the Presence, and displayed the face of weakness and humility before the threshold of compassion.

The Auspicious Amir gave orders to shackle and imprison Sudun and Timurtash. The old and new money and treasuries, that which bygone kings had placed there and that which the city notables had brought there, were all placed at the disposal of the officers of the high *dīwān*. . . . He divided this money and effects among the amirs and the soldiers and left the remainder of the treasures in the citadel.

Niẓām al-Dīn Shāmī, *Ẓafarnāma,* pp. 224–228.

7

Muslim Spain

For a while Spain was the remote far western frontier of Islam, where soldiers, frontiersmen, and settlers brought civilization to the barbarians and reaped the familiar rewards for themselves. At first the conquered territories were ruled by a governor sent from the East. After the supersession of the Umayyads by the ʿAbbasids, an Umayyad prince fleeing from Syria established an independent amirate, later Caliphate, in Cordova, which lasted until ca. 1031. After its collapse Muslim Spain broke up into a number of small principalities, many of them ruled by Berber dynasties.

The first of the following excerpts is from an Eastern Arabic chronicle and gives an account, semihistorical and semilegendary, of the Arab conquest. The remainder, from Spanish Arab sources, deal with the arrival of a group of Syrian Arab settlers, with some events during the reign of an Umayyad amir of Cordova, and with life at the court of a Berber prince of Granada, as described in the memoirs of a member of the princely family.

31. The Conquest of Spain (710–715)

Mūsā ibn Nuṣayr sent his son Marwān ibn Mūsā toward Tangier to garrison the coast. He and his companions found themselves overtaxed, and he therefore left, placing Ṭāriq ibn ʿAmr in command of his army. They numbered 1,700 men. According to another version, Ṭāriq had 12,000 Berbers and only 16 Arabs, but this is not authentic.

It is also said the Mūsā ibn Nuṣayr left Ifrīqiya on an expedition against Tangier. He was the first governor to occupy Tangier, which was inhabited by Berbers of the tribes of Butr and Barānis who had not yet submitted. When he was near Tangier, he sent out flying columns, and his horsemen reached the lower Sūs. He treated them roughly and took many captives, and they submitted to him. Mūsā appointed a governor who treated them well. He sent Busr ibn Abī Arṭā against a fortress three days' distance from the town of Qayrawān. Busr captured it, took the children into captivity, and sacked the place. It came to be called Qalʿat Busr [Busr's Castle] and is known by no other name to this day. Mūsā then dismissed the governor whom he had appointed in Tangier and appointed Ṭāriq ibn Ziyād in his place. He then left for Qayrawān. Ṭāriq took with him one of his slave-girls, called Umm Ḥakīm. He stayed there on frontier duty for some time. This was in the year 92 [710–711].

The straits between him and Spain were commanded by a foreigner called Julian, the lord of Ceuta and of a town in Spain, called al-Khaḍrā' [Algeciras], on the Spanish side of the straits facing Tangier. Julian was subject to Rodrigo, the ruler of Spain, who lived in Toledo. Ṭāriq corresponded with Julian and by blandishment brought him to the point of exchanging gifts.

Now Julian had sent one of his daughters to Rodrigo, the ruler of Spain, for him to educate and instruct her, but Rodrigo made her pregnant. When Julian heard of this, he said, "I can see no punishment and no retribution other than to send the Arabs against him." He therefore wrote to Ṭāriq saying, "It is I who will bring you into Spain." Ṭāriq was then at Tlemcen, and Mūsā ibn Nuṣayr was at Qayrawān. Ṭāriq replied, "I cannot trust you unless you send me hostages." Julian then sent him two daughters, as he had no other children. Ṭāriq installed them in Tlemcen, and having made sure of them, he went to meet Julian, who was then at Ceuta on the straits. Julian was delighted when he came and said to him, "It is I who will bring you into Spain."

In the straits between Ceuta and Spain there is a rock which is today called Jabal Ṭāriq [the Mountain of Ṭāriq]. At nightfall Julian brought ships and took him across the straits. They hid during the day, and at nightfall he sent the ships back to bring the rest of his men. They ferried them across until none remained, while the Spaniards noticed nothing. They thought that all this was the usual movement of ships about their business. Ṭāriq himself sailed with the last party and joined his men. Julian and the merchants who were with him stayed behind at al-Khaḍrā to please his companions and his countrymen. The Spaniards had by now heard of Ṭāriq and his men and of their position.

Ṭāriq set out on his way. With his men, he crossed a bridge which led from the mountain to a village called Qarṭajanna [Carteya]. Then, advancing towards Cordova, he passed near an island in the sea, where he left his slave-girl, Umm Ḥakīm, with a few of his men. From that day onward the island was called Jazīrat Umm Ḥakīm [the Island of Umm Ḥakīm]. When the Muslims landed on this island, they found some wine growers and no one else. They made them prisoners. Then they picked on one of the wine growers, killed him, cut him to pieces, and cooked him while his surviving companions watched. Now the Muslims had already prepared meat in other pots. When this meat was ready, they threw away the cooked human flesh unbeknown to the Spaniards, and substituted and ate the meat which they had previously cooked. The surviving wine growers saw this and had no doubt but that they were eating the flesh of their friend. Then they released them, and they told the Spaniards that they ate human flesh and told them what had happened to the wine grower.

According to what my father ʿAbdallāh ibn ʿAbd al-Ḥakam and Hishām ibn Isḥāq told me, there was in Spain a house closed with many locks, to which every king on his accession added another lock of his own. This continued until the time of the king who was invaded by the Muslims. When he succeeded, they asked him to add a lock as all the kings before him had done. He refused and said, "I shall add nothing until I know what is inside." He gave orders to open it, and inside there were pictures of the Arabs, with this inscription, "When this door is opened, these people will enter this country."

When Ṭāriq had crossed the straits, the army of Cordova came to meet him and were emboldened when they saw how few were his men. They joined battle and after fierce fighting were put to flight. Ṭāriq pursued them and killed them all the way to Cordova. Rodrigo heard of this defeat and marched against them from Toledo. They met at a place called Shadhūna, by a river which is today called Wādī Umm Ḥakīm. They fought fiercely, and Almighty God caused Rodrigo and his men to perish. Mughīth al-Rūmī, a *ghulām* in the service of al-Walīd ibn 'Abd al-Malik who commanded Ṭāriq's cavalry, advanced on Cordova, and Ṭāriq proceeded to Toledo, which he entered. His only concern was to ask about the table which had belonged to Solomon the son of David, according to what the People of the Book claim.

Yaḥyā ibn Bukayr says on the authority of al-Layth ibn Sa'd: Spain was conquered under the orders of Mūsā and the table of Solomon the son of David, peace be upon him, was taken, as was the crown. Ṭāriq was told that the table was in a fortress called Firas, a two days' journey from Toledo, and that the fortress was commanded by a nephew of Rodrigo. Ṭāriq sent to him, offering him safe-conduct for himself and for his family. He came to Ṭāriq, who gave him his safe-conduct and confirmed it. Then Ṭāriq said, "Give me the table," and he gave it to him. It was adorned with gold and jewels, the like of which had never been seen. Ṭāriq tore off one of the legs, with its gold and jewels, and put another leg in its place. This table, because of its jewels, was assessed at 200,000 dinars. Ṭāriq seized whatever there was of jewels, arms, gold, silver, and vessels, as well as other property, the like of which has never been seen. Having put all this together, he went to Cordova and stayed there. He wrote to Mūsā ibn Nuṣayr, informing him of the conquest of Spain and of the booty he had gathered. Mūsā wrote to the Caliph al-Walīd ibn 'Abd al-Malik, informing him of this and ascribing it to himself. Mūsā also wrote to Ṭāriq, ordering him not to go beyond Cordova until he himself had joined him and insulting him in scurrilous language.

Mūsā ibn Nuṣayr set out for Spain in Rajab of the year 93 [April–May 712], accompanied by leading Arabs and *mawālī* and by Berber chiefs. When he left he was furious with Ṭāriq. He took Ḥabīb ibn Abī 'Ubayda al-Fihrī with him and left his eldest son, 'Abdallāh ibn Mūsā, in charge at Qayrawān. He landed at al-Khaḍrā' and proceeded to Cordova. Ṭāriq went to meet him and tried to conciliate him. "I am only your *mawlā*," he said, "this conquest is yours." Mūsā then collected riches beyond description, and Ṭāriq handed all that was booty over to him.

According to another version, Rodrigo came to meet Ṭāriq, who was then in the mountains. When Rodrigo was near by, Ṭāriq went out against him. Rodrigo was seated that day on his royal throne, which was carried by two mules. He was wearing his crown, his gloves, and all the adornments which the kings before him used to wear. Ṭāriq and his men attacked on foot; there was not a single horseman among them. They fought from sunrise to sunset, and it seemed that all were doomed. But God caused Rodrigo and his men to perish, and gave the victory to the Muslims. Never had there been greater carnage in the Maghrib. For three days the Muslims did not rest their swords from the enemy, and then they advanced on Cordova.

It is also said that it was Mūsā who sent Ṭāriq to Toledo after his entry into Spain. Toledo is halfway between Cordova and Narbonne, which is the furthest limit of Spain. The writ of ʿUmar ibn ʿAbd al-Azīz reached as far as this town, which the polytheists later captured and which is in their hands today. It was at Narbonne that Ṭāriq found the table. Rodrigo had possessed 200 miles of the coasts on this side.

The Muslims took great booty in gold and silver. ʿAbd al-Malik ibn Maslama related the following on the authority of al-Layth ibn Saʿd: There were carpets woven with gold thread, with their gold chains strung with pearls, rubies, and topaz. When the Berbers found one of these and could not carry it away, they brought an axe and split it down the middle, and two of them took half each for themselves. Some went with them while the men were otherwise engaged.

ʿAbd al-Malik ibn Maslama told us on the authority of Al-Layth ibn Saʿd: During the conquest of Spain a man came to find Mūsā ibn Nuṣayr and said, "Send someone with me and I will show you a treasure." Mūsā sent someone with him. The man said, "Break in here." They did so and were flooded with topaz and rubies such as they had never seen before. When they saw this they were afraid and said, "Mūsā ibn Nuṣayr will not believe us." They sent to fetch him, and he came and saw for himself.

. . . .

ʿAbd al-Malik ibn Maslama told us on the authority of Mālik ibn Anas, on the authority of Yaḥyā ibn Saʿīd: When Spain was conquered the men found much booty and misappropriated a good deal of it. They took it on-board ship and set sail. When they were out at sea, they heard a voice crying, "O God, drown them." They prayed to God and girded themselves with Qurʾāns, but at once a storm wind struck them, and the ships collided, broke, and sank with them. The Egyptians reject this story and say that it was not Muslims coming from Spain, but from Sardinia, who were drowned. According to Saʿīd ibn ʿUfayr, when the Muslims came to Sardinia, the Sardinians went to one of their ports, blocked the entrance, drained away the water, and put all their gold and silver vessels into it. Then they let the water flow back and reach its usual level. They also went to one of their churches, built a false ceiling under the real ceiling, and put their possessions between the two ceilings. A Muslim happened to go and bathe in the place which they had emptied and then refilled with water. His foot touched something; he took it out, and it was a silver platter. He dived in again and brought out other things. When the Muslims heard about this, they drained away the water and seized all the vessels. Another Muslim, with a crossbow, entered the church where they had hidden their riches between the two ceilings. Seeing pigeons, he shot a bolt at them, but missed and hit a wooden plank, it broke, and the money rained down on them. On that day the Muslims misappropriated much booty. Sometimes a man would catch a cat, kill it, remove its entrails, stuff it with his loot, sew it together, and throw it on the road so that anyone who saw it would think it was just a dead animal. On his way out he would pick it up again. Sometimes a man would detach the blade of his sword, throw it away, fill his scabbard with loot, and then put the hilt in the scabbard. When they embarked and were on their way they heard a voice cry out, "O God, drown them." They girded themselves with Qurʾāns, but they were all drowned except for Abū ʿAbd al-Raḥmān al-Ḥubulī and Ḥanash ibn ʿAbdallāh al-Sabāʾī, who had not misappropriated anything.

ʿAbd al-Malik ibn Maslama told us on the authority of Ibn Lahīʿa, who said: I heard Abūʿ Aswad say: I heard ʿAmr ibn Aws say: Mūsā ibn Nuṣayr sent me to search the companions of ʿAtāʾ ibn Rāfiʿ, a *mawlā* of the tribe of Hudhayl, when their ships were wrecked. It happened that I found a man who was hiding dinars in a rag put between his testicles. Another man, he said, passed by me, leaning on a cane. I went up to search him and he tried to resist. I became angry, seized his cane, and hit him with it. The cane broke, scattering the dinars which were hidden in it. I collected them all.

ʿAbd al-Malik told us on the authority of al-Layth ibn Saʿd: I heard that a man on a raid led by ʿAṭāʾibn Rāfiʿ, or someone else, in the Maghrib misappropriated part of the booty and hid his gains in pitch. At the moment of his death he cried out, "From the pitch! The pitch!"

Mūsā ibn Nuṣayr had Ṭāriq ibn ʿAmr arrested, loaded him with chains, threw him in prison, and intended to kill him. Mughīth al-Rūmī was a *ghulām* in the service of al-Walīd ibn ʿAbd al-Malik. Ṭāriq sent him a message, saying, "If you will tell al-Walīd of my predicament, that the conquest of Spain was my work, and that Mūsā has imprisoned me and intends to kill me, I will give you a hundred slaves." He gave him his bond to do this. When Mughīth was leaving, he went to take leave of Mūsā ibn Nuṣayr and said to him, "Do not act in haste against Ṭāriq, for you have enemies and the Commander of the Faithful knows about him. I fear lest his feelings turn against you." Mughīth left, and Mūsā remained in Spain. When Mughīth called on the Caliph al-Walīd, he informed him that the conquest of Spain was the work of Ṭāriq and that Mūsā had imprisoned him with the intention of killing him. Al-Walīd then wrote to Mūsā swearing by God, "If you strike him, I will surely strike you. If you kill him, I will surely kill your son to avenge him." He sent the letter with Mughīth al-Rūmī, who took it to Mūsā in Spain. When he read it he released Ṭāriq, who gave Mughīth the hundred slaves he had promised.

Mūsā ibn Nuṣayr left Spain with his booty, jewels, and the table, leaving his son 'Abd al-Azīz ibn Mūsā in charge. He had stayed in Spain for the years 93, 94, and several months of 95 (711–714). When Mūsā reached Ifrīqiya, the Caliph al-Walīd ibn 'Abd al-Malik wrote, summoning him to come and see him. Mūsā went and left his son 'Abdallāh ibn Mūsā in charge of Ifrīqiya. He set out with all the booty and gifts and had reached Egypt when the caliph al-Walīd ibn 'Abd al-Malik fell ill. He wrote to Mūsā urging him to hurry, but at the same time Sulaymān wrote, telling him to delay and remain where he was until al-Walīd died so that Mūsā's booty would come to him. But Mūsā went on, and at Tiberias he heard of the death of al-Walīd. He therefore appeared with all his gifts before Sulaymān, who was delighted. It is also said that on his return journey from Spain Mūsā did not stop at Qayrawān but passed right by it and halted at Qaṣr al-Mā', where he celebrated the Feast of Sacrifice. He then continued his journey, taking Ṭāriq with him.

Yaḥyā ibn 'Abdallāh ibn Bukayr told us, on the authority of al-Layth ibn Sa'd: Mūsā ibn Nuṣayr left Spain to go to the Commander of the Faithful in the year 96 [714–715]. He arrived in Fusṭāṭ on Thursday, when six nights remained of the month of Rabī' I. While Sulaymān was inspecting these gifts, one of Mūsā ibn Nuṣayr's companions came forward. He was called 'Īsā ibn 'Abdallāh al-Ṭawīl, a man from Medina who had been in charge of the booty. "O Commander of the Faithful," he said, "God has given you enough lawful booty to make unlawful booty superfluous. I am in charge of the division, and Mūsā did not remove a fifth part from all that he brought you." Sulaymān rose in anger from his throne, went to his residence, then came out again, and said before the people, "It is true. God has given me enough that is lawful to make the unlawful needless." He then gave orders for the booty to be placed in the public treasury. Sulaymān ordered Mūsā ibn Nuṣayr and his companions to provide for their needs and then to return to the Maghrib.

According to another version, Mūsā ibn Nuṣayr appeared before al-Walīd ibn al-Malik while he was ill and presented the table to him. "It was I who took it," said Ṭāriq, and Mūsā gave him the lie. "Have the table brought," said Ṭāriq to Walīd, "and see if anything is missing." Al-Walīd had it brought and examined it. One of the legs was unlike the others. "Ask him why, O Commander of the Faithful," said Ṭāriq, "and see if he can give you an answer which will convince you of his truthfulness." Al-Walīd questioned Mūsā about this leg, and he replied, "That is how I found it." Then Ṭāriq produced the leg which he had torn off when he discovered the table, and said, "This leg should convince the Commander of the Faithful of the truth of what I told him. It was I who found this table." Al-Walīd believed him, accepted what he said, and rewarded him munificently.

Ibn 'Abd al-Ḥakam, *Futūḥ*, pp. 204–211.

32. Syrians in Spain (742)

When the Syrians with their amir, Balj, entered Spain, in pride and strength, like the lions of al-Sharā, those who had come earlier to Spain, that is the local Arabs [*baladī*], felt that they were crowding them and demanded that the newcomers leave the country, which they had conquered and which they thought could not hold both of them. They gathered to fight them, and warfare continued between the two groups until Abū'l-Khaṭṭār Ḥusām ibn Dirār al-Kalbī arrived in Spain. Traveling in secret, he crossed the sea from the coast of Tunis and appeared suddenly in Cordova while they were still fighting. They all submitted to his orders, in accordance with the mandate of Hanẓala ibn Ṣafwān, the governor of Ifrīqiya. He arrested the chiefs of the Syrians and, as is well known, induced them to go away. To forestall a resumption of civil war, he decided to scatter the Syrian tribes in the provinces of Spain. He did this and assigned them one-third of the revenue from the remaining Roman *dhimmīs*. The Syrian tribes therefore left Cordova.

Abū Marwān said: Ardabast, the Count of Spain, the chief of the native *dhimmīs* and the collector of the tax due from them to the amirs of the Muslims, had suggested this to Abu'l-Khaṭṭār. The count was famous for his knowledge and cleverness, and it was his idea to send the Syrian tribes of 'Alam away from Cordova, the capital, where there was no room for them, and settle them in the provinces where they could live as they had lived in the provinces of their native Syria. The governor did this, allowing them a choice. He settled the *jund* of Damascus in the province of Elvira, the *jund* of Jordan in the province of Reiya, the *jund* of Palestine in the province of Sidona, the *jund* of Ḥimṣ in the province of Seville, the *jund* of Qinnasrīn in the province of Jaen, and some of the *jund* of Egypt in the province of Beja and some in the province of Todmīr. These are the dwellings of the Syrian Arabs. He assigned them one-third of the revenue from the native *dhimmīs* as grants. The local Arabs and the Berbers remained their partners. The Syrians were happy and became great and rich. . . . Those of them, however, who, when they first arrived in Spain, had established themselves in places which pleased them, did not leave them, but stayed there with the local Arabs, and when pay was distributed or the troops were mobilized for a campaign, they went to the *jund* to which they belonged. They were known at that time as the detached ones [al-Shādhdha].

Aḥmad ibn Mūsā said: The Caliph normally appointed two chiefs in each *jund,* one who went to war [*ghazw*] and one who stayed in the *jund.* The warchief received 200 dinars during his command, whereas the other received no pay for three months, after which he changed places with a warchief, either of the same tribe or of another. The Syrian warriors who were brothers, sons, or nephews of the chief, each received ten dinars at the end of the campaign. The chief used to sit by the side of the commander [*qā'id*] and declare who had fought and earned pay, and pay was given on his declaration in deference to him. He was responsible for their service in the regular army and for reviewing them. Syrians who went to war but were not kinsmen of the chief were each paid five dinars at the end of the campaign. Among the local Arabs no pay was given to anyone other than the chief. They, too, had two chiefs, one of whom went to war and the other stayed at home. The warchief received one hundred dinars' weight of gold and remained chief for six months, after which he changed places with the opposite chief of his tribe or of another tribe. The *dīwān* and the secretariat existed exclusively for the Syrians. They were on call for military service, but were exempt from the tithe and subject only to a fixed tax [*muqāta'a*] on the money of the Romans that came into their hands. The local Arabs paid the tithe like everybody else. Some families among them went to war in the same way as the Syrians, but without pay, and they were then treated as described above. The local Arabs were mustered for war only when the Caliph dispatched two armies in two directions, in which case he made use of them. There was also a third group known as the reserves [*naẓīr*, literally equivalent], consisting of both Syrian and local Arabs, who would go to war in the same conditions as the two main groups with which they were connected.

Ibn al-Khaṭīb, *Kitāb al-Iḥāṭa fī Akhbār Gharnāṭa*, i, pp. 17–19.

33. Episodes in the Reign of al-Ḥakam of Cordova (796–822)

A group of Cordovan chiefs disapproved of certain actions of the amir, which disquieted them, and tried to depose him. They approached one of his cousins, called Ibn al-Shammās of the line of Mundhir ibn 'Abd al-Raḥmān ibn Mu'āwiya. They approached him on this and wanted to enthrone him and depose al-Ḥakam. He pretended to agree and said, "Tell me who is with you in this business," and they promised to tell him on a day which they appointed. Then he, himself, went to al-Ḥakam and informed him of this. "You are trying," al-Ḥakam said to him, "to turn me against the chiefs of my city. By God, you will prove this to me or I will cut off your head." "Send me someone you trust on such and such a night," said Ibn al-Shammās, and al-Ḥakam sent his page Vicent and his secretary, Ibn al-Khadā, the ancestor of the Banu'l-Khadā, and Ibn al-Shammās hid them in a place where they would hear what was said between him and them. They came and discussed the matter, and he asked them, "Who is with you in this?" And they gave names, which the secretary, hidden behind the curtain, wrote down. They named so many that the secretary, fearing that he himself would be named, made a noise with his pen on the parchment. The conspirators were startled, and said, "What have you done, enemy of God?" Those who left at once and fled were saved; those who stayed were captured. Among those who fled were 'Isā ibn Dīnār, the chief jurist of Spain, Yaḥyā ibn Yaḥyā, and others. Six prominent men were arrested; of these Yaḥyā ibn Naṣr al-Yaḥsubī, who lived in Secunda, Mūsā ibn Sālim al-Khawlānī, and his son were crucified.

Because of this the people of the suburbs rose in arms and fought against the army [*jund*], but being heavily outnumbered, they cried out that they would submit. Some of the viziers advised him to refuse, while others advised him to accept it, saying that among them there were good as well as bad. He accepted the opinion of those who advised leniency and allowed them to leave Cordova. They scattered and reached the Barbary coast and some settled there, but a large group of them, about 5,000 to 10,000, parted from them and sailed to Alexandria, which they seized at the beginning of the reign of al-Rashīd. They treated the inhabitants abominably and put most of them to the sword—all because a butcher had struck one of them, a Muslim, in the face with the stomach of an animal. They were so offended at this that they massacred most of the townspeople. When al-Rashīd heard of this, he sent the chamberlain Harthama ibn A'yan to settle things with them. He ransomed the city from them for a considerable sum of money and gave them the choice of settling wherever they wished, either in Egypt or in the islands. They chose the island of Crete where they landed. They are still there to this day.

. . . .

One of those who abetted the rising in the suburbs was Ṭālūt ibn 'Abd al-Jabbār al-Ma'āfirī, who had studied under Mālik and other great jurists. When the rising failed, he fled from his house, which was in the city near the mosque and ditch which bear his name, and remained hidden for a whole year in the house of a Jew until things became quiet and passions were calmed. There was friendship between him and the vizier, Abu'l-Bassām, the ancestor of the Banū'l-Bassām, the keepers of the granary, and as he was growing weary of his stay in the house of the Jew, he went at nightfall to the house of Abu'l-Bassām the vizier. When he arrived, the vizier asked him where he had been, and Ṭālūt replied, "With a certain Jew." The vizier promised him safety and reassured him and said, "The amir, may God preserve him, has regretted what happened." Ṭālūt stayed the night with him, and the following morning, having left his guest in safekeeping, the vizier went to al-Ḥakam and said, "What would you say to a fat sheep that has been kept at the manger for a whole year?" "The flesh of a foddered animal is heavy," replied al-Ḥakam. "That of a free-grazing animal is lighter and tastier." "I mean something else," said Abu'l-Bassām. "I have Ṭālūt in my hands." "How did you get hold of him?" asked al-Ḥakam. "I caught him with kindness," replied the vizier.

He was then summoned and given a chair. The old man was brought, overcome with fear. He made obeisance, and al-Ḥakam said, "O Ṭālūt, tell me, if your father or your son had ruled in this palace, could they have shown you more generosity and more honor than I did? Did you ever ask me for anything, for yourself or another, that I did not hasten to grant you? Did I not, when you were sick, go to see you several times? Did I not, when your wife died, go to the door of your house? Did I not walk at her funeral as far as the suburbs and then walk back with you to your own house? Then what happened to you? What is the matter with you, that nothing would content you but to shed my blood, to disgrace and dishonor me?" "At this moment," said Ṭālūt, "I can find nothing that will serve me better than the truth. I hated you for God's sake, and all that you did for me availed you nothing with me."

Al-Ḥakam was shocked into silence and then said, "I sent for you, and there is no punishment on earth which I did not think of in order to inflict it on you. But know that He for whose sake you hated me diverted me from punishing you. Go safe and sound, in God's care! By God, I shall never cease to honor you and treat you as I did before, for the rest of my life, please God. But I wish that what happened, had not happened." "Had it not happened," said Ṭālūt, "it would be better for you."

Then al-Ḥakam asked him, "How did Abu'l-Bassām get hold of you?"

"He did not get hold of me," said Ṭālūt. "I put myself in his hands and sought him because of the friendship between us."

"And where have you been all the year?" asked al-Ḥakam. "In the house of a certain Jew," he replied.

Then al-Ḥakam said to the vizier, "O Abu'l-Bassām, a Jew protected him out of respect for his eminence in religion and scholarship and endangered himself, his wife, his possessions, and his children at my hands—and you wanted to involve me again in something which I have already regretted!" Then he said to Abu'l-Bassām, "Leave me! By God, I never want to see your face again!" He gave orders to remove his carpet [i.e., his place in the council] and dismissed him, and his descendants are decayed and degraded to this day. Ṭālūt was honored and respected until he died, as the amir had undertaken, and Al-Ḥakam attended his funeral.

After this, the Caliph was stricken by a long sickness which lasted seven years until he died, in contrition and penitence for what he had done. In sickness he grew gentle, and he spent the nights reading the Qur'ān until he died.

Ibn al-Qūṭiyya, *Ta'rīkh Iftitāḥ al-Andalus*, pp. 50–55.

34. Death of a Jew in Granada (1066)

[The Jewish vizier[1]] informed the elders of the Jews that Sayf al-Dawla had turned against him. The shrewdest of them, with the keenest judgment, said to him, "Don't expect to prosper when the *shaykh* [Sultan al-Muẓaffar Bādīs ibn Ḥabbūs[2]] is no more and hope for nothing from Sayf al-Dawla. Consider, rather, whom you will enthrone if your sovereign dies. Have you found him? Contrive to poison Sayf al-Dawla. His brother, Māksan, is now a nonentity. If you kill the one and enthrone the other, you will render him a service which he will not forget."

The vizier let himself be tempted to poison Sayf al-Dawla. He was well able to do so because my father often used to drink with

[1] The Jewish vizier in question is Yūsuf (Joseph) ibn Nagrella, son and successor of the more famous Samuel ibn Nagrella, known as Samuel ha-Nagid. They served the (Berber) Zirid ruler of Granada.

[2] Reigned 1038–1073; grandfather of the author of these memoirs.

him and was often in his house. One day he drank with him as usual in his house. He had hardly left his house when he vomited up all that was in his stomach and fell on his back on the ground. It was only with a great effort that he was able to walk back to his own house. He lingered for two days and then died. May God have mercy on him.

I heard one of Bādīs's chief eunuchs tell this story: One day Sayf al-Dawla sent for me and said: "Go and find my lady Mothers[3] and tell them that I intend to kill the Jew." I said to him, "I will not take this message, for he would undoubtedly hear of it. If you really intend to kill him, then you should not inform me or anyone else among God's creatures." I realized that it was his condition which led him to such actions.

Another thing which had previously helped to make trouble was that my father was on terms which were the very opposite of confidence with the palace ladies who had brought up his son, al-Mu'izz, my brother. The reason was that they lavished money on his son while he was still a small child and refused it to him, so that he had to have recourse to the Jew to get money. The ladies complained to him and tried to prevent him from associating with the Jew, until the latter became aware of this, and my father and he agreed to charge the women before the sovereign and accuse them of having stolen the money and sent it out into the country. When my grandfather became aware of the matter and of the quarrel which had arisen between the palace ladies and their son, Sayf al-Dawla, the latter was at the same time blamed by both his father and the women, while the women contrived to exculpate themselves from the slanderous accusation which had been made against them. With his father on the side of the women, Sayf al-Dawla was obliged to make peace with them, and, in the end, the whole story rebounded on the head of the Jew. All this increased the Jew's hatred and vindictiveness, until, at the appointed time, God's decree made him the instrument of the death of Sayf al-Dawla.

When the quarrel was just beginning, the Jew had retained for himself a large part of the tax revenue from Guadix. Sayf al-

[3] The ladies of the palace, the mothers of the princes.

Dawla complained of this to his father. The swine, therefore, contrived to invite my father to his house to drink until he was drunk, whereupon he gave orders to bring out his sons and his women dressed in mourning. My father was shocked by their condition and by their weeping and asked the vizier, "Has someone died in your house?" "A large sum of money has died in my house," he replied. "It is withheld from you only because of the slowness of the subjects in paying their taxes. But today is a good day. Comfort my family, therefore, by writing a quittance in which you hold me innocent of this sum until your money reaches you. My family are in fear and terror. Complete your benevolence by writing this quittance." Thus he seized his opportunity and my father wrote him this quittance. Then the Jew took this quittance to his father [Bādīs] and said to him, "He spends his money for the viziers and on constant drinking. Here is a document in which he gives me quittance. Of what, then, does he complain?" Sayf al-Dawla again fell into even greater disfavor with his father and lost the day against both the vizier and the women, since it was God's will to put a term to his existence. May God reward him [in the other world] for his good intentions and his sincere behavior toward both the nobles and the common people.

When my father died it was a great calamity for the people, who had hoped that he would make justice prevail. The people were in turmoil and wanted to kill the Jew. These were the first signs of his downfall, but they expected my grandfather, the sovereign, to punish him. The Jew continued his campaign against the Qarawī family and alleged to al-Muẓaffar [Bādīs] that members of this family had so extolled wine-bibbing to his son that he had died of it. Because of this the Qarawī family suffered great misfortunes. They were expelled from their lands, their property was seized, and some of them, viziers attached to the person of my father, were put to death because of accusations brought against them, and the real culprit remained undetected.

After the death of Sayf al-Dawla the Jew acted as if he were a Barmecide[4] and tried to install my uncle, Māksan, as heir to

[4] The Barmecides was a famous family of viziers under the early 'Abbasid Caliphs. Their power and authority became legendary.

the succession. At this time my grandfather was very old. He was inclined to repose and, because of his age and the death of his son, he undertook no further conquests, leaving the reins of government to the Jew to serve in his place. He was thus able to command and forbid as he pleased. My grandfather's sole desire, the object of his greatest endeavors, was the capture of Malaga. Indeed, whenever he captured some castle in Spain, they brought him this message from al-Muʿizz ibn Bādīs, "The prince of Granada has written to inform me that he has taken country districts and villages. If he had captured Cordova, Malaga, or such like cities, then I would make obeisance to him for it." These words drove Bādīs to make a special effort against Malaga. He was, moreover, aware of the weakness of the sultans of that city and feared lest someone else capture it and cause him trouble. For several years he pursued his campaigns against Malaga, without weariness or intermission, until finally he took it. He then built a casba in the city, such that no one in his time could build. He equipped and supplied it with what was needed, using all the money which he had inherited from his son and more besides. He feared the greed of the sultans of Spain and the possibility that they might make an alliance against him. His aim, therefore, was, in case of necessity, to hold out in Malaga as long as he could or, if this failed, to cross with his family and his treasures to the shore of his cousins' realm [in Africa].

After the capture of Malaga my grandfather retired from active life. Ibn ʿAbbād tried to wrest Malaga from him and was obeyed by the inhabitants outside the casba. My grandfather sent troops and routed Ibn ʿAbbād near Malaga, who returned the city to him after he had given up hope of recovering it. No sultan ever endured as much for a city as he did for Malaga, in struggles and in expenditure of money. When he finally achieved the fulfillment of his hopes there, he withdrew from active life and sought to enjoy his kingship. Many troubles befell him because of his blind faith in the viziers and governors of the country, as I shall relate in due course. . . .

For a time, there was peace and well-being. The treasury was filled, and for several years no dissension was heard and no disorder seen. Then things went wrong. The Jew, may God curse him, played false, and Guadix and all its territory passed into the power of Ibn Ṣumādiḥ. The other princes pounced on our lands until nothing was left to us but Granada, Almuñecar, Priego, and Cabra. The rumor spread among the subjects that the great sovereign was dead. He had, indeed, disappeared from sight. The castles were evacuated by their garrisons, and the populace took the opportunity to move into them, in circumstances which I shall describe later, please God. . . .

It was at the peak of Bādīs's power and glory that al-Nāya came to seek him. He had been a slave of al-Mu'taḍid ibn 'Abbād, may God have mercy on him, and was one of the group who had plotted treason against him, in collusion with his son, whose story is well known. Al-Nāya came to Granada, driven by his inescapable destiny, and a group of the chiefs of the [black] slaves befriended him and asked the Sultan to bestow gifts on him. The Sultan granted their request, desiring to please them and thus increase their zeal and loyalty in his service. "This man," they said, "has come to seek you, breaking with another and counting on you. He has placed his hopes in you. Whatever you do for him, you do for us."

He entered Granada at a time most fortunate for him and most troublous for the state. At first he behaved excellently and with modesty in his dealings with officials, so that they praised his conduct and helped him by commending him to the Sultan, who took him into his service and gave him a military appointment. Because of his desire for vengeance on the 'Abbadids, he acquitted himself well in the struggle for Malaga and won over some units of the army in the town where he held a command, which was under Muqātil ibn Yaḥyā, the commanding general [*qā'id*]. This Muqātil, whenever a raiding party went out against the territory of 'Ibn Abbād, did not fail to report favorably to al-Muẓaffar [Bādīs] on al-Nāya's role in it, almost to the point of giving him the whole credit, so much so that he received a letter from the Sultan, making them associates. Al-Nāya thus became *qā'id* in Malaga with Muqātil. His activity increased and his reputation grew. The Sultan redoubled his favors toward him, and when

[5] Al-Mu'taṣim ibn Ṣumādiḥ was the ruler of Almeria and a rival of the Zirids of Granada.

he went to Malaga he stayed at al-Nāya's house and drank in his company. As time passed, he favored and advanced him still further. Thanks to his intimacy with the Sultan, he would turn his mind against the Jew when he was alone with him or could take advantage of his drunkenness and say to him, "He has eaten your money, he has possessed himself of the greater part of your fortune, and he has built a finer palace than yours. By God! You must get rid of him and earn the love of the Muslims by his removal." Al-Muẓaffar then made promises to him and said, "I must, indeed, do this, and I will give you the job of killing him." No doubt he uttered this in the hearing of some of his slaves or palace staff, to whom he paid no attention, and who, at once, went, to report it to the Jew.

That swine's rage and hatred only increased all the more, and he was almost dying with worry and anger, as well as his envy of al-Nāya for the high rank which he had attained to his own disadvantage. What he desired, above all, was to call him to account before the Sultan, but the Sultan was not willing. Seeing that al-Nāya's position became ever stronger and fearing that he would induce the Sultan to kill him, he lost all hope and said to himself, "It is only for the glory of the Sultan that I have treated the people with scorn, counting for my safety on his protection and care. But now, all hope is lost, and I cannot turn to the Sultan for protection. An evil companion incites him against me, the common people desire my death, and we [Jews] are few and feeble in the land."

He had already, before this time, tried to gain a hold over my uncle Māksan, in the hope of being able to lean on him. But Māksan responded with the greatest hostility, having no one at his side to guide and instruct him in discretion. He even said to him, face to face, "Do you want to kill me as you killed my brother?" These words worked on the Jew's mind. In addition to all this, Māksan displayed abominable conduct, little charity, and foul language. He uttered so many threats that the people of his father's court loathed and detested him, and there were many complaints about him to his father. His mother ceased to have dealings with the vizier who had tried to gain a hold over her son; instead, she preferred his maternal uncle, another Jew called

Abu'l-Rabī' ibn al-Māṭūnī, the collector of revenue. She wrote to him all the time, asking for advances of money without interest. The vizier became jealous and decided to take action against him, which would also be against Māksan's mother and entourage. He, therefore, brought a false accusation against them to the Sultan, and it was attested by a group of courtiers who were already hostile to Māksan, as I said above. The Sultan was incited against him to such effect that, revolted by what had been reported to him, he ordered the execution of Māksan's mother, his nurses, and some others connected with them. The vizier had his uncle killed by treachery, in his own house and while drinking, for having opposed him in this and other matters and for fear that he would advise the Sultan. He gave the Sultan a very large sum of money so that he should not condemn him for this murder. The Sultan accepted it from him and would have been glad for him to murder another Jew every day and pay him money for it.

Some time later al-Muẓaffar ordered his son's banishment. One of the chief causes of this banishment was the following incident: One day the Sultan went out to review the troops at the time of the conflict with Ibn Ṣumādiḥ. One of the shaykhs of the army went up to him and said, "It is not fitting for you to place black slaves or other such at our head and to set aside your own son. Send him with us, and we shall follow him through every calamity." He was speaking of Māksan. This was too much for the father, already angry with him because of what he had seen and of what was reported to him about his son. He feared that behind these words there was a plan to put him aside and transfer power to his son. The Jew was also very alarmed at this and remarked later, "On that day I was sure that I would be put to death." He put the matter to the Sultan, who at once ordered his son's banishment from the country. He sent one of his slaves with him to escort him outside his territory. The Jew, whom God curse, advised this slave to take him to a certain place which he named and there, in secret, cut off his head. My brother al-Mu'izz had been brought up by our grandfather and had been well-treated by him, and the people of his father's household loved him. They all agreed with the Jew to kill Māksan and appoint al-Mu'izz as heir, fearing for themselves, lest Māksan turn on them and punish them for loving his nephew and bringing him up. His banishment was, therefore, what they had hoped. My uncle thus left Granada in the worst circumstances, in fear and trembling. Some advised that he be put to death and others objected, demanding only that he be forbidden to remain in any part of the realm. In the end, he went by a certain route and was delivered from his troubles by the death of the Jew, which I shall relate in due course.

When this swine, whom God curse, saw the turbulence of the palace women, each group of them desiring the appointment as heir of whichever of the princes she had brought up, and seeing the change in his master's attitude toward him, the growing strength of al-Nāya, and his determination to destroy him, he could no longer find any escape in the world nor any way to save himself. He consulted the wise elders of his people and one of them said, "Save yourself and send ahead of you the greater part of your fortune to whatever part of the country you choose. You can then go to live there, rich and safe."

"That would be possible," he replied, "except that my exalted sovereign would send a message about me to the ruler of the country in which I had taken refuge, saying to him, 'My vizier has run away with my money. Either you return him or I make war against you.' Do you really think that he would then prefer me to the Sultan? It would only work if I could give him territory so that war would break out between the two of them. This would secure my safety with the ruler to whom I go. He would not be able to hand me over when I have brought him new territory and great glory."

They therefore agreed to approach Ibn Ṣumādiḥ, since he was the most suitable, being a neighbor and close at hand in case of need.

Ibn Ṣumādiḥ's envoy, Ibn Arqam, whom they had chosen for this mission, said: I was received one day by al-Muẓaffar [Bādīs], may God have mercy on him, in one of his pleasure palaces to which he had gone. Al-Nāya was with him, and the Jew was behind him. Al-Nāya noticed a Jewish doctor of the vizier. He gave orders that he should be insulted and forced to dismount in the presence of the sovereign. He behaved very insolently in this and subjected the Jew to violent abuse. The Jew was outraged and said to Ibn Arqam, "What do you think of this intolerable insult? If you can't help me, I shall have to look elsewhere." Ibn Arqam then said to him, "You are well able to stand firm in this affair. What need have you to turn to us when you control the population and the collection of taxes? The Sultan has changed nothing in your situation; these are no more than pinpricks from this slanderer. Contrive to be patient until the shaykh al-Muẓaffar [Bādīs] dies, the more so since he is already old. Then you will get a hold over his grandson, al-Mu-ʿizz, and have the same position with him as you had with his grandfather. That is the best way to save yourself."

To this the Jew replied, "I would do what you say, but al-Muʿizz is still very young. He is under the influence of the palace ladies, as well as of a large number of palace women of various kinds and their retinues. How can I hope to prevail against them? My situation in that case would be even worse because of their conflicting desires. What is more, I have sure knowledge that the young man hates me because of what people say about my having poisoned his father. I have already pondered on all these aspects of the matter, and I can see no better course before me than to offer myself to al-Muʿtaṣim."

Ibn Arqam said: I went to see al-Muẓaffar, gave him some hint of this conversation, and said to him," God help you—be on your guard! You are not all that old, and you have not yet reached an age which obliges you to neglect your affairs of state." I hoped by this to induce him to question me further about the conversation, so that I could tell him more of it. But he sent for the Jew and said to him, "Go find Ibn Arqam and ask him why he has just told me to be on my guard. Get him to explain it to you."

Ibn Arqam continued: The Jew came to me and informed me of the matter. I was appalled and could have dropped dead; I did not know what answer to give. The swine then suspected me, wrote to al-Muʿtaṣim [Ibn Ṣumādiḥ] about me, and advised him to relieve me of my mission and send someone else whom he could trust. Al-Muʿtaṣim chose his milk-brother and ordered him to concert with the Jew in devising a scheme to get the government of Granada into his hands, in spite of the fact that the city was a mine of troops and contained Ṣanhāja Berbers,[6] who would never acquiesce in this. The envoy said to the Jew, "Do not involve yourself and al-Muʿtaṣim in something which cannot be carried through to the end and discredit yourself in the eyes of al-Muẓaffar, who is rich and able to wage war. You would be the cause of your own destruction and al-Muʿtaṣim's ruin." The swine, on this advice, decided to expel from Granada all those whose resistance he feared.

He therefore chose certain prominent persons among the Ṣanhāja and certain slaves from whom he expected trouble and advised the Sultan to send them to the principal castles with letters of appointment to them. He said to them in secret, "You are my brothers, for you have been thrust aside as I have; you have seen it yourselves. I see in the rule of this Sultan things which you are right to disapprove. He puts at your head men who are not of your kind or of your station. His rule will continue to bring you shame and dishonor for as long as it lasts. I have given the Sultan good advice on his affairs, but he has not accepted my advice, though he cannot refute it. Now danger threatens this noble land and he will hand over these fine castles to al-Nāya's men. We would all suffer by this, and we would not be able to prevail against them for the control of the state. They would have dominion over us, and we would have no recourse, except to al-Nāya himself. But if we hold firm in the castles while your kinsmen are at court, he will not dare to scatter you and he will soon lose all power. If he tries to change things, we shall kill him. If the Sultan becomes angry with one of us and orders his banishment, he can come to a friend's castle."

They approved his words, the more readily because of their greed for governorships, and they hurried off to their posts. He sent Yaḥyā ibn Ifrān to the city al Almuñecar, Musakkan ibn Ḥabbūs al-Maghralī to Jaen, and the rest to other provincial centers. The Jew persuaded the Sultan that this was to his advantage, that only leading men could defend important centers, and that the negligence and incompetence of the dismissed

[6] A Berber tribe, from which the Zirid monarchy emerged. See p. 60ff.

governors had been proved to him, for so great was his confidence in the Jew that he listened to no one but him on such matters.

The Jew then wrote to Ibn Ṣumādiḥ to inform him that he had removed the troublemakers from the city, that no one was left there but people without importance whom his sword would mow down as when he entered, and that he was ready to open the gates of Granada to him as soon as he would venture his way. He deliberately neglected all the castles other than the provincial centers, and he omitted, as if by oversight, to send them the supplies and reinforcements which they needed, so that they were evacuated.

Meanwhile, al-Muẓaffar knew nothing of this and devoted himself to drink and idleness. Then the garrisons evacuated the castles, seeing that no one cared for them and that the Sultan no longer showed himself to them, accepting as truth the rumor that he was dead. Calling out to one another, they abandoned the castles and regions which they controlled. Ibn Ṣumādiḥ's troops seized the opportunity and occupied them, until the only castle which remained was that of Cabrera, near Granada, on the road to Guadix. The Jew at once sent a message to Ibn Ṣumādiḥ, urging him to march against the city, since there was no one to prevent him from doing so. But Ibn Ṣumādiḥ backed out of the enterprise, not daring to attack a city like Granada. Meanwhile, the breech grew wider and the upheavals increased. The Jew moved from his house to the casba to protect himself from the common people until his hopes were fulfilled. People held this against him as also his building the Alhambra with the intention of going there with his family when Ibn Ṣumādiḥ entered the city, and staying until order was restored. Both the common people and the nobles were disgusted by the cunning of the Jews, the notorious changes which they had brought about in the order of things, and the positions which they occupied, in violation of their pact. God decreed their destruction on Saturday, Ṣafar 10 [459 December 31, 1066]. The previous night the Jew had been drinking with some of al-Muẓaffar's slaves, some who were his allies and confederates and some who secretly hated him. He told them about Ibn Ṣumādiḥ, who, he said, was coming and who would assign them such and such villages in the plain of Granada. One of those slaves who had concealed his enmity went up to him and said, "We know all that! Instead of assigning us estates, tell us if our master is alive or dead." Some of the Jew's followers restrained him and rebuked him for having spoken thus. The slave went out in disgust and ran away, drunken and shouting to the people, "All you who are loyal to al-Muẓaffar! The Jew has betrayed him and this Ibn Ṣumādiḥ is entering the city! Everybody, the common people and the nobles alike, listened to these words, and they came determined to kill the Jew. He contrived to get al-Muẓaffar to appear before them and said to them," Here is your Sultan, alive!" The sovereign tried to calm them, but could not, and the situation got out of hand. The Jew fled into the interior of the palace, but the mob pursued him there, seized him, and killed him. They then put every Jew in the city to the sword and took vast quantities of their property.

After this, the Ṣanhāja became bold and insolent toward their sovereign, who was faced with rebellion on every side. They became the viziers and the real rulers of the state. As a result of all this, al-Muẓaffar was full of fear and ignominy. He hated them for what they had done to his vizier, knowing nothing of his misdeeds and not believing what they said about him. He put up with them as best he could, with fair words and with patience, until his lands were conquered and his authority restored, as I shall relate later, please God.

Sultan ʿAbdallāh of Granada, *Kitāb al-Tibyān . . . in Andalus*, iii (1935), pp. 265–274.

8

The Rise of the Ottomans

At first the newly acquired Turkish territories in Anatolia were politically and culturally dependent on the older centers in the East. The Seljuq Sultanate of Rūm was subordinate to the Great Sultanate and then, after an interval of independence, to the Mongol rulers of Iran. After the breakup of the Seljuq state, Anatolia was divided into a number of Turkish principalities. One of these, the frontier-march of the Ottomans, became the nucleus of a vast empire, and the last of the great Islamic Sultanates. The four following excerpts, all drawn from early Turkish chronicles, depict the growth and transformation of the Ottoman state, as seen from the point of view of the frontiersmen.

35. The Good Old Days (1360–1389)

At that time [the reign of Murād I (1360–1389)] the tax was low. Conditions were such that even the unbelievers were not oppressed. It was not the practice to seize their purse [clothes?] or their ox or their son or their daughter and sell them or hold them as pledges. At that time the rulers [*Pādishāh*] were not greedy. Whatever came into their hands they gave away again, and they did not know what a treasury was. But when Hayreddin Pasha came to the Gate [of the government] greedy scholars became the companions of the rulers. They began by displaying piety and then went on to issue rulings [*fetva*]. "He who is ruler must have a treasury," they said. At that time they won over the rulers and influenced them. Greed and oppression appeared. Indeed, where there is greed there must also be oppression. In our time it has increased. Whatever oppression and corruption there is in this country is due to scholars. They are the cause of it. If they would act in accordance with wisdom, the ignorant common people would also follow them. But about this there is a story.

In Anatolia, in the neighborhood of Yenishehir, lived Akbïyïk Dede. One day while he was sitting in Bursa with Mevlana Yiken, Akbïyïk Dede said, "Mevlana![1] Whatever sins these ignorant common people commit, the cause is the ulema. God may well call you to account for these sins." "Why should He call us to account?" asked Mevlana Yiken. To this Akbïyïk Dede replied, "For this reason: The common people have seen how you commit adultery and pederasty, lend money on interest, and make no difference between permitted and forbidden. They have seen you do this and have done the same, imitating you. If they did not see you do these things, they would not do them. Because you do not eat pig meat, the common people do not eat it. If you did not do all these other things, they would not do them either." And let us be fair–is it not in fact so? At the present time is there one of the ulema who refuses to accept anything on the grounds that it is unlawful? Whatever comes to them, there is no such thing as unlawful or even doubtful. If there is anything unlawful or doubtful, for them it becomes necessary. If once in his lifetime, one of them were to refuse something! But to refuse is out of the question. Let it be permitted, let it be forbidden, as long as he gets hold of it. Yes, indeed, the wonder is that they even begrudge eating. To give alms or feed others, for the men of learning, is a sin. Do not mention such words in their presence.

Anonymous Ottoman Chronicle, pp. 25–26.

36. Sultan Bāyezīd Yïldïrïm (1389–1402)

When Gāzī Murād,[1] may God's abundant mercy be upon him, was killed in that battle, the Begs, as soon as they had heard about it, consulted together. Finally, they got Ya'qūb Čelebi to

[1] Literally, our master; an honorific title often applied to religious scholars.

[1] Sultan Murād I; reigned 1362–1389. He was killed at the battle of Kossovo.

come by, saying to him, "Come, your father wants you!" When
he came, they seized him, disposed of him, and put Yîldîrîm
Bāyezîd[2] on the throne as Pādishāh. Lazoghlu[3] was also captured
in the battle. They brought him before Yîldîrîm Khan and killed
him, may he stay in the fire in Hell. Murād Gāzī ruled for thirty
years and then died. They built a monument [türbe] in the
place where he fell and marked it clearly. His monument still
stands today in that place. Then they carried his body to Kaplîja
and buried him there. This happened in the year 791 of the
Hijra [1389]. Then Bāyezîd left for Edirne.

. . . .

In that year Bāyezîd Yîldîrîm conquered the mines of Karatova
and the surrounding region. There was a bold warrior called
Fīrūz Beg, whom he sent forward. He went and conquered
Viddin. Then Yîldîrîm Khan stayed in Edirne. Then they entrusted
the raid to Fīrūz Beg, who attacked and raided Walachia and
took his fill of booty. Also Pasha Yigit, the tutor of Ishaq Beg,
attacked and raided Bosnia and conquered the land of Bosnia.
Then Yîldîrîm Khan went to Bursa, where he began and completed the construction of a mosque, a medrese, and a hospital.
Then he also built a hospice in Edirne, which he also completed.
Then he went back to Bursa, gathered an army, and set out
against Karaman. The Karamanlis came to meet him. Then Yîldîrîm Khan conquered Alashehir. They themselves handed over
the land of Aydîn and Ayasoluk. From there Yîldîrîm Khan went
to the land of Sārukhān and conquered it. After that the beg
of Aydîn, the beg of Sārukhān, and the beg of Germiyān, their
time having come, all died. All these lands came to Yîldîrîm
Khan. . . . Then he gave the region of Sārukhān to his son
Ertogrul. The date of these conquests is the year 792 of the
Hijra. Then Sultan Bāyezîd marched against Constantinople,
attacked it, and made war. While they were at war, the accursed
king of the Hungarians attacked, fell upon Nicopolis, and laid
siege to it. When the news reached Yîldîrîm Khan, he withdrew
from Constantinople, and when he was nearby, he assembled
his troops by night, made a night attack, threw the king with

2 Sultan Bāyezîd I was known as Yîldîrîm, the Thunderbolt.
3 Lazar, the king of the Serbs.

his army into the Danube, and destroyed him. This happened in the year 793 of the Hijra. Then Yíldírím renewed his attack on Constantinople. Up above Galata there is a high rampart. There he erected watch posts, overtopping and surrounding them, so that the unbelievers were helpless. Finally, in despair, the emperor sent an envoy and made peace with Sultan Yíldírím Khan. Yíldírím Khan appointed a qāḍī there; he brought the garrison of Taraqlí Yenijesi and settled them inside Istanbul. They formed a city quarter and built a mosque. This happened in the year 794 [1391–1392] of the Hijra. Then Yíldírím Khan took Nicopolis and Silistria. Then he marched on the Morea. He paused in Karaferia, sent raids in all four directions, and gathered much money. He also built a hospice in Karaferia. Then he went to Edirne and stayed there. Vulkoglu[4] gave Yíldírím Khan his daughter. They became brothers-in-law. Until Vulkoglu's daughter came to him, Yíldírím Khan did not know what drinking parties were. He did not drink and held no carouses. In the times of Osmān, Orkhān Gāzī, and Murād, wine was not drunk. At that time there were ulema who made their words effective. At that time the Sultans were ashamed before the ulema and did not depart from whatever words they uttered. If in the house of Osmān any sin or injustice arose, they stopped it. Had they not stopped it, the ulema of that time would have left them, and none would have come to such a Pādishāh. The ulema of that time were not sinners like the ulema of today. They were men of standing who came to the gate of the Pādishāh. If anything contrary to the law occurred, they knew very well how to make their words effective.

. . . .

Qāḍīs

At that time, to fill the office of qāḍī, they used to seek a scholar from among the professors. A qadiship might remain vacant for a long time, and when a suitable scholar was found, he was not happy to accept appointment as qāḍī. They used

[4] The Serb despot George Vuković Branković (b. 1375), reigned 1427–1456), son of Vuk Branković. It was in fact the daughter of King Lazar who was sent by George Branković to Bāyezīd.

to say that qadiship is a matted seat in hell, and they fled from appointment as qāḍī. It is remarkable that at the present time they are willing to destroy one another for a qadiship if it comes their way. Because of this, at the present time, unqualified persons, after serving someone for a while, seek and obtain posts as qāḍīs. If their own name is written down and handed to them, they cannot read it. In these days we have even found qāḍīs who, when a document is needed, say, "I cannot write. If there is anyone here who can, let him write," By God, is such a one fit to be a qāḍī and apply the Holy Law? Woe to the land in which the scholars of today become qāḍīs and enforce the Holy Law. In bygone times they used to seek out a scholar for a qadiship.

. . . .

When the Persians and the Karamanlis became the companions of the princes of the house of Osmān, these princes committed all kinds of sins. Čandarlî Kara Halīl and the Karamanian Turk Rüstem were both at that time considered as great and learned. When these two came to the Ottoman princes, they filled the world with all kinds of cunning tricks. Until then nothing was known of keeping account books. When they came to the Ottoman princes, they compiled account books. The practice of accumulating money and storing it in a treasury comes from them. They had no thought of the end and did not remember that they would have to leave it all behind them, but were very proud of themselves.

. . . .

When 'Alī Pasha, the son of Kara Halīl, became vizier, sin and wickedness increased. He gathered pretty boys around himself and called them pages [*ičoglan*]. When he had misused them for a while, he let them go and gave them posts. Before that time there were the old-timers who were the heads of families; these held all the posts; they were not sent away and not dismissed, and their positions were not given to others. When a *sipāhī* died, his post was given to his son, and when there was no son and only a daughter or a widow, they were given to a slave of the Porte so that they should not suffer privation, and he was given the fief [*timar*] of the dead man.

The *ičoglan* was then lower than a dog. The high regard for the *ičoglans* dates from ʻAlī Pasha.

When ʻAlī Pasha became vizier, the number of scholars also increased in his time. They came to the doors of the begs, one to each beg, and desiring to be useful to them, gave them the answers they wanted and abandoned God's command and the words of the Prophet. The house of Osmān was a sturdy people, but these outsiders came to them and introduced all kinds of tricks so that they put aside piety [*taqvā*] and brought in the *fetvā*. From their time, when new money was struck, the old could no longer be used. They banned the old money so that it should not go outside the country.

ʻAlī Pasha was a very deceitful man and most people followed him. Among the qāḍīs, too, corruption began to appear. When Bāyezīd Khan became aware of this, he gave orders to collect all the qāḍīs, as many as there were, and put them in a house in Yenishehir. Then he said, "Set the house on fire. Let them all burn." The vizier ʻAlī Pasha was at a loss and could find no way to save the qāḍīs.

Now the Pādishāh had a black jester, an Ethiopian. One word from him was enough; as boon companion he had no equal. When Yı̊ldı̊rı̊m Khan was angry, no one else could say a word to him.

. . . .

ʻAlī Pasha called the black man and said, "Hey black, I will give you what you ask for if you can save the qāḍīs from Yı̊ldı̊rı̊m." The black man waited awhile and put on a traveler's kilt and a cap, and thus attired, went to Yı̊ldı̊rı̊m Khan. When the Pādishāh saw him, he said, "Hey black, have you now become a traveler?"

"I ask a favor of my Sultan," said the black.

"Ask for what you will," said the Pādishāh.

"I ask that you send me as envoy to Istanbul," said the black, "so that I may go there."

"Hey black," said the Pādishāh, "what do you want to do in Istanbul?"

"I want to go and ask the Emperor to give me forty or fifty monks," said the black.

"Hey black," said the Pādishāh, "what will you do with all these monks?"

"My Sultan," replied the black, "let us kill the qāḍīs and set up the monks in their place."

"Hey black," said the Pādishāh, "instead of the monks, I would rather make my own servants qāḍīs."

"My Sultan," said the black, "to be qāḍī an educated man is needed. These servants of yours are not educated."

"Hey black," said the Pādishāh, "are these qāḍīs educated?"

"My Sultan," said the black, "can there be a qāḍī who is not educated?"

"If they are educated," said the Pādishāh, "why don't they practice what they have learnt?"

The black thought a while and did not know what to say. Then Yïldïrïm sent for 'Alī Pasha and asked, "Are these qāḍīs educated?"

"My Sultan," 'Alī Pasha replied, "can there be a qāḍī who is not educated?"

"Since they are educated," said the Pādishāh, "why do they behave like this?"

"My Sultan," said 'Alī Pasha, "these judges have no income, that is why they behave like this." Then Yïldïrïm Khan said, "Well, what shall we do with these qāḍīs?" And 'Alī Pasha replied, "Now, my Sultan, they must have an income."

"Then find them an income," said the Pādishāh. Then 'Alī Pasha assigned twenty aspers out of every thousand aspers of the estate of a dead man for the qāḍīs, and two aspers for every letter. This fee for the qāḍīs dates from that time. 'Alī Pasha introduced this innovation. He set the qāḍīs free. This fee remains in force for the qāḍīs and qāḍī'askers [military judge].

Anonymous Ottoman Chronicle, pp. 27–33.

37. The Battle of Varna (1444)

Thereupon Sultan Murād[1] dismissed the janissaries and his other men, renounced his dominion, settled in Manisa, and put

[1] Sultan Murād II, reigned 1421–1451.

Sultan Meḥmed on the throne. Halīl Pasha became vizier, and Mevlana Husrev became military judge [*qāḍī'asker*]. They placed Sultan Meḥmed on the throne. This happened in the year 847 of the Hijra [1443–1444].

Again the accursed king[2] and the polluted Yanko[3] attacked. The Hungarians had assembled, the soldiers of the Saxons, Germans, Czechs, Latins, Bosniaks, and Apulians, and the Vlachs, Franks, and Karamanians were all in alliance. Except for the Karamanians they were all with the king. The armies thus assembled amounted to 70,000 to 80,000 men. They brought some thousands of cannon with them, such that the troops were submerged in the blue iron. In such splendor they passed by Belgrade and Severin and came to Madara; they devastated the district of Shumla, came to Nicopolis, and besieged Pravadia, but could not take it, passed it by, and continued their advance. The bey of the Sanjak of Nicopolis, Meḥmed Bey, the son of Fīrūz Bey, followed the unbelievers with the troops in Nicopolis, and those Akïnjïs who were present, attacked and destroyed some of the unbelievers and captured some mailed, armored, and accoutred unbelievers. Then news from this side reached Sultan Murād in Manisa.

But Sultan Murād did not come. "Your bey is there," he said, "go and fight." In the end the beys said, "Without you we cannot attack. You are our bey, and surely you must come with us." They persisted and perforce induced Sultan Murād to leave his place and come to Gallipoli. The accursed Franks had sent many ships and commanded the sea. In the end Sultan Murād crossed in the neighborhood of Galata, by Yenihiṣār, on a Frankish ship and came to Rumelia. The army of Anatolia also crossed. While it was in Edirne, Meḥmed Bey, the son of Fīrūz Bey, sent the armored unbelievers. The Sultan said "This victory comes as a good sign. Our cause is just." Under God's care, he gave great thanks to God and girded his loins with the intention of waging holy war. Moving out of Edirne, he led a great number of janissaries, Rumelian and Anatolian troops,

[2] Vladislav, king of Hungary and Poland.
[3] John Hunyadi, the Hungarian commander.

akînjîs, azabs, and serakhors,[4] and the Muslims gathered from all parts as to a general call to arms. Sultan Murād marched against the accursed Hungarian and met him by Varna. It was a great battle. They shot each other with cannons, muskets, and cross-bows, like a rain of death. The accursed king stood in the middle, the accursed Yanko on one side, and Kara Mikhal on the other side and attacked Sultan Murād and overwhelmed him, carried both his wings away, and grappled with the Anatolian troops. It was a very great battle. The *beylerbey* of Anatolia, Güvegü Karaja, was killed. When the Anatolians saw this they scattered. When the Rumelian troops and the akînjîs saw that the Anatolians had scattered, they, too, fled before the unbelievers had even attacked them. Not one remained; they ran away without looking behind them. Sultan Murād saw this, looked up to heaven, and prayed to God, "O God, give the religion of Islam strength and bestow victory on the religion of Islam out of respect for the light of Muḥammad, for the sake of the light of Muḥammad." So he prayed and humbly implored. Before even the arrow of prayer had reached the target of response, God granted his prayer. Through the blessing of the miracles of Muḥammad, through the intercession of holy men, through the blessing of the belief of the warriors in the holy war, Almighty God gave him victory. He caused temptations to enter the heart of the accursed king so that he became over-weening and attacked Sultan Murād. In his pride he thought himself a mighty hero and thought, "I alone will destroy this army," and hurled himself against Sultan Murād's people. Through God's grace the king's horse stumbled and he himself fell head over heels on his face. There were two janissaries there. One was called Koja Hizir, a man of great courage. At once he cut off the king's head and brought it to Sultan Murād. When Sultan Murād saw it, he thanked God greatly and had the head stuck on a spear and held aloft. Criers cried in all four directions, saying, "The king's head has been cut off and stuck on a spear!" The whole scattered army reformed around Sultan

[4] The akînjîs were light irregular cavalry, used as raiders or skirmishers; the term "azab" was variously used of marines, light archers, and of certain fortress troops. The serakhors were a corps attached to the Sultan's stables.

Murād. When the unbeliever troops saw this, they brought the news to the accursed Yanko. He saw the position. His army began to scatter. He tried to prevent them from scattering. The following is related. When the accursed Yanko saw that the armies were beginning to scatter, he said to the unbelievers, "We came here for the sake of our religion, not for the sake of the king!," and thus he brought the army to order again. Then he turned and made two or three attacks. He saw that the Muslims had increased in numbers and thought it best to flee without further ado. When the army of the unbelievers was beaten, they turned to flee. When the army of Islam saw this, they pursued the unbelievers on every side. The soldiers of Islam had beaten the soldiers of the unbelievers and began to kill them. The troops who had previously scattered now came back. Then the janissaries, *azabs,* and other soldiers who were present came to the unbelievers' wagons. There was hard fighting. In the end they plundered the wagons and took rich booty. They came to Sultan Murād and congratulated him, saying, "May your festival be happy." They stayed on the battlefield for three days. On the fourth day they went with their goods and booty to Edirne.

Ottoman Anonymous Chronicle, pp. 68–70.

38. The Capture of Constantinople (1453)

What Sultan Meḥmed Khan Gāzī[1] *Did When He Had Returned from Karaman, and What Buildings He Raised*

He wanted to cross to Rumeli at Gallipoli, but they said to him, "O mighty Sultan! Infidel ships have come and have closed the straits at Gallipoli."

So they took the Sultan and led him to Kojaeli. They made camp at Akčahisar, on the shore of the Bosphorus above Istanbul.

There, where his father had crossed, he crossed to Rumeli and made camp opposite Akčahisar.

He said to Halīl Pasha, "Lala,[2] here I need a fortress!" In

[1] Sultan Meḥmed II, known as the Conqueror, reigned 1451–1481.

[2] Tutor or guardian, a form of address used by princes to their tutors and ministers.

short, he gave orders at once and had the fortress built, and it was completed.

Then he despatched Akčayluoglu Meḥmed Bey, saying, "Make haste and besiege Istanbul."

Meḥmed Bey came, cleared the people from the city gates, and drove away the sheep and goats from the adjoining villages. The Emperor was told, "The Turk has struck us to the heart and pulled our house down on our heads."

The Emperor said, "Neighborliness between them and us is like the neighborliness of the falcon and the crow."

Then he said, "If there is any way of saving ourselves from this Turk, we must appeal again to our friend Halil Pasha. Now we must send Halīl Pasha some little fish."

He filled the bellies of these fish with florins and sent them to Halīl Pasha. The Emperor had a vizier whose name was Master Luke.[3] He said, "Ha! Halīl Pasha will swallow the fish and it won't do you any good. He is no longer concerned about helping you. Look to your own resources."

They brought Halīl the fish. He ate the fish and put the contents in his money chest. Then he acted for the infidels. He went to the Sultan and spoke many words to him about the infidels. The Sultan said, "Ha Lala, let the summer come and then we shall see. What God commands, that we shall do."

They had been busy for some time with preparations for the conquest of the city. When all was ready and summer came, Sultan Meḥmed said, "We shall spend this summer in Istanbul."

They came and made camp around the walls of Istanbul. From the land side and with ships on the sea they enclosed the city all around. There were 400 ships on the sea, and 70 ships sailed over Galata across the dry land. The warriors stood ready and unfurled their flags. At the foot of the walls they went into the sea and made a bridge over the water. They attacked.

The fighting went on, day and night, for fifty days. On the fifty-first day the Sultan ordered free plunder. They attacked. On the fifty-first day, a Tuesday, the citadel was captured. There was good booty and plunder. Gold and silver and jewels and

[3] The Byzantine *Megadux* Lucas Notaras.

fine stuffs were brought and stacked in the camp market. They began to sell them. They made the people of the city slaves and killed their Emperor, and the *gāzīs* embraced their pretty girls. On Wednesday they arrested Halīl Pasha and his sons and his officers and put them in prison. Theirs is a long story, but I have cut it short, because all this is well known, concerning what they did to Halīl Pasha.

In short, on the first Friday after the conquest, they recited the communal prayer in Santa Sofia, and the Islamic invocation was read in the name of Sultan Meḥmed Khan Gāzī, the son of Sultan Murād Khan Gāzī, the son of Sultan Meḥmed Khan Gāzī, the son of Sultan Bāyezīd Khan, the son of Murād Hünkâr Gāzī, the son of Orkhan Gāzī Khan, the son of Osmān Gāzī Khan, the son of Ertugrul Gāzī Khan, the son of Sultan Süleymānshāh Gāzī Khan of the house of Gökalp, the son of Oguz Khan. I have set forth their family tree in the first chapter.

This victory was achieved by Sultan Meḥmed Khan in the year 857 of the Hijra [1453].

How Istanbul Was Destroyed When It Was Captured and How It Again Became a Flourishing City

When Sultan Meḥmed Khan Gāzī had captured Istanbul, he made his servant Süleymān Bey city commandant. Then he sent messengers to all his lands saying, "Whoever wishes, let him come, and let him become owner of houses, vineyards, and gardens in Istanbul." And they gave them to all who came.

This was, however, not enough to repopulate the city. This time, therefore, the Sultan gave orders to dispatch families, both rich and poor, from every province. The Sultan's servants were sent with orders to the qāḍīs and the military commandants of every province and, in accordance with these orders, conscribed and brought very many families. These newcomers were also given houses, and this time the city began to flourish.

On the houses which were given to these newcomers a rental [*muqāṭa'a*] was imposed, which bore heavily upon them. They said, "Did you remove us from our own property and bring us here just to pay rent for these infidel houses?" And some abandoned their wives and children and ran away.

Sultan Meḥmed had a servant called Kula Shahin who had served his father and grandfather and had been a vizier. Kula Shahin said to the Pādishāh, "O mighty Sultan! Your father and your grandfather conquered so many lands but in none did they impose a rental. It would be more fitting for my Sultan not to do this."

The Pādishāh accepted what he said and forewent the rental. He issued orders, "Every house which you assign, assign as freehold [*mülk*]." Henceforth, with every house which was assigned, they gave a letter that it was to be their freehold. In this way the city again began to flourish. They began to build mosques. Some of them built dervish convents, some of them private houses, and the city returned to its previous state.

Then a new vizier, who was the son of an infidel, came to the Pādishāh and became the Pādishāh's close confidant. The father and friends of this vizier were infidels, old residents of Istanbul. They came to him and said, "Hey, what are you doing? The Turks have repopulated this city. Have you no loyalty? They have taken your father's home and our home and make free with it before our eyes. But you are the confidant of the Pādishāh; therefore, do all you can so that these people should give up the rebuilding of this city, and then it will remain in our hands as before."

The vizier said, "We shall reimpose that rental which they had imposed at the time. Then these people will stop building private houses, and in this way the city will again fall in ruins and finally be left in the hands of our community."

One day this vizier found an occasion to persuade the Pādishāh, and he reintroduced the rental. . . . Whatever this scheming infidel said, he did, and they wrote it down.

Question: Who then was this vizier?

Answer: It was the Greek Meḥmed Pasha, whom he later had strangled like a dog.

Question: What buildings did Sultan Meḥmed Khan Gāzī build in Istanbul?

He built eight *medreses*, with a great cathedral mosque in their midst, and facing the mosque a fine hospice and a hospital, and at the side of the eight *medreses* he built eight more small *medreses,* to house the students. Apart from this, he had a fine mausoleum built over the grave of the holy Eyyūb-ī Enṣārī,[4] with a hospice, a *medrese,* and a mosque nearby.

. . . .

Because of this rental people began to flee the rebuilding of Istanbul. . . . The imposing of this rental, which still stands, was the fault of this Greek Meḥmed.

'Āshiḳpāshāzāde, *Tevārīh-i Āl-i Osmān,* ed. Nihal Atsız, pp. 191–194, ed. Ālī, pp. 141–144.

[4] Abū Ayyūb al-Anṣārī, a Companion of the Prophet believed to have fallen in an attack on Constantinople.

2 Government

9
Religion and Sovereignty

In strict juristic theory, the only legitimate political authority in Islam is that of the Caliphate, as required and regulated by the law. The realities of politics, however, compelled jurists to make some adjustments to their formulations of the law so as to accommodate the new forms of government while preserving the principle that what the community as a whole does, is right. Some excerpts illustrate the changing interpretation of the legal doctrines. The first, from the Qur'ān, contains two of the most frequently cited passages of political content. The second contains a selection of ḥadīths *which reflect the different interests, factions, and issues of the early centuries of Islam. The third is an exhortation to the Caliph Hārūn al-Rashīd, written by an eminent jurist as an introduction to a book on the land tax which the Caliph had asked him to compile. The fourth, by a Ḥanbalī author, gives reasons for submission to tyranny, subject to religious safeguards. The fifth is an extract from a classical legal treatise on the law concerning government. The last, written after the Mongol invasions, reflects the despairing but generally accepted view that any tyranny, however bad, is better than anarchy and must be obeyed as a duty of holy law.*

39. Islam and Government: From the Qur'ān

O you who believe! Obey God and obey the Prophet and those of you who hold authority.

iv, 59.

It is by God's grace that you [the Prophet] have dealt gently with them. Had you been harsh and hard-hearted, they would have dispersed from around you. Therefore, forgive them and pardon them and consult them in affairs [or "in this affair"]. When you have made a decision, put your trust in God, for God loves those who put their trust in Him.

iii, 159.

40. Sayings Ascribed to the Prophet

I charge the Caliph after me to fear God, and I commend the community of the Muslims to him, to respect the great among them and have pity on the small, to honor the learned among them, not to strike them and humiliate them, not to oppress them and drive them to unbelief, not to close his doors to them and allow the strong to devour the weak.

The Imams are of Quraysh; the godly among them rulers of the godly, and the wicked among them rulers of the wicked. If Quraysh gives a crop-nosed Ethiopian slave authority over you, hear him and obey him as long as he does not force any of you to choose between his Islam and his neck. And if he does force anyone to choose between his Islam and his neck, let him offer his neck.

Hear and obey, even if a shaggy-headed black slave is appointed over you.

Whosoever shall try to divide my community, strike off his head.

If allegiance is sworn to two Caliphs, kill the other.

He who sees in his ruler something he disapproves should be patient, for if anyone separates himself from the community, even by a span, and dies, he dies the death of a pagan.

Obey your rulers, whatever happens. If their commands accord with the revelation I brought you, they will be rewarded for it, and you will be rewarded for obeying them; if their commands are not in accord with what I brought you, they are responsible and you are absolved. When you meet God, you will say, "Lord God! No evil." And He will say, "No evil!" And you will say, "Lord God! Thou didst send us Prophets, and we obeyed them by Thy leave; and Thou didst appoint over us Caliphs, and we obeyed them by Thy leave; and Thou didst place over us rulers, and we obeyed them for Thy sake." And He will say, "You speak truth. They are responsible, and you are absolved."

If you have rulers over you who ordain prayer and the alms tax and the Holy War for God, then God forbids you to revile them and allows you to pray behind them.

If anyone comes out against my community when they are united and seeks to divide them, kill him, whoever he may be.

He who dies without an Imam dies the death of a pagan, and he who throws off his obedience will have no defense on the Day of Judgment.

Do not revile the Sultan, for he is God's shadow on God's earth.

Obedience is the duty of the Muslim man, whether he like it or not, as long as he is not ordered to commit a sin. If he is ordered to commit a sin, he does not have to obey.

The nearer a man is to government, the further he is from God; the more followers he has, the more devils; the greater his wealth, the more exacting his reckoning.

He who commends a Sultan in what God condemns has left the religion of God.

Al-Muttaqī, *Kanz al-'Ummāl,* iii, pp. 197–201.

41. Advice to a Caliph (Late Eighth Century)

This is what Abū Yūsuf, may God have mercy on him, wrote to the Commander of the Faithful Hārūn al-Rashīd [reigned 786–809].

May God lengthen the lifetime of the Commander of the Faithful, prolong his glory in the plenitude of delight and the continuance of honor, and cause what He had bestowed upon him to continue with the good things of the world to come, which neither fail nor pass away, and with the companionship of the Prophet, may God praise and save him!

The Commander of the Faithful, may Almighty God strengthen him, asked me to compose for him a comprehensive book that may be acted upon in the collection of land tax, tithes, poor tax, and poll tax and in other matters requiring supervision and action. His only wish in this was to remove oppression from his subjects and to promote their well-being. May Almighty God give success to the Commander of the Faithful, guide and help him in these tasks that he has undertaken, and preserve him from that which he fears and against which he guards. He asked me to clarify for him those matters about which he questioned me concerning the actions which he wishes to take and to explain and interpret them for him. So I have explained this, and I have interpreted it.

O Commander of the Faithful, Almighty God has girded you with a mighty task, whose reward is the greatest of rewards and whose punishment is the direst of punishments. He has girded you with authority over this community. Morning and evening, you build for many people, and God has made you their shepherd, has entrusted them to you, has visited you with them, and has given you authority over them. If the building is based on anything but piety, it will not be long before God strikes at the foundations and destroys it over him who built it and sought aid in it. Do not squander the authority which God has given you over this community and flock, for power in action is by God's consent alone.

Do not put off today's work until tomorrow, for if you do this, you are wasteful and death interposes before hope. Therefore, let your work precede death, for there is no work after death. The shepherds [of men] are answerable to their Lord, as the shepherd [of flocks] is answerable to his lord. Cause right to prevail in those matters where God has empowered and authorized you, if only for an hour of the day, for the happiest of shepherds before God on Judgment Day is the shepherd who made his flock happy. Do not stray, lest your flock stray. Beware of command by caprice and of punishment in anger. If you look upon two things, one of this world and one of the other, choose that of the other world rather than of this, for the other world endures and this world passes. Be cautious in the fear of God, and in God's command let all men, near or far, be equal before you. In God's work do not fear the blame of any man. Be cautious, with the caution of the heart, not the tongue; fear God, for the fear of God is a safeguard, and God protects those who fear Him. Work according to a determined end, a traveled path, a followed way, a remembered act, a frequented watering place, for this destination is the right and the great station, at which hearts tremble and arguments are cut short before the Majesty of the King Whose might overwhelms them, in Whose hands mankind is humble, awaiting His judgment and fearing His punishment, as if it had already been. For him who knew but did not act, there will only be regret and repentance at that great station on that day, the day when feet will stumble and faces pale, when the trial will be long and the reckoning hard. God, may He be blessed and exalted, said in His book, "Indeed, a day with your Lord is like a thousand years as you count them." [Qur'ān, xxii, 46/47]. And He said, "This is the Day of setting apart, for which We have assembled both you and the ancients" [Qur'ān, lxxvii, 38]. And He said, "The Day of setting apart, the appointed time for all of them" [Qur'ān, xliv, 40]. And He said, "On the day when they see what is promised them, it will be as if they had only stayed for an hour in the grave" [Qur'ān, xlvi, 34–35]. And He said, "On the day when they see, it will be as if they had only stayed [in the grave] for an evening or its morning" [Qur'ān, lxxix, 46]. Alas for the error that cannot be undone; alas for the regret that does not avail. There is only the alternation of night and day by which the new grows old, the far draws near, the promised time arrives, and God recompenses every soul as it deserves, for God is swift in reckoning. God is God! Life is short; the task is great; the world is mortal, as is he that dwells in it; the other world is the abode of eternity. Do not meet God tomorrow while you are following the path of the transgressors, for the Judge of the Day of Judgment judges men only by their deeds, not by their ranks. God has warned you; therefore be warned. You were not created without aim, and you will not be abandoned without purpose. God will question you about what you are at and what you have done; therefore, look to the answer. Know, that the steps of no man shall pass from before Almighty God save after questioning. As the Prophet, God bless and save him, has said, "On the Day of Judgment, no creature shall pass beyond until he has been asked four questions concerning his knowledge and the use he made of it, his life and the way he passed it, his wealth and the way he earned and spent it, his body and the way he used it." Prepare, therefore, O Commander of the Faithful, an answer for each question, for what you have done and established will be read out against you tomorrow. Remember that the veil between you and God will be removed at the gathering of witnesses.

I counsel you, O Commander of the Faithful, to guard what God has entrusted to your guardianship and protect what God has placed under your protection, looking only to Him in this and caring only for Him. If you do not do this, the straight and easy path of God's guidance will become hard for you, your eyes will be blind to it, its signs will be obscured and its breadth narrow for you; you will not recognize what you see and you will see what you do not recognize. Contend with your soul, but seeking to strike a blow for it, not against it. For the bad shepherd is answerable for what is lost through his default, for those whom, had he wished, he could have removed with God's permission from the places of destruction and led to the places of life and salvation. If he neglected to do this, he failed in his duty, and if he was occupied with other things, the destruction comes now swiftly upon him and is more grievous to him. But if he has acted rightly, he will thereby be happier, and God will multiply his recompense. Take care not to lose your flock, lest their Master lay claim for them against you and make you lose your wages for your default. A building can only be underpinned before it collapses. To your credit, you have only what you have done for the good of those whom God placed in your care; to your debit, what has harmed them. Do not forget to attend to those whom God has entrusted to you, and you yourself will not be forgotten. Do not neglect them and their welfare, and you will not be neglected. Your portion in this world will not be lost, in these days and nights, while your tongue is busy uttering the glory and praise of God and the blessings of His Prophet, God bless and save him, the guide in the right path.

God in His benevolence and mercy has appointed the holders of authority as deputies [*khalīfa*] on His earth and has given them a light to illuminate for the subjects those of their affairs that are obscure to them and to clarify those duties about which they are in doubt. The illumination of the light of the holders of authority consists of enforcing the penalties for offenses as laid down in the holy law and the rendering of what is due to those to whom it is due, resolutely and by clear command. The maintenance of the traditional practices [*sunan*] established by worthy men is of the greatest importance, for the maintenance of traditions is one of those good deeds which lives and does not die. The oppression of the shepherd is the ruin of the flock; if he relies on men other than the worthy and the good, this is the ruin of the commonalty. O Commander of the Faithful, complete the benefactions which God has vouchsafed to you by using them well, and seek to increase them by gratitude for them; for God, may He be blessed and exalted, says in His book, "If you are grateful, I shall add to My gifts, but if you disbelieve, My punishment will be severe" [Qur'ān, xiv, 7]. Nothing is dearer to God than good deeds or more hateful to Him than evil-doing. To commit sins is to deny His benefactions. There are few, indeed, who were ungrateful for God's benefactions and were not then frightened into penitence, who were not despoiled of their might and subjected by God to the dominion of their enemy. I ask God, O Commander of the Faithful, Who granted you the honor of knowing Him when He gave you authority, that He should not leave you to yourself in any part of your task, but should befriend you as He befriended His saints and His friends, for in this He is Master, and that which is sought for is in Him.

I have written for you as you commanded and have explained it to you and interpreted it. Study it and reread it until you know it by heart. I have striven for you in this and have not withheld advice from you and from the Muslims, who aspire to the countenance of God and His reward and fear His punishment. I hope that, if you act in accordance with my explanations, God will increase for you the yield of your land tax, without the oppression of any Muslim or tributary ally [*mu'āhad*], and that He will prosper your subjects for you, for their prosperity lies in the enforcement of the legal penalties [*ḥudūd*] and the prevention of oppression and injustice arising from uncertainties concerning their obligations. I have written down for you some fine traditions, in which there is inspiration and encouragement in the matters about which you asked and in that which you intend to do, please God. May God keep you to that which will win you His favor, and may He grant you success.

Abū Yūsuf said, may God have mercy on him: Yaḥyā ibn Saʿīd told me, on the authority of Abu'l-Zubayr, on the authority of Ṭā'ūs, on the authority of Muʿādh ibn Jabal, who said: The Prophet of God, God bless and save him, said, "No deed done by a human being is more effective in saving him from hellfire than reciting God's name." They said to him, "O Prophet of God, what of the Holy War for God's cause?" He answered, "Not the Holy War for God's cause, what though you strike with your sword until it break, strike with your sword until it break, strike with your sword until it break." He said it three times. Yet, O Commander of the Faithful, the merit of the Holy War is very great, and its reward is bounteous.

Abū Yūsuf said: One of our shaykhs told me, on the authority of Nāfiʿ, on the authority of Ibn ʿUmar, that [the Caliph] Abū Bakr al-Ṣiddīq, may God be pleased with him, sent Yazīd ibn Abī Sufyān to Syria. He walked with them for about two miles and then someone said to him, "O deputy of the Prophet of God, should you not go back?" And Abū Bakr replied, "No. I heard the Prophet of God, God bless and save him, say, 'Whose feet grow dusty on God's way, God will preserve his feet from hellfire.' "

Abū Yūsuf said: Muḥammad ibn ʿAjlān told me, on the authority of Abū Ḥāzim, on the authority of Abū Hurayra, who said: The Prophet of God, may God bless and save him, said, "A morning or an evening on God's way is better than this world and all that is in it." It has also reached us, on the authority of Makḥūl, that the meaning of the saying "a morning or an evening in God's way" is that to go out yourself in one morning or evening is better than to spend the world and its fullness, but not to go out yourself.

Abū Yūsuf said: Abān ibn Abī ʿAyyāsh told me, on the authority of Anas, who said: The Prophet of God, may God bless and save him, said: "Who invokes one blessing for me, God will repay him with ten blessings and unburden him of ten evils."

Abū Yūsuf said: One of our shaykhs told me, on the authority of ʿAbdallāh ibn al-Sā'ib, on the authority of ʿAbdallāh, that is, ibn Masʿūd, may God be pleased with him, who said: The Prophet of God, may God bless and save him, said, "God has angels who travel about in the world and bring me greetings from my community."

Abū Yūsuf said: Al-A'mash told me, on the authority of Abū Ṣāliḥ, on the authority of Abū Sa'īd, on the authority of the Prophet of God, may God bless and save him, who said, "How can I take pleasure when the trumpeter has put the trumpet to his lip, inclined his brow, bent his ear, and awaits the command?" We asked, "O Prophet of God, what should we say?" And he answered, "Say: 'God suffices us and is a good protector; in Him we trust.'"

He said: and Yazīd ibn Sinan told me, on the authority of 'Ā'idhallāh ibn Idrīs, who said: Shaddād ibn Aws preached to the people and praised God and glorified Him, and then he said: Indeed, I heard the Prophet of God, may God bless and save him, say, "Good in its entirety is in heaven, and evil in its entirety is in hell. But heaven is surrounded with abominations, and hell is surrounded with delights. When a veil of abomination is raised before a man and he stands firm, he looks upon paradise and becomes one of its people; when a veil of delight and desire is raised before a man, he looks upon hell and becomes one of its people. Therefore, do what is right in preparation for the day when judgment will be given in accordance only with what is right so that you may repose in the abode of right."

He said: Al-A'mash told me, on the authority of Yazīd al-Raqāshī, on the authority of Anas, who said: At the time of the Prophet's ascension by night, when he was drawing near to heaven, he heard a bang, and asked, "O Gabriel what is this?" He answered, "It is a stone that was flung from the rim of hell; it has been falling inward for seventy years, and now it has reached the bottom."

He said: Al-A'mash told me, on the authority of Yazīd al-Raqāshī, on the authority of Anas ibn Mālīk, who said: The Prophet of God, may God bless and save him, said, "The people of hell will be stricken with weeping until the tears run dry. Then they will weep until their faces are full of furrows."

He said: Muḥammad ibn Isḥāq told me: he said: he said: 'Abdallāh ibn al-Mughīra told me, on the authority of Sulaymān ibn ʿAmr, on the authority of Abū Saʿīd al-Khudarī, may God be pleased with him, who said: I heard the Prophet of God, may God bless and save him, say, "The path of the righteous shall be placed through the midst of hell, and on it prickles like the prickles of the *saʿdān* plant, and people will seek leave to pass. Some will be whole and saved, some torn but saved, some caught and thrown headlong into hell."

He said: Saʿīd ibn Muslim informed me, on the authority of ʿĀmir, on the authority of ʿAbdallāh ibn al-Zubayr, on the authority of ʿAwf ibn al-Ḥārith, on the authority of ʿĀʾisha, may God be pleased with her, who said: The Prophet of God, may God bless and save him, said, "O ʿĀʾisha, beware of petty and contemptible acts, for God will inquire about them."

He said: ʿAbdallāh ibn Wāqid told me, on the authority of Muḥammad ibn Mālik, on the authority of al-Barrāʾ ibn ʿĀzib, who said: We were with the Prophet of God, may God bless and save him, at a funeral, and when we reached the grave, the Prophet of God, may God bless and save him, knelt. I turned and faced him and saw that he wept until the earth was wet. Then he said, "Brothers, prepare yourselves for a day like this."

He said: Muḥammad ibn ʿAmr told me, on the authority of al-Faḍl, on the authority of ʿUbayd ibn ʿUmayr, who said: The grave says, "O son of Adam, what have you prepared for me? Do you not know that I am the house of exile, the house of worms, the house of solitude?"

He said: Muḥammad ibn ʿAmr told me, on the authority of Abū Salama, on the authority of Abū Hurayra, on the authority of the Prophet of God, may God bless and save him, who said: God, may he be glorified and exalted, said: I have prepared for My righteous servants that which no eye has seen and no ear has heard and no mind has conceived. Read if you wish, "No soul knows what joys have been hidden for them as a reward for what they do" [Qurʾān xxiii, 17]. There is a tree in Paradise such that a rider may ride for a hundred years and not leave its shadow. Read if you wish, "An extended shadow" [Qurʾān, lvi, 29]. A whip-length of Paradise is better than the world and all that is in it. Read if you wish, "He who is removed from hell and placed in

Paradise shall be triumphant, while the life of this world is but an illusory joy" [Qur'ān, iii, 182/185].

Abū Yūsuf said: Al-Faḍl ibn Marzūq told me, on the authority of 'Aṭiyya ibn Sa'd, on the authority of Abū Sa'īd, who said: The Prophet of God, may God bless and save him, said, "The dearest of men to me, and the nearest to me in station on the Day of Judgment, is a just Imam. The most hateful of men to me on the Day of Judgment and the recipient of the severest punishment is the tyrannical Imam."

He said: Hishām ibn Sa'd informed me, on the authority of Al-Ḍaḥḥāk ibn Muzāḥim, on the authority of 'Abdallāh ibn 'Abbās, who said: The Prophet of God, may God bless and save him, said, "If God wishes a people well, he puts them in charge of the wise, and their property in the hands of the generous. And if God wishes a people ill, he puts them in charge of fools, and their property in the hands of misers. He who has any authority over my community and deals kindly with their needs, God will deal kindly with him on the day of his need. But he who is aloof from their needs, God will be aloof from his needs and wants."

He said: 'Abdallāh ibn 'Alī told me, on the authority of Abu'l-Zinād, on the authority of Al-A'raj, on the authority of Abū Hurayra, on the authority of the Prophet of God, may God bless and save him, who said, "The Imam is a shield behind which one fights and protects oneself. If he ordains piety and acts justly, he will have a reward for it, but if he does otherwise, he will bear an offense."

He said: Yaḥyā ibn Sa'īd told me, on the authority of al-Ḥārith ibn Ziyād al-Ḥimyarī, that Abū Dharr asked the Prophet, may God bless and save him, to appoint him to a position of command and the Prophet replied, "You are weak and this is a trust which, on the Day of Judgment, will bring shame and regret, save only to him who took it rightly and discharged the duties it imposed on him."

Abū Yūsuf said: Isrā'īl told me, on the authority of Abū Isḥāq, on the authority of Yaḥyā ibn al-Ḥusayn, on the authority of his grandmother Umm al-Ḥusayn, who said: I saw the Prophet of God, may God bless and save him, wrapped in his cloak which he had caught under his armpit, and he said, "O people, trust in God, hear and obey. And if a crop-nosed Ethiopian slave is in command over you, hear him and obey."

He said: Al-A'mash told me, on the authority of Abū Ṣāliḥ, on the authority of Abū Hurayra, who said: The Prophet of God, may God bless and save him, said: "Who obeys me obeys God, and who obeys the Imam obeys me. Who disobeys me disobeys God, and who disobeys the Imam disobeys me."

He said: One of our shaykhs told me, on the authority of Ḥabīb, that is, Ibn Abī Thābit, on the authority of Abu'l-Bakhtarī, on the authority of Ḥudhayfa, who said: There is nothing in the tradition [*sunna*] which authorizes you to draw a weapon against your Imam.

Abū Yusūf said: Muṭarrif ibn Ṭarīf told me, on the authority of Abu'l-Jahm, on the authority of Khālid ibn Wahbān, on the authority of Abū Dharr, who said: The Prophet of God, may God bless and save him, said, "He removes himself by a handspan from the community and Islam has removed the bond of Islam from his neck."

He said: Muḥammad ibn Isḥāq told me, on the authority of 'Abd al-Salām, on the authority of al-Zuhrī, on the authority of Muḥammad ibn Jubayr ibn Muṭ'im, on the authority of his father, who said: The Prophet of God, may God bless and praise him, rose up in the mosque of al-Khayf, at Minā, and said, "May God prosper the man who heard my words and passed them on as he heard them. Many a man carries learning [*fiqh*], though he himself is not learned; many a man carries learning to one more learned than he. In three things the heart of a believer is protected from error: sincerity in works for God, good counsel for the rulers of the Muslims, and solidarity with them, for their bidding encompasses and protects them."

He said: Ghaylān ibn Qays al-Hamadānī told me, on the authority of Anas ibn Mālik, who said, "Our elders among the companions of Muḥammad, may God bless and save him, ordered us not to abuse our rulers, nor to deceive them, nor to disobey them, but to trust in God and be patient."

He said: Ismā'il ibn Ibrāhīm ibn Muhājir told me, on the authority of Wā'il ibn Abī Bakr, who said: I heard al-Ḥasan al-

Baṣrī say: The Prophet of God, may God bless and praise him, said, "Do not abuse rulers, for if they treat you well, they will be rewarded and you must be grateful, but if they treat you badly, theirs is the burden and you must be patient. They are a punishment by which God punishes whom He wishes; therefore, do not receive God's punishment with heat and anger, but with calm and humility."

He said: Al-A'mash told me, on the authority of Zayd ibn Wahb, on the authority of 'Abd al-Raḥmān ibn 'Abd Rabb al-Ka'ba, who said: I went up to 'Abdallāh ibn 'Umar, when he was sitting in the shadow of the Ka'ba, with people gathered around him, and I heard him say: The Prophet of God, may God bless and save him, said, "He who has sworn homage to an Imam and has given his handshake and his heart, must obey him to the limit of his capacity; if another rises to challenge him, strike off the head of that other."

He said: One of our shaykhs told me, on the authority of Makḥūl, on the authority of Mu'ādh ibn Jabal, who said: The Prophet of God, may God bless and save him, said, "O Mu'ādh, obey every amir, and pray behind every Imam, and do not abuse any of my companions."

He said: Ismā'īl ibn Abī Khālid told me, on the authority of Qays, who said: Abū Bakr, may God be pleased with him, rose up and praised God and glorified Him, and then he said, "O people, you read this verse, 'O you who believe, you must take care for yourselves! He who is in error cannot harm you if you are rightly guided' [Qur'ān, v. 104]. And we have heard the Prophet of God, may God bless and save him, say, 'If men see evil and do not change it. God will swiftly blind them with His punishment.' "

He said: Yaḥyā ibn Sa'īd told me, on the authority of Ibrāhīm, on the authority of Ismā'īl ibn Abī Ḥakīm, on the authority of 'Umar ibn 'Abd al-'Azīz, who said, "God will not hold the commonalty [*al-'āmma*] guilty for the acts of the people of rank [*al-khāṣṣa*], but if wrongdoing becomes manifest and is not denounced, they all of them deserve punishment."

Abū Yūsuf said: Ismā'īl ibn Abī Khālid told me, on the authority of Zubayd ibn al-Ḥārith or ibn Sābit, who said: When death came to Abū Bakr, may God be pleased with him, he sent for

'Umar to appoint him as his successor. People said to him, "Will you appoint over us a crude, coarse man, who when he reigns over us will became cruder and coarser? What will you say to your Lord when you meet Him, after having appointed 'Umar (may God be pleased with him) as Caliph over us?" He answered, "Are you trying to frighten me with my Lord? I will answer Him, 'O God, I have given authority over them to the best of Your people.' Then he sent for 'Umar and said to him, "I shall give you advice such that if you observe it, nothing will be more welcome to you than death when it comes for you, and if you disregard it, nothing will be more hateful to you than inevitable death. God has claims on you by night which He will not accept by day, and claims by day which He will not accept by night. A work of supererogation will not be accepted before the task that is obligatory has been performed. If a man's scales are light on the day of Judgment, then they are light because they record the vanity of the world and its lightness on them, and scales on which nothing but vanity is put, will rightly be light; if a man's scales are heavy on the Day of Judgment, then they are heavy because they record the truth in this world and its heaviness on them, and scales on which nothing but truth is put, will rightly be heavy. If you follow this my advice, then there will be no future event that is dearer to you than inescapable death; but if you disregard my advice, there will be no future event more hateful to you than unrelenting death."

Mūsā ibn 'Uqba said that Asmā the daughter of 'Uways said that Abū Bakr also said to 'Umar, "O son of Al-Khaṭṭāb! I have appointed you to come after me only because of what I have left behind me. I was a companion of the Prophet of God, may God bless and save him, and I saw how he preferred us to himself and our families to his family, to such a point that we always used to give his family some of the excess of what came to us from him. You have been my companion, and you have seen that I only followed the path of him who was before me. By God, I did not sleep and then dream, I did not daydream and become negligent, and I did not turn away from the path. The first against whom I warn you, O 'Umar, is yourself, for every soul has a desire, and if that is granted, it goes on to another. Beware of those of the companions of the Prophet, may God bless and save him, whose bellies are puffed up, whose eyes are avid, and of whom each loves himself best. They are astonished when one of them stumbles; beware lest you be that one. Know that they will not cease to fear you as long as you fear God and will be straight with you as long as your way is straight. This is my advice, and I bid you farewell."

He said: 'Abd al-Raḥmān ibn Isḥāq told me, on the authority of 'Abdallāh al-Qurashī, on the authority of 'Abdallāh ibn Ḥakīm, who said, Abū Bakr, may God be pleased with him, addressed us and said, "I advise you to fear God and to praise Him, as is His meet, to mix fear with desire, and to join adjuration to importunity. For God, may He be exalted, praised Zakariyā and his house, saying, "They hastened to do good, and they prayed to Us in both desire and fear, and they were humble before Us" [Qur'ān, xxi, 90]. Therefore, know, O servants of God, that God, may He be exalted, has accepted your souls as a pledge and has received your bonds for this; He bought from you what is small and mortal and paid what is great and everlasting. Here you have the book of God, whose wonders do not fade and whose light is not dimmed. Believe God's word, be advised by His book, and be illuminated by it on the day of darkness, for you were created only to worship, and He appointed over you noble scribes who know what you do. Know, O servants of God, that you are approaching, morning and evening, your predestined end, knowledge of which is hidden from you. If you can, let your time come while you are doing God's work, but you can only achieve this through God. Therefore, try in this to outpace your destinies before they come to you, lest God throw you back to your evil deeds. There are people who made over their destinies to others, and forgot themselves. I forbid you to be like them. Hurry! Hurry! Escape! Escape! For behind you there is a swift seeker whose orders are urgent."

Abū Yūsuf said: Abū Bakr ibn 'Abdallāh al-Hudhalī told me, on the authority of al-Ḥasan al-Baṣrī, that a man said to 'Umar ibn al-Khaṭṭāb, "Fear God, O 'Umar!" and repeated it several times. Someone said to him, "Be silent, you are nagging the Commander of the Faithful." And 'Umar said to him, "Let him be. It is not good for them not to say this to us; it is not good for us not to accept it." He was almost ready to reply to [?reward] the man who had said it.

He said: 'Ubaydallāh ibn Abī Ḥamīd told me, on the authority of Abu'l-Malīḥ ibn Abī Usāma al-Hudhalī, who said: 'Umar ibn al-Khaṭṭāb, may God be pleased with him, was giving an address and said, "We have a duty to you of advice concerning the unknown and help toward what is good, O shepherds. There is no forbearance dearer to God and more generally useful than the forbearance and gentleness of an Imam; and there is no ignorance more hateful to God and more generally harmful than the ignorance and roughness of an Imam. He who deals kindly with those who are in his care will be given kindness from above."

He said: Dā'ūd ibn Abī Hind told me, on the authority of 'Āmir, who said: 'Abdallāh ibn 'Abbās said: I went in to 'Umar when he had been stabbed, and said to him, "Rejoice in paradise, O Commander of the Faithful. You accepted Islam when men denied it and fought with the Prophet of God, may God bless and save him, when men forsook him. The Prophet of God, may God bless and save him, died content with you. There was no dispute when you became Caliph, and you die a martyr." He said, "Repeat that," and I repeated it. Then 'Umar said, "By God, other than Whom there is no God, if all the gold and silver in the world were mine I would ransom myself with it from the fear of the Day of Judgment."

He said: One of our shaykhs told me, on the authority of 'Abd al-Mālik ibn Muslim, on the authority of 'Uthmān ibn 'Aṭā' al-Kalā'ī, on the authority of his father, who said, 'Umar was addressing the people, and he praised God and glorified Him and then he said, "I advise you to fear God, Who lives while others than He perish; obedience to Whom profits His friends while disobedience harms His enemies. If a man perishes he can have no excuse that he followed error thinking it right or abandoned truth thinking it error. The most authentic responsibility of the shepherd for his flock is to see that they fulfill their obligations to God in the duties of the religion to which God guided them. Our duty is but to command what God has commanded you to do in obedience to Him and to forbid what God has forbidden you to do in disobedience to Him and to establish God's command among men both near and far. I do not care whether anyone tells the truth [?]. Thus, God ordained prayer and laid down conditions for it, among which are ablution, humility, bowing, and kneeling. Know, O people, that covetousness is poverty and renunciation is riches and that in solitude there is rest from evil company. Know that he who does not willingly accept God's decree which displeases him will not be given that for which he would be thankful. And know that God has servants who kill vanity by avoiding it and revive truth by proclaiming it. Desire was put in them, and they desire; they were frightened and they were afraid. If they fear and do not feel safe, they will perceive a certainty which they did not see and will be saved by what they did not leave. Fear saved them and removed them from the transitory to the enduring. Life for them is a trial, and death a boon."

He said: Ismā'īl ibn Abī Khālid told me, on the authority of Zubayd al-Iyāmī, who said: When 'Umar, may God be pleased with him, gave his final advice, he said: "I advise the Caliph after me to fear God; I advise him to recognize the rights and honor of the first Emigrants; and I advise him, in dealing with the Helpers who previously held to the house and faith, to accept those of them who do good and overlook those who do evil; I advise him concerning the people of the garrison cities, who are the prop of Islam, the bane of the enemy, and the gatherers of wealth, only to take from them their excess and with their consent; I advise him concerning the Bedouin, who are the root of the Arabs and the stuff of Islam, to take only the fringes of their wealth and to return what he takes to the poor among them. I advise him, concerning those who are protected by the pact of God and the pact of His Prophet, may God bless and save him, to carry out his undertakings to them and to fight those behind them and not to load them beyond their ability."

He said: Sa'īd ibn Abī 'Arūba told me, on the authority of Qatāda, on the authority of Sālim ibn Abi'l-Ja'd, on the authority of Ma'dān ibn Abī Ṭalḥa al-Ya'murī, that 'Umar ibn al-Khaṭṭāb, may God be pleased with him, rose on Friday to preach and praised God and glorified Him; then he mentioned the Prophet of God, may God bless and save him, and Abū Bakr al-Ṣiddīq, may God be pleased with him; and then he said, "O God, I call Thee as witness against the governors of the garrison cities. I sent them only to teach the people their religion and the custom [*sunna*] of their Prophet, may God bless and save him, to share out their booty among them and to deal justly with them; and if anything was too difficult for them, to refer it to me."

He said: 'Abdallāh ibn 'Alī told me, on the authority of al-Zuhrī, who said: A man came to 'Umar ibn al-Khaṭṭāb, may God be pleased with him, and he said, "O Commander of the Faithful, would it be better for me, in what concerns God, to disregard the censure of anyone who censures me or to accept it upon myself?" He answered, "He who has any part of authority over the Muslims should not fear, in what concerns God, the censure of any man; but he who is free from this responsibility should accept it upon himself and take counsel with his ruler."

He said: 'Abdallāh ibn 'Alī told me, on the authority of al-Zuhrī, who said: 'Umar, may God be pleased with him, said, "Do not interfere with what does not concern you, avoid your enemy, and beware of your friend unless he is faithful, for the faithful are beyond evaluation; do not frequent the evildoer, lest he teach you his evil; do not reveal your secret to him, but consult in your affairs with those who fear God."

He said: Ismā'īl ibn Abī Khālid told me, on the authority of Sa'īd ibn Abī Burda, who said: 'Umar ibn al-Khaṭṭāb, may God be pleased with him, wrote to Abū Mūsā, as follows: "The happiest of shepherds before God is he who has made his flocks happy, and the most wretched of shepherds he who has made his flocks wretched. Beware lest you go astray and your officials go astray, and you will be before God like a beast that looks for greenstuff on the ground and gorges itself aspiring to grow fat, yet its fatness causes its death. Farewell."

He said: Mis'ar told me, on the authority of a man, on the authority of 'Umar, may God be pleased with him, who said, "The command of God can only be established by a man who does not fawn and does not flatter and does not pursue ambition. The command of God can be established by a man whose energy does not diminish and who is not sparing with the truth for his followers."

Abū Yūsuf said: One of our shaykhs told me, on the authority of Hāni', the *mawlā* of 'Uthmān ibn Affān, who said: When 'Uthmān, may God be pleased with him, stood by a grave, he wept until his beard was wet. Someone said to him, "You do not weep when you speak of heaven and hell, yet you weep for this?" And he replied, "The Prophet of God, may God bless and save him, said: 'The grave is the first stage of the journey to the other world. If one is delivered from it, what follows is easier; if one is not delivered from it, what follows is harder.' And the Prophet of God, may God bless and save him, said, 'I have seen no sight that is as dreadful as the grave.'"

Abū Yūsuf said: I heard Abū Ḥanīfa, God have mercy on him, say: 'Alī said to 'Umar, may God be pleased with both of them, when 'Umar became Caliph, "If you wish to equal your predecessor patch your shirt, turn your belt, mend your sandals, cobble your shoes, limit your hopes, and do not eat your fill."

He said: One of our shaykhs told me, on the authority of 'Aṭā' ibn Abī Rabāḥ, who said: When 'Alī ibn Abī Ṭālib, may God be pleased with him, appointed a man to command an expedition, he used to say to him, "I advise you to fear God, Whom you must inevitably meet, and other than Whom you have no final destination, for He rules both this world and the next. Attend to the mission on which you are sent, and attend to that which will bring you nearer to God, may He be glorified and magnified; for in what is with God there is a replacement for this world."

He said: Ismā'īl ibn Ibrāhīm ibn al-Muhājir al-Bajalī told me, on the authority of 'Abd al-Malik ibn 'Umayr, who said: A man of the tribe of Thaqīf said to me: 'Alī ibn Abī Tālib, may Almighty God be pleased with him, appointed me collector of 'Ukbarā and said to me, while the people of the place were with me and listening, "See to it that you collect all the land tax [*kharāj*] that is owing from them. Beware lest you let them off anything, beware lest they see any weakness in you." Then he said, "Come to me at noon." So I went to him at noon, and he said to me, "I only gave you the advice which I gave you in the presence of your charges because they are rogues. But take care, when you come to them, not to sell up any garment in winter or summer, nor any foodstuffs which they eat, nor any animal which they use. Do not strike any one of them a single stroke of the whip to extract a dirham, nor make him stand on his feet to get a dirham out of him. Do not sell goods belonging to any of them to cover any part of the land tax, for we are commanded to collect only their superfluity. If you disobey my commands, God will punish you if I do not, and if I hear that you have disobeyed, I will dismiss you." He said, "Then I will return to you as I left you." 'Alī asked, "And what if you do return as you left?" The man said: Then I took my departure, and I acted as he had commanded me, and when I returned, I had not reduced the yield of the land tax at all.

Abū Yūsuf said: One of our shaykhs told me, on the authority of Muḥammad ibn Ka'b al-Quraẓī, who said: When 'Umar ibn 'Abd al-'Azīz,[1] may God be pleased with him, became Caliph, he summoned me from Medina. When I came into his presence, I stared at him fixedly in astonishment. He said to me, "O Ibn Ka'b, you are looking at me as you have never looked at me before." Then I said, "In astonishment." He asked, "What astonishes you?" I answered, "How your color has changed, your body wasted, your beard grown thin." He said, "And how would it be if you saw me three days after I am lowered into my grave, with my eyeballs spilling on my cheeks and my nostrils flowing with pus and blood. You would find me even harder to recognize!"

He said: One of our shaykhs told me, on the authority of 'Umar ibn Dharr, who said: The sole concern of 'Umar ibn 'Abd al-'Azīz was to remedy injustice and to distribute among the people.

He said: An old man from Syria told me: When 'Umar ibn 'Abd al-'Azīz became Caliph he spent two months absorbed in his grief and sadness at the affliction that had befallen him with the acquisition of authority over the affairs of the people. Then he began to look into their affairs and to remedy injustices until his concern for the people was greater than his concern for himself, and he continued in this way, until his time came, may Almighty God have mercy on him. When he died the *faqīhs* came to his wife to condole with her and to tell her how great was the disaster

[1] Umayyad Caliph, reigned 717–720. He alone, among the Umayyads, is accorded the title "Caliph" by 'Abbasid historical and religious writers and is cited, after the Prophet and the patriarchal Caliphs, as a model to be followed.

which had befallen the people of Islam through his death. They said to her, "Tell us about him, for it is a man's family that knows him best." She answered, "By God, he was not one of those among you who prayed and fasted more than the rest, but by God, I never saw any one of God's servants who feared God more deeply than 'Umar. May God have mercy on him, he wore out his body and his soul for the people; he used to spend the whole day on their needs, and if anything was left over at evening, he used to continue into the night. One evening he had settled all their affairs and sent for a lamp, which he kept at his own expense. He prayed two prostrations and then he squatted, with his hand under his chin and tears flowing down his cheeks, and remained like this until dawn and fasted the next day. I asked him, 'O Commander of the Faithful, surely what I saw this night was something you have never done before?' He answered, 'Yes indeed! I am in authority over this people, both the black and the red among them; I remembered the mendicant wandering stranger, the needy poor, the crushed captive, and their like all over the land, and I knew that Almighty God would question me about them and that Muḥammad, may God bless and save him, would reason with me about them. Then I feared that I would have no excuse before God and no evidence for Muḥammad, may God bless and save him, and I feared for my soul.' By God, if 'Umar was in a situation in which a man's joy with his wife reached its utmost, and he thought of something of God's command, he would become as agitated as a bird falling into the water, and then his weeping would reach such a point that I would throw off the coverlet from me and from him out of pity for him." Then she said, "By God, I wish we had been as far from this authority as the East is from the West."

He said: One of our shaykhs from Kūfa said to me: A shaykh in Medina said to me, "I saw 'Umar ibn 'Abd al-'Azīz in Medina, and he was the best dressed of men, the most fragrantly scented, the haughtiest in bearing. Then I saw him after he had taken over the Caliphate, and he bore himself like a monk." He said: If anyone tells you that bearing is part of a man's character, do not believe it after 'Umar ibn 'Abd al-'Azīz.

He said: One of our shaykhs told me, on the authority of

Ismā'īl ibn Abī Ḥakīm, who said: One day 'Umar ibn 'Abd al-'Azīz became very angry—he had a hot temper—in the presence of his son 'Abd al-Malik. When his anger calmed down, his son said to him, "O Commander of the Faithful, given the extent of God's benevolence to you, the position in which God has placed you, and the authority which He has given you over His servants, how can anger overcome you to such a degree?" And 'Umar asked, "What did you say?" And his son repeated it; and 'Umar said to him, "Don't you ever get angry, O 'Abd al-Malik?" He answered, "My belly is of no use to me if I cannot force my anger down into it so that nothing of it shows."

Abū Yūsuf, *Kitāb al-Kharāj*, pp. 3–17.

42. On Submission to Authority (Tenth Century)

You will hate, for the sake of God, whoever has disobeyed Him and has befriended His enemies, even if he be your near relative and even if he favor your ambitions in this world. You will adopt this position and you will declare it with certitude, neither uttering a personal opinion nor inclining to anyone who does so, for personal opinion may be wrong as well as right.

You will not keep company with the people of controversy, for they argue about God's signs. Beware, too, of wrangling and disputation in religion, for this gives rise to rancor and leads one who adopts it, even if he be a Sunnī, toward innovation [*bid'a*]. The first weakening of his religion to which a Sunnī is exposed, when he engages in controversy with an innovator, arises from his associating with the innovator and entering into discussion with him. One cannot be sure that he will not be affected by some subtle word or evil doctrine, which may or may not seduce him. He will feel the need, in order to refute his opponent, to exercise his personal judgment so that he will maintain things for which there is no basis in exegesis, no authority in revelation, and no trace in the acts and utterances of the Prophet, may God bless and save him.

You must therefore abstain and refrain from sedition [*fitna*]. You must not rise in arms against the Imams, even if they be unjust. 'Umar ibn as-Khaṭṭāb said, may God be pleased with him, "If he oppress you, be patient; if he dispossess you, be patient."

The Prophet, may God bless and save him, said to Abū Dharr, "Be patient, even if he be an Ethiopian slave."

All the ulema, whether jurists, scholars, devotees, pietists, or ascetics, from the beginnings of this community until our time, have agreed unanimously that the Friday prayers, the two festivals, the ceremonies of Minā and of 'Arafāt, warfare against the infidels, the pilgrimage, and the sacrifices are incumbent under every amir, whether he be upright or an evildoer; that it is lawful to pay them the land tax, the legal alms, and the tithe [*'ushr*]; to pray in the cathedral mosques which they build and to walk on the bridges which they construct. Similarly, buying and selling and other kinds of trade, agriculture, and all crafts, in every period and under no matter what amir, are lawful in conformity with the Book and the *Sunna.* The oppression of the oppressor and the tyranny of the tyrant do not harm a man who preserves his religion and adheres to the *Sunna* of his Prophet, provided that he himself acts in conformity with the Book and the *Sunna,* in the same way that if a man, under a just imam, makes a sale contrary to the Book and the *Sunna,* the justice of his imam will be of no avail to him.

Similarly, it is lawful to resort to the jurisdiction of their judges, to secure the enforcement of legal punishments and penalties, to seek redress for wrongs from their amirs or their police authorities, and to obey any officer whom they appoint, even if he be an Ethiopian slave—except in disobedience to Almighty God, for there is no duty of obedience to a creature against his creator.

Ibn Baṭṭa, *Kitāb al-Sharḥ wa'l-Ibāna 'alā uṣūl al-Sunna wa'l-diyāna,* pp. 66–68.

43. The Contract of the Imamate (Eleventh Century)

The office of Imam was set up in order to replace the office of Prophet in the defense of the faith and the government of the world. By general consensus [*ijmā'*], from which only al-Aṣamm dissents, the investiture of whichsoever member of the community exercises the functions of Imam is obligatory. But there is disagreement as to whether this obligation derives from reason or from Holy Law. One group says it derives from reason, since it is in the nature of reasonable men to submit to a leader who will prevent them from injuring one another and who will settle quarrels and disputes, for without rulers men would live in anarchy and heedlessness like benighted savages. As the pre-Islamic poet Al-Afwah al-Awdī said.

Anarchy, with no chiefs, is not good for men
And there are no chiefs when the ignorant rule.

Another group says that the obligation derives from the Holy Law and not from reason, since the Imam deals with matters of Holy Law to which, in reason, he would be allowed not to devote himself, since reason does not make them obligatory. All that reason requires is that a reasonable man should refrain from mutual injury and conflict with his neighbor and act equitably in mutual fairness and good relations, conducting himself in accordance with his own reason, and not with someone else's. But it is the Holy Law which intervenes to entrust these affairs to its religious representative. God said, "O you who believe, obey God, obey the Prophet, and obey those among you who are in authority" [Qur'ān, iv, 62]. He thus explicitly enjoined us to obey those among us who are in authority, and they are the Imams who hold sway over us.

Hishām ibn 'Urwa related, on the authority of Abū Ṣāliḥ, on the authority of Abū Hurayra, that the Prophet of God, may God bless and save him, said: Other rulers after me will rule over you, the pious according to his piety, the wicked according to his wickedness. Hear them and obey in all that accords with the truth. If they do good, it will count for you and for them. If they do evil, it will count for you and against them.

The obligation of the Imamate, which is thus confirmed, is a collective duty, like the Holy War and the pursuit of knowledge, so that when it is performed by those whose charge it is, the general obligation of the rest of the community lapses. If no one discharges it, then two groups of people must be distinguished from the rest; first, the electors, who choose an Imam for the community; and second, those eligible for the Imamate, one of whom must be made Imam. The rest of the community, who belong neither to the one nor to the other group, commit no sin or offense if there is a delay in filling the Imamate. When these two groups are constituted and take over the collective obligation, each group must conform to the prescribed conditions. The conditions required in the electors are three:

1. Rectitude [*'adāla*] in all respects.
2. The knowledge to recognize the required qualifications for the Imamate.
3. The discernment and wisdom to choose the candidate best suited to the Imamate, the most capable and the best informed of the conduct of public affairs.

He who is in the city of the Imam has no privilege or precedence, because of this, over those in other places. That those who are present in the city of the Imam undertake the appointment of the new Imam is custom, not law; this happens because they are the first to hear of his death and because those who are best qualified to succeed him are usually to be found in his city.

The conditions of eligibility for the Imamate are seven:

1. Rectitude in all respects.
2. The knowledge to exercise personal judgment [*ijtihād*] in cases and decisions.
3. Soundness of hearing, sight, and tongue so that he may deal accurately with those matters which can only be attained by them.
4. Soundness of limb so that he has no defect which would prevent him from moving freely and rising quickly.
5. The discernment needed to govern the subjects and conduct public affairs.
6. The courage and vigor to defend the lands of Islam and to wage holy war against the enemy.
7. Descent, that is to say, he must be of the tribe of Quraysh, as is prescribed by a text and accepted by consensus. No credit should be given to the opinion of Ḍirār, who dissents

and considers all mankind as eligible; for Abū Bakr al-Ṣiddīq, may God be pleased with him, used this as an argument against the Anṣār on the day of the Porch,[1] so as to withhold the Caliphate from them when they had invested Sa'd ibn 'Ubāda, quoting against them the words of the Prophet, may God bless and save him, "The Imams are of Quraysh." The Anṣār then gave up their attempt to take over the Imamate and even abandoned their proposal to share it, as when they had said, "An amir from among you, and an amir from among us." Thus they submitted to what he told them, accepting its authenticity and approving his saying: We are the amirs and you are the viziers. The Prophet also said, may God bless and save him, "Give precedence to the Quraysh and do not precede them." This text is beyond doubt and leaves no room for dispute or opposition.

The Imamate is conferred in two ways: one is by the choice of the electors [literally, those competent to bind and to loosen], and the other is by the nomination of the previous Imam. Regarding appointment by the choice of the electors, scholars are divided into several schools as to the number of electors needed for the appointment of an Imam. One group says that a valid appointment can only be effected by all electors in all countries, so that consent may be general and submission to his Imamate be accepted by consensus. This opinion is refuted by the investiture [*bay'a*] of Abū Bakr, may God be pleased with him, as Caliph by the choice of those who were present, without awaiting the arrival of those who were not present. Another group says that the smallest number of electors needed for the appointment of an Imam is five, either all acting together or by the action of one with the consent of the other four. This opinion rests on two arguments: First, that the appointment of Abū Bakr, may God be pleased with him, was made by five persons acting in agreement and the rest of the community following their choice, the five being 'Umar ibn al-Khaṭṭāb, Abū 'Ubayda ibn al-Jarrāḥ, Usayd ibn Ḥuḍayr, Bishr ibn Sa'd, and Salīm, the freedman of Abū Ḥudhayfa, may God be pleased with them; and, second, that 'Umar, may God be pleased with

[1] See above, p. 2ff.

him, appointed a committee of six persons to choose one among themselves with the consent of the other five. This is the view of most of the jurists and theologians of Basra. Others, the scholars of Kūfa, however, say that an appointment can be effected by three, of whom one becomes Imam with the consent of the other two, acting as a judge with two legal witnesses [*shāhid*] in the same way as a marriage is validly contracted by a guardian [*walī*] and two witnesses. Another group says that an appointment can be made by a single elector, since al-'Abbās said to 'Alī, may God be pleased with them both, "Stretch out your hand so that I can swear allegiance to you, so that the people may say that the uncle of the Prophet, may God bless and save him, has sworn allegiance to his cousin and that there may not be two people to oppose you." They say that this amounts to a judicial decision and that the decision of a single judge is valid.

When the electors meet, they scrutinize the qualified candidates and proceed to appoint that one among them who is the most worthy, who best meets the required conditions, and to whom the people are most willing to give obedience. They recognize him without delay. If the exercise of their judgment leads them to choose a particular person from the community, they offer him the Imamate. If he accepts, they swear allegiance to him, and the Imamate is vested in him by this procedure. Allegiance to him and obedience to him then become binding on the entire community. If he holds back and refuses the Imamate, it cannot be imposed upon him, since it is a contract by consent and choice and may not involve compulsion or constraint. In such case the Imamate is offered to another qualified candidate.

If two candidates are equally well qualified, the elder takes precedence in choice; however, seniority, where the parties are of age, is not a necessary condition, and if the younger is appointed, it is still valid. If one is wiser and the other braver, the choice should be determined by the needs of the time. If the need for courage is more urgent because of the disorder of the frontiers and the appearance of rebels, then the braver has a better claim. If the need for wisdom is more urgent because of the quiescence of the populace and the appearance of heretics, then it is the wiser who has a better claim.

If the choice falls on one of two candidates and they dispute the Imamate, some jurists hold that this is a flaw which disqualifies both of them and that the Imamate must be given to someone else. But the view of most scholars and jurists is that such a dispute does not disqualify and that seeking for the Imamate is not in itself reprehensible, since the members of 'Umar's committee competed for it and this did not disqualify any candidate or exclude any aspirant.

Jurists disagree on how to settle a dispute between two candidates who are equally qualified. One group says that lots should be cast and the winner preferred. Others say that the electors may choose freely and appoint whichever they prefer without drawing lots.

If the electors choose someone who is the worthiest and invest him as Imam and then someone else emerges who is worthier, the Imamate of the first one, established by their investiture, remains valid, and it is not lawful to set him aside in favor of one who is worthier than he. If they begin the investiture of the candidate of their choice while another, worthier, exists, then the case is arguable. If this happens for some good reason, such as that the worthier candidate is absent or sick or that the appointed candidate commands readier obedience and greater affection among the people, then his investiture is effective and his Imamate valid. But if he was invested without any such excuse, there may be disagreement concerning the effectiveness of this investiture and the validity of his Imamate. Some jurists, including al-Jāḥiẓ, take the view that his investiture is not valid, since in a choice requiring the better of two, it is not lawful to reject the better in favor of one that is not the better, following the rule used in the exercise of independent judgment [*ijtihād*] in matters of Holy Law. But most jurists and theologians consider that his Imamate is lawful and his investiture valid and that the existence of a worthier candidate does not invalidate the Imamate of the chosen candidate, provided that he does not lack any of the required qualifications for the Imamate. This follows the principle according to which it is lawful to appoint as judge a man who is preferred, although a worthier may exist, since superior merit is supererogatory in election and is not considered a necessary qualification.

If at any time there is only one person possessing the necessary qualifications for the Imamate and no other person is equally qualified, the Imamate must be conferred upon him, and it is not lawful to set him aside in favor of another. But scholars disagree as to whether his Imamate is established and his authority inaugurated without contract and choice. Some jurists of Iraq consider that his authority is established and his Imamate inaugurated *ipso facto,* thus imposing on the community the duty of obeying him, even if the electors have not appointed him, since the purpose of the choice is to designate the one who is most fit to rule, and this one is designated as such by his attributes. The generality of jurists and theologians maintain that his appointment as Imam can only take place by consent and choice, but that the electors are bound to choose him as Imam.

. . . .

The duties of the Imam in the conduct of public affairs are ten:

1. To maintain the religion according to established principles and the consensus of the first generation of Muslims. If an innovator appears or if some dubious person deviates from it, the Imam must clarify the proofs of religion to him, expound that which is correct, and apply to him the proper rules and penalties so that religion may be protected from injury and the community safeguarded from error.
2. To execute judgments given between litigants and to settle disputes between contestants so that justice may prevail and so that none commit or suffer injustice.
3. To defend the lands of Islam and to protect them from intrusion so that people may earn their livelihood and travel at will without danger to life or property.
4. To enforce the legal penalties for the protection of God's commandments from violation and for the preservation of the rights of his servants from injury or destruction.
5. To maintain the frontier fortresses with adequate supplies and effective force for their defense so that the enemy may not take them by surprise, commit profanation there, or shed the blood, either of a Muslim or an ally [*muʿāhad*].

6. To wage holy war [*jihād*] against those who, after having been invited to accept Islam, persist in rejecting it, until they either become Muslims or enter the Pact [*dhimma*] so that God's truth may prevail over every religion [cf. Qur'ān, ix, 33].
7. To collect the booty and the alms [*ṣadaqa*] in conformity with the prescriptions of the Holy Law, as defined by explicit texts and by independent judgment [*ijtihād*], and this without terror or oppression.
8. To determine the salaries and other sums due from the treasury, without extravagance and without parsimony, and to make payment at the proper time, neither in advance nor in arrears.
9. To employ capable and trustworthy men and appoint sincere men for the tasks which he delegates to them and for the money which he entrusts to them so that the tasks may be competently discharged and the money honestly safeguarded.
10. To concern himself directly with the supervision of affairs and the scrutiny of conditions so that he may personally govern the community, safeguard the faith, and not resort to delegation in order to free himself either for pleasure or for worship, for even the trustworthy may betray and the sincere may deceive. God said, "O David, we have made you our vicegerent [*khalīfa*] on earth; therefore, judge justly among men and do not follow your caprice, which will lead you astray from God's path." [Qur'ān, xxxviii, 25]. In this, God was not content with delegation, but required a personal performance and did not excuse the following of passions, which, He says, lead astray from His path, and this, though He considered David worthy to judge in religion and to hold His vicegerency [*khilāfa*]. This is one of the duties of government of any shepherd. The Prophet of God, may God bless and save him, said, "You are all shepherds, and you are all answerable for your flocks."

. . . .

The rules of the Imamate and its general jurisdiction over the interests of religion and the governance of the community, as we have described them, being established, and the investiture of an Imam being duly confirmed, the authority which comes from him to his deputies is of four kinds:

1. Those who have unlimited authority of unlimited scope. These are the viziers, for they are entrusted with all public affairs without specific attribution.
2. Those who have unlimited authority of limited scope. Such are the provincial and district governors, whose authority is unlimited within the specific areas assigned to them.
3. Those who have limited authority of unlimited scope. Such are the chief qāḍī, the commander of the armies, the commandant of the frontier fortresses, the intendant of the land tax, and the collector of the alms, each of whom has unlimited authority in the specific functions assigned to him.
4. Those with limited authority of limited scope, such as the qāḍī of a town or district, the local intendant of the land tax, collector of tithes, the frontier commandant, or the army commander, every one of whom has limited authority of limited scope.

Al-Māwardī, *Al-Aḥkām al-Sulṭāniyya,*
pp. 3–6, 14–15, and 19–20.

44. Imamate by Compulsion (Thirteenth–Fourteenth Centuries)

As regards the third method, that by which the *bay'a* is contracted by compulsion, this arises from the compulsion of the holder of power. At a time when there is no Imam and an unqualified person seeks the imamate and compels the people by his power and his armies, without any *bay'a* or succession, then his *bay'a* is validly contracted and obedience to him is obligatory, so as to maintain the unity of the Muslims and preserve agreement among them. This is still so, even if he is barbarous or vicious, according to the best opinion. When the imamate is thus contracted by force and violence to one, and then another arises, who overcomes the first by his power and his armies, then the first is deposed and the second becomes imam, for the welfare of the Muslims and the preservation of their unity, as we have stated. It was for this reason that the son of 'Umar said at the battle of al-Ḥarra, "We are with the victors."

Ibn Jamā'a, *Taḥrīr,* p. 357.

10

Persian Statecraft

Not all political writing was juristic. These two excerpts, translated from the Persian, express the views of two officials, one employed by the Ghaznavids, the other by the Seljuqs.

45. A Sermon on Kings and Prophets (Eleventh Century)

Know that God has bestowed one power on prophets, may the blessings of God be on all of them, and another power on kings, and He imposed on mankind the duty to accept and obey both these powers and by them to know God's true path. Whoever seeks to know this from the spheres and stars and heavenly mansions eliminates the Creator and becomes a Muʿtazilī,[1] a heretic [*zindīq*], and a materialist, and his place is in Hell, may God preserve us.

The power of Prophets, peace be upon them, comes from miracles, that is to say, things the like of which mankind is unable to perform. The power of kings lies in subtle thought, a long arm, triumph and victory over enemies, and the justice which they provide in accordance with God's commands. This is the difference between kings supported and favored by God and kings who are pretenders and usurpers. To kings who are just and beneficent, of good life and good deeds, obedience must be given and their rightful authority must be recognized. Those who seize power and are oppressors and evildoers must

[1] A follower of the Muʿtazila (see *EI*[1], s.v.), a theological school in medieval Islam regarded as deviant from the mainstream of Sunnī belief and practice. It is now extinct.

be denounced as usurpers, and holy war must be waged against them. These are the scales in which the doer of good and the doer of evil are weighed and discovered, so that, of necessity, it may be known which of these two persons should be chosen.

May God forgive those of our kings who have passed and preserve those who are still living! We must observe their ways and see how they went and how they go on the paths of justice, beneficence, virtue, religion, and purity, how they subdue the bold and the sly and cut off the hands of usurpers and oppressors, so that it becomes clear that they are the chosen of the Creator and that obedience to them was and continues to be an obligation.

If, in the meantime, some deficiency affects our kings, so that they suffer a setback, or some incident occurs of a kind often seen in this world, the wise man must observe them with the eye of wisdom and not involve himself in error, for God's decree is inscribed on the hidden tablet and cannot be changed, and there is no rebellion against His decision. Truth must always be known as truth, and falsehood as falsehood, for as it is said, "Truth is truth though men do not know it, the day is the day though the blind do not see it." I ask God to safeguard us and all the Muslims from sin and stumbling by His patience, His generosity, and the vastness of His mercy.

Bayhaqī, *Tārīkh*, pp. 99–100.

46. On Kings (Eleventh Century)

In every age God chooses one among mankind, adorns him with the kingly virtues, and entrusts to him the affairs of the world and the welfare of His servants. By him, He closes the doors of corruption, upheaval, and sedition. He gives him reverence in the hearts of men and magnificence in their eyes so that they may live under his justice, enjoy security, and desire to see his reign continue. But if the subjects should disobey or make light of the holy law and fall short in obeying God's commandments, and if God should wish to punish them and let them taste retribution for their deeds—may God not show us such a time and keep such calamities far from us—then certainly from such ill-fated disobedience the wrath of God would fall upon these people. The good king would go from among them, swords would be drawn in conflict, and blood would be shed, and he whose arm is stronger would do whatever he pleases until those sinners perish in the disasters and the bloodshed. It is like a reed bed when fire breaks out. All that is dry is consumed, and because of nearness to the dry reeds, much that is moist is also consumed.

Then one of Gods' servants, by God's grace, acquires happiness and power, and God grants him good fortune, according to his deserts, and gives him wisdom and knowledge, by which wisdom and knowledge he keeps his subordinates under his control, treating each according to his merits and assigning each a rank and post according to his worth. He chooses their servants and henchmen among the people, and he gives each of them a status and position and relies on them for the conduct of both religious and worldly affairs. His subjects follow the path of obedience and busy themselves with their own affairs, and he keeps them safe from troubles, so that they may pass their lives in peace, under the shadow of his justice.

Should one of his servants or officers commit an impropriety or an act of oppression, then if, after correction, exhortation and punishment, he mends his ways and awakes from the sleep of negligence, he may be kept in his post. But if he does not awake, he should not keep him in his post, but should replace him by another who is worthy.

If any of the subjects are ungrateful and do not appreciate the measure of security and repose which they enjoy, but meditate treachery, display rebelliousness, and overstep their limits, he must admonish them according to their offenses and punish them in the measure of their crimes so that they desist.

The sovereign should also concern himself with all that conduces to the prosperity of the world, such as preparing underground watercourses for irrigation, digging canals, building bridges over great rivers, fostering villages and hamlets, constructing fortifications, founding new cities, erecting lofty buildings and splendid residences, and building caravanserais on the highways. By these works he will secure lasting fame and receive reward in this world and blessings in the next.

Niẓām al-Mulk, *Siyāsat-nāma,* pp. 5–6.

11
Administration

The medieval Islamic states developed a complex bureaucratic apparatus, headed by the viziers or their equivalents, and staffed by a great army of secretaries, who often played an important role in the conduct of affairs. They also produced a considerable literature, of which the following are specimens. The first contains a selection of maxims from the section on government in a famous work of literary scholarship. The second, written by the chief secretary of the last Umayyad Caliph, formulates a general ethos of the secretarial profession. The third is extracted from a history of viziers and secretaries. The fourth contains some dicta ascribed to a well-known vizier. The last, taken from a medieval Egyptian bureaucratic encyclopedia, contains part of a detailed description of the court and government of the Fatimid Caliphs.

47. Maxims on Statecraft (Seventh–Ninth Centuries)

Al-Ḥasan used to say: Islam assigns four things to government: adjudication, booty, the Friday prayer, and the Holy War.

Ka'b said: Islam, the government and the people are like the tent, the pole, the ropes, and the pegs. The tent is Islam; the pole is the government; the ropes and the pegs are the people. None will do without the others.

The Prophet said: God has His guards. His guards in heaven are the angels, and His guards on earth are the keepers of the *dīwān*.

They used to say: Government and religion are two brothers; neither can stand without the other.

Ziyād heard a man revile the time, and said, "If he knew what time was, I would punish him, for the time means the government."

Chosroes said: Do not stay in a country which lacks these five things: a strong rule, a just judge, a fixed market, a wise physician, and a flowing river.

They used to say: Obedience to the government is of four kinds: through desire, fear, love, or religion.

When Anūshirwān appointed a man to a position of authority, he ordered the scribe to leave four lines blank in the brevet of appointment so that he might write something in his own hand. And when the brevet was brought to him, he wrote, "Govern the best of the people by love; mingle desire and fear for the common people; and govern the lowest by terror."

'Umar ibn al-Khaṭṭāb said: No one is fit to govern, save he who is mild without weakness and strong without harshness.

Mu'āwiya said, "I do not use my sword where my whip will do; I do not use my whip where my tongue will do. If there were no more than a hair between me and the people, it would not be broken." He was asked, "How so?" and he answered, "If they stretch it I let go, and if they let go I stretch it."

They used to say: There can be no government without men, no men without money, no money without prosperity, and no prosperity without justice and good government.

Walīd said to 'Abd al-Malik, "Father, what is statecraft?" He answered, "To win the respect and sincere affection of the upper classes; to bind the hearts of the common people by just dealing; to be patient with the lapses of your underlings."

In the books of the Persians it is said: The hearts of the subjects are the treasure houses of their kings. Whatever they deposit in them, they know it is there.

A certain king described his statecraft thus: I was never in jest when I promised or threatened or commanded or forbade; I never punished in anger; I employed for reward, which I fixed according to effort, not caprice; in their hearts I stored respect untainted with hate and love untainted with disrespect; I provided food for all but avoided a glut.

Al-Manṣūr said in audience to his commanders: That Bedouin was right who said, "Starve your dog and he will follow you."

Then Abu'l-Abbās al-Ṭūsī rose and said, O Commander of the Faithful, I fear lest someone else tempt him with a morsel, and he follow him and leave you."

The mother of the Jabghu, the king of Tukhāristān, said to Naṣr ibn Sayyār al-Laythī: There are six things which a ruler ought to have: a vizier whom he can trust and to whom he can reveal his secrets; a fortress in which he can take refuge when he flees and which will save him, that is, a horse; a sword such that when he attacks his enemies with it he need not fear that it will fail him; a treasure, light to carry, which he can take when misfortune befalls him; a woman such that when he comes to her, his cares are dispelled; a cook who, when he has no desire for food, will make him something that will arouse his appetite.

Ibn Qutayba, *Uyūn al-akhbār*, i, pp. 2, 5–11, 110–111.

48. A Letter to Secretaries (Eighth Century)

May God protect you, O you who practice the art of writing, and may He guard you and help you and guide you. For Almighty God has divided mankind, after the prophets and apostles, may God bless and save them all, and after the honored kings, into classes, these being in fact equal, and has disposed them among different kinds of crafts and sorts of endeavor, by which they gain their livelihood and earn their keep. He made you secretaries in the most distinguished positions, men of culture and virtue, of knowledge and discernment. By your means the excellences of the Caliphate are well-ordered, and its affairs uprightly maintained. By your counsel God fits government to the people, and the land prospers. The king cannot do without you, nor can any competent person be found, save among you. You are, therefore, for kings the ears with which they hear, the eyes with which they see, the tongues with which they speak, the hands with which they strike. May God let you profit from the merit of the craft which He has assigned to you, and may He not withdraw from you the grace which He has vouchsafed to you.

There is no one among the practitioners of all the crafts who is in greater need than you, O secretaries, to combine the diverse virtues which are praised and the various merits which are spoken and reckoned if you are to fit the description of you that follows in this letter. For the secretary owes it to himself and owes it to his master who trusts him in his important affairs to be magnanimous at the time for magnanimity, wise at the time for judgment, bold at the time for boldness, cautious at the time for caution, to prefer virtue, justice, and fairness, and to be discreet in keeping secrets, faithful in adversity, and resourceful in emergencies. He should put affairs in their proper places and deal with events in their situations. He should study every branch of knowledge and master it, or if he does not master it, take from it sufficient for his needs. By his natural intelligence, his good education, and his valuable experience, he should know what will happen to him before it happens and the consequence of his acts before he enacts them. For every task he should have the appropriate tools and instruments ready; for every eventuality, the right posture and usage.

Vie with one another, O secretaries, in the different branches of culture, and instruct yourselves in religion. Begin with knowledge of the book of Almighty God and of the religious duties; then of the Arabic language, for it is the hone of your tongues; then acquire a fine handwriting, for it is the adornment of your letters. Learn poetry and its rare words and their meanings, and know the ancient battles of the Arabs and the Persians and their stories and heroic deeds, for this will help you in achieving that to which you aspire. Do not neglect the study of arithmetic, for it is the foundation of the scribes of the land tax. Turn your minds away from covetousness for objects great or small and from trivial and paltry things, for they are a degradation and a cause of evil for secretaries. Keep your art far from base things, and raise yourselves above slander, tale bearing, and the ways of the ignorant and vulgar. Beware of arrogance, vainglory, and haughtiness, for they arouse hostility even where there is no real enmity. Work together with affection, before Almighty God, in your craft, and enjoin in it that which is most worthy of your virtuous, just, and noble predecessors.

If fate deals a blow to one of you, treat him with compassion and give him help until his position is restored. If old age makes one of you incapable of earning his living and meeting his friends, visit him, show him honor, ask his advice, and seek help from the fullness of his experience and the length of his knowledge. Let each of you be more solicitous for his patron who relies on him in time of need than he is for his own son and brother. If anything goes well in his work, he should attribute it only to his chief; if anything goes badly, he should take the blame himself. Let him avoid errors and oversights and not be downcast when fortune frowns, for shame, O secretaries, strikes you more swiftly than it strikes women and does you more harm than it does them.

You know that if one of you is taken into employment by a man who bestows on him, of his own accord, favors which he is [not] entitled to expect, then he owes that man loyalty and gratitude, endurance and patience, counsel and discretion, and the wise conduct of his affairs which are the fulfillment of his master's claims on him; and he should confirm this with his deeds when he is needed and when his abilities are required.

Make these qualities, may God give you success, your watchword in the time of prosperity and of adversity, of privation and sufficiency and affluence, in joy and in sorrow. How excellent is such a character in any man who among the practitioners of this noble craft is stamped with it.

If any man among you is given a position of authority or is empowered to deal with the affairs of God's creatures and children, let him fear God and delight in obedience to Him; let him be kindly to the weak and fair to the oppressed, for the people are all God's children, and the dearest to God are those who are kindest to His children. Let him judge with justice, give honor to the noble, cause the booty to be plentiful, make the country prosper, be friendly to the subjects, and refrain from injuring them. Let him be modest and magnanimous when he gives audience and kindly in recording his taxes and demanding what is due.

If one of you accompanies a man as secretary, let him study his character, for if he understands its good and evil sides, then he can help that man to realize his good intentions and contrive to divert him from his evil urges, and this with the subtlest of stratagems and the aptest of expedients. For you know that the man who handles a beast, if he is perceptive in his task, will try to understand the beast's character. If it kicks, he takes care of its rear legs; if it rears, he watches its forelegs; if it bolts, he does not spur it when he rides; if he fears that it will bite, he keeps a watch on its head; if it is stubborn, he curbs its caprices gently on the way; if it persists, he turns it slightly to the side so that it becomes easier to guide. In this description of the care of a beast, there are also indications for those who handle men and who manage, test, and have dealings with them. Now the secretary, by virtue of his education, his noble profession, his subtle arts, and his handling of those with whom he talks and argues, whom he understands or whose power he fears, is better able to charm and to meet the needs of his master than the handler of a beast that gives no answer, does not know right from wrong, and understands no communication, save what the rider conveys to it when he rides it. Therefore, may God have mercy on you, study this attentively and devote to it as much reflection and thought as you can so that, by God's leave, you will be safe from rejection, dislike, and estrangement on the part of him whom you serve. From you he will gain acquiescence; from him you will attain brotherhood and compassion, may it please Almighty God.

Let no man among you exceed the measures of what is his due, in his audience, his dress, his mount, his food, his drink, his household, his servants, and other appurtenances. For you, notwithstanding the nobility of the craft with which God has distinguished you, are servants, who must not fall short in your service, and guardians, in whom no waste or squandering can be endured. Seek help for your probity in frugality and in all that I have mentioned to you and related to you; guard yourselves against the perils of extravagance and the evil consequences of luxury, for they both lead to poverty and degradation and bring dishonor to those who indulge in them, especially to secretaries and men of education. There are similarities between things, and some therefore can serve as indications for others. Be guided, when you begin any undertaking, by your previous experience, and choose among the different ways of doing your work that way in which the goal is clearest, the evidence soundest, the result most praiseworthy.

Know that secretarial efficiency is subject to a pernicious evil, and that is wordiness, which distracts him who is addicted to it from using his mind and doing his work. Therefore, let each man among you, at his audience, be expertly moderate in his eloquence and brief in his exordium and his reply, and let him use the syntheses of his arguments, for this is conducive to effectiveness in his work and preventive of distraction through prolixity. Let him beseech God for the boon of His help, His aid, and His guidance for fear lest he fall into some error harmful to his body, his mind, or his education. If any one of you thinks or says that his outstanding skill in his craft and effectiveness in action are due only to his own shrewdness or efficiency, then he is running the risk by such a thought or statement that Almighty God will abandon him to himself and that as a result he will become incompetent. This is not hidden from any one who reflects.

Let none of you say that he is more perceptive in affairs or better able to bear the burdens of administration than his colleague in his profession and his companion in his work. The wiser of two men, for the discerning, is he who throws conceit behind his back and holds his master wiser than himself and more praiseworthy in his way. Each of the two sides must recognize the value of God's grace without being opinionated, self-justificatory, or overbearing against his comrade or equal, his master or colleague. All must praise God in modesty before His might and in humility before His glory and give utterance to His grace.

And I say, in this my letter, as the proverb has already said, "Who keeps to the truth, his work will keep him!" This is the essence of this letter and the main point of what it says, after the mention of Almighty God, which it contains. Therefore, I have put it at the end and concluded with it. May God care for us and for you, O students and secretaries, as He cares for those of whose divine guidance and felicity He has foreknowledge, for this is His and by His hand. Peace be with you and the mercy of God and His blessings.

'Abd al-Ḥamīd, *Risāla ila'l-kuttāb,* in Aḥmad Zakī Ṣafwat, *Jamharat Rasā'il al-'Arab,* ii, pp. 534–540.

49. Caliphs and Secretaries (Eighth Century)

Qabīṣa ibn Dhu'ayb died, and ['Abd al-Malik][1] appointed 'Amr ibn al-Ḥārith al-Fahmī, a *mawlā* of the Banū 'Āmir ibn Lu'ayy, in his place. When 'Amr died, ['Abd al-Malik] appointed his *mawlā* Janāḥ to the *dīwān* of the seal and contented himself with the remainder of his secretaries.

At that time there were still two *dīwāns* in Kūfa and Basra, one in Arabic to count the men and their pay (this was the one established by 'Umar), and the other in Persian for financial matters. The same applied in Syria, where one was in Greek and the other in Arabic. So it continued until the days of 'Abd al-Malik ibn Marwān.

When he made al-Ḥajjāj[2] governor of Iraq, his secretary was Ṣāliḥ ibn 'Abd al-Raḥmān, called Abū'l-Walīd. The man in charge of the Persian *dīwān* at that time was Zādhānfarrūkh, whom Ṣāliḥ ibn 'Abd al-Raḥmān succeeded. Ṣālih stood well with al-Ḥajjāj and was favored by him. He said to Zādhānfarrūkh, "I stand well with al-Hajjāj, and I am not sure whether I should replace you in your post, for he prefers me, yet you are my chief." Zādhānfarrūkh replied, "Don't do it, for he needs me more than I need him."

"How so?" asked Ṣāliḥ, and he replied, "He will not find anyone who can deal satisfactorily with the accounts for him." To which Ṣāliḥ said, "If I wish, I can put it into Arabic." Zādhānfarrūkh said, "Try just one line of it!"

Ṣāliḥ put a great deal of it into Arabic, and Zādhānfarrūkh said to his colleagues, "You had better look for some other situation."

Al-Ḥajjāj ordered Ṣāliḥ to convert the *dīwāns* to Arabic in

1 Umayyad Caliph, reigned 685–705.
2 Al-Ḥajjāj was appointed governor of Iraq in 694. See p. 23.

the year 78 [697–698], and all the secretaries of Iraq were Ṣāliḥ's pupils.

Such was al-Mughīra ibn Abi Qurra, who served as secretary to Yazīd ibn al-Muhallab; such, too, were Quḥdhum ibn Abī Sulaym and Shayba ibn Ayman, who were secretaries to Yūsuf ibn Umar; al-Mughīra and Sa'īd, the sons of 'Aṭiyya (Sa'īd was secretary to 'Amr ibn Hubayra); Marwān ibn Iyās, secretary to Khālid al-Qaṣrī and others.

One day al-Ḥajjāj said to Ṣāliḥ, "I was thinking about you, and I find that your property and your blood are lawful to me; if I take them, I shall be blameless." Ṣāliḥ replied, "The worst of it, may God strengthen the amir, is that you say this after thinking about it." Al-Ḥajjāj laughed at this and made no answer.

When al-Ḥajjāj came to Iraq, his rule weighed heavily on the people of the country. The local gentry [*dihqān*] came in a group to Jamīl ibn Buṣbuhrī, a resourceful and prominent man, and complained of their fear of the evils of al-Ḥajjāj.

He asked them, "Tell me where he was born?"

"The Ḥijāz," they answered.

"Weak and vain," he said. "And where was he brought up?"

"In Syria," they replied.

"That is bad," he said, and then he continued, "How much better off you would be if you were not afflicted, in addition to him, with a secretary who is one of your own people." They were afflicted with Zādhānfarrūkh, who was one-eyed and nasty. Then Jamīl quoted a parable to them: An axehead was thrown among some trees. One tree said to another, "This was not thrown here for any good purpose." An older tree said to them, "Unless something from you [i.e., a wooden handle] goes into this thing, you need not fear it."

The man who ran the *dīwān* of Syria in Greek for 'Abd al-Malik and for his predecessor was Sarjūn ibn Manṣūr the Christian. One day 'Abd al-Malik ordered him to do something which he could not be bothered with and, therefore, kept postponing. 'Abd al-Malik repeated his request, pressed it upon him, and found him remiss and dilatory. 'Abd al-Malik said to Abū Thābit Sulaymān ibn Sa'd al-Khushanī, the head of his *dīwān* of chancery, "Do you see how Sarjūn takes liberties with us?

I think he sees that we are dependent on him and his skill. Can you suggest any way of dealing with him?" To which Abū Thābit replied, "If you wish, I will change the accounts to Arabic." Abd al-Malik said, "Do so." He changed it, and 'Abd al-Malik transferred all the *dīwāns* of Syria to him.

It is related that 'Abd al-Malik had a Christian secretary called Sham'al. He was angry with him for some reason and threw at him a stick which he had in his hand. The stick struck his foot and marked it. Sham'al saw some of his enemies among 'Abd al-Malik's courtiers show their joy, and he recited these verses:

Do my enemies pounce because my foot is struck, when I am neither at fault nor blamed?
The Commander of the Faithful and what he does are like fate; there is no shame in the blow of fate.

When al-Ḥajjāj appointed 'Ubaydallāh ibn al-Muhārib as governor of the two Fallūjas and when 'Ubaydallāh asked, on arrival, whether there was a *dihqān* by whose counsel one could live, they referred him to Jamīl ibn Buṣbuhrī. He summoned him and asked his advice.

Jamīl asked, "Have you come here to please your God, to please him who sent you, or to please yourself?" 'Ubaydallāh replied, "My only reason for consulting you is to enable me to please all three." Jamīl said, "Then observe these principles which I give you. Do not make distinctions between your subjects, but be magnanimous to the noble and the humble alike. Do not employ a doorkeeper, so that anyone under your protection can come to you in full confidence that he will have access to you. Prolong your audiences for your subjects, and let your officials stand in awe of you. Do not accept gifts, for he who gives a gift will not be satisfied with a thirty-fold return; but if you do, then flay their skins from horns to heels."

'Ubaydallāh said, "I followed his advice and collected eighteen million dirhams in tax."

. . . .

One day al-Ḥajjāj asked one of his secretaries, "What do people say about me?" He asked to be excused from answering, but al-Ḥajjāj would not excuse him, and he said, "They say that you are an oppressor, a tyrant, a murderer, a despot, and a liar." Al-Ḥajjāj answered, "They are right in all that they say, except liar, since I have learned that falsehood dishonors those who practice it."

Yazīd ibn Abī Muslim (Abū Muslim's name was Dīnār, and he was a *mawlā* of Thaqīf,[3] not a *mawlā* by manumission. He was a foster brother of al-Ḥajjāj.) served as head of the *dīwān* of chancery under al-Ḥajjāj. His *kunya* was Abu'l-'Alā'. Al-Ḥajjāj assigned him 300 dirhams a month. Of this, he used to give 50 dirhams to his wife, spend 45 dirhams on the cost of meat, and the rest for flour and other expenses. If anything was left over, he bought water with it and gave it to the poor. Sometimes he also bought clothes, which he distributed among them. With all this he used to kill people for al-Ḥajjāj. It is related that al-Ḥajjāj visited him when he was sick and found that he had only a mud oven and a wooden lamp. Al-Ḥajjāj said to him, "O Abu'l-'Alā'! I don't think your stipend is enough for you." To which he replied, "If 300 is not enough for me, then 30,000 would not be enough for me."

. . . .

'Abd al-Malik ibn Marwān heard that one of his secretaries had accepted a gift. He asked him, "Have you accepted any gift since I appointed you?" The secretary answered, "Your affairs are orderly, your finances are abundant, the officials are praiseworthy, and your tax receipts are overflowing."

The Caliph said, "Answer the question I asked you."

The secretary said, "Yes, I have."

The Caliph said, "By God, if you have accepted a gift and do not intend to reward the giver, you are blameworthy and vile; if you have accepted it and will do something for a man which you would not have done without the gift, then you are a traitor; and if you intend to compensate the giver for his gift, neither betraying his trust nor remaining in his debt, then you have done something which will make you the talk of your colleagues and the prey of your neighbors and deprive you of the respect of your

[3] Thaqīf was the Arabian tribe to which al-Ḥajjāj belonged. A *mawlā* by manumission was a freedman, a liberated slave. One could also be a *mawlā*, or client-member, of a tribe.

office. What should be done to a man who takes up a charge in which he is not free from blame or vileness or betrayal or feigned ignorance?" And he dismissed him from his post.

. . . .

It is told on the authority of 'Abdallāh ibn Abī Bakr [ibn 'Amr] ibn Ḥazm that his father served as secretary to 'Umar ibn 'Abd al-Azīz. Once he asked him for more papyrus, and 'Umar replied, "Sharpen your pen and write less; it will be more swiftly understood." He also wrote to another official, who had written asking for papyrus and complaining that he had very little of it, "Cut your pen fine and your words short, and make do with what papyrus you have."

. . . .

It is related that Hishām,[4] before he became Caliph, was granted the revenues [*iqṭā'*] of a place called Dūrayn. He sent to collect them and found that the place was ruined and uninhabited. He said to Dhuwayd, who was then secretary in Syria, "Woe, what can you do about it?" Dhuwayd asked, "What will you give me?" Hishām said, "400 dinars." Thereupon Dhuwayd wrote, "Dūrayn and its villages." He registered it accordingly in the *dīwāns*, and Hishām received much money. When Hishām became Caliph, Dhuwayd came to him, and Hishām said to him, "Dūrayn and its villages! By God, you will never hold any authority from me!" and he sent him out of Syria.

. . . .

When the cause of the 'Abbasids grew strong and appeared openly, Marwān[5] said to 'Abd al-Ḥamīd, "We see from our letters that sovereignty is departing from us, and nothing can prevent it. These people [meaning the 'Abbasids] will have need of you. Therefore, go to them, and I hope that you will gain a position of influence with them which will enable you to be of use to me, for my estate and heirs and for many of my affairs." 'Abd al-Ḥamid answered, "How could I arrange matters so that everyone would know that this was done at your suggestion? They would all say

[4] Reigned 724–743.

[5] The last Umayyad Caliph, reigned 744–750. On his secretary 'Abd al-Ḥamīd, see p. 186ff.

that I had betrayed you and gone over to your enemy." Then he recited this verse:

Shall I conceal loyalty and display treachery?
Who then will provide me with an excuse, the display of which will satisfy people?

He also recited:

My guilt is manifest, he who condemns it is justified; my excuse is concealed.

When Marwān heard this, he knew that he would not do it. Then ʿAbd al-Ḥamīd said to him, "What you have asked me is the more useful of the two courses for you and the worse for me. You can count on me to endure with you until either God gives you victory or I am killed with you."

When ʿĀmir ibn Ismāʿīl al-Maslamī killed Marwān, he seized his secretary ʿAbd al-Ḥamīd and displayed the heads of the dead to him, for Marwān was killed together with six or seven of his intimates who were with him. ʿAbd al-Ḥamīd identified Marwān's head, and then he was sent to Abu'l-ʿAbbās,[6] who handed him over to ʿAbd al-Jabbār ibn ʿAbd al-Raḥmān. He heated a basin, put it on his head, and continued doing this until he killed him.

I found this in the handwriting of Abū ʿAlī Aḥmad ibn Ismāʿīl: Al-ʿAbbās ibn Jaʿfar al-Iṣfahānī told me. They came to look for ʿAbd al-Ḥamīd the secretary, who was a friend of Ibn al-Muqaffaʿ. The search surprised the two of them when they were together in a house. Those who came in upon them asked, "Which of you is ʿAbd al-Ḥamīd?" and both of them answered "I," fearing lest some harm come to his friend. ʿAbd al-Ḥamīd feared lest they hasten away with Ibn al-Muqaffa,' and he said, "Go gently! I have certain signs. Let one of you stay with us, and let another go and mention these signs to him who sent you." This was done, and ʿAbd al-Ḥamīd was taken.

Al-Ḥusayn ibn Muḥammad ibn al-Qāsim al-Nakhaʿī served as secretary to ʿĀmir ibn Ismāʿīl.

ʿAbd al-Ḥamīd used to say: Give honor to secretaries, for Al-

[6] The first ʿAbbasid Caliph, reigned 750–754.

mighty God arranges the sustenance of His creatures through their hands.

Ziyād ibn Abi'l-Ward al-Ashja'ī served Marwān as secretary for expenditure. His name is inscribed on the harbor at Tyre and on the harbor at Acre, and [the inscription says that] the Commander of the Faithful Marwān ordered repairs, and they were executed by the hand of Ziyād ibn Abi'l-Ward.

'Alī ibn Sirāj the Traditionist said that he had seen an inscription on the treasury in Adharbayjān, saying that it was ordered by the servant of God al-Manṣūr[7], Commander of the Faithful, and executed by the hand of Ziyād ibn Abi'l-Ward, because he also carried out these duties for al-Manṣūr.

Makhlad ibn Muḥammad ibn al-Ḥārith, who was one of Marwān's secretaries until he was killed and who then joined 'Abdallāh ibn 'Alī, said that he was at 'Abdallāh's audience one day, and 'Abdallāh asked him about Marwān and said, "Tell me about him." Makhlad answered, "On the day of the battle he said to me, 'Estimate their army for me,' and I replied, 'I am a man of the pen, not a man of war.' Then he looked to the right and to the left, scrutinized them, and said to me, 'They are 12,000.' 'Abdallāh, who was lolling, sat up and said, 'Bravo! On that day our register counted just 12,000.' "

A governor presented Marwān with a black slave. He said to 'Abd al-Ḥamīd, "Write to him and disparage what he has done." 'Abd al-Ḥamīd wrote to the governor, "Had you found a worse color than black and a smaller number than one, you would have sent that." This is adapted from the saying of a Bedouin who was asked what children he had, and replied, "Little and bad." When asked what he meant, he replied, "Not less than one, not worse than a daughter."

. . . .

'Abd al-Ḥamīd had descendants who live in Egypt. Among the earlier ones there were none who achieved fame. Then when Aḥmad ibn Ṭūlūn[8] went to Egypt, four of 'Abd al-Ḥamīd's descendants joined him. They were known as the "sons of the migrants"

[7] The second 'Abbasid Caliph, reigned 754–775.

[8] A governor of Egypt who founded an independent dynasty. He ruled from 868 to 884.

[*Banū'l-Muhājir*] and had previously worked as secretaries for Ḥusayn the eunuch, nicknamed the "sweat of death" ['Araq al-mawt].

Aḥmad ibn Ṭūlūn employed al-Ḥasan ibn Muḥammad ibn Abi'l-Muhājir as secretary (his brother 'Alī ibn Muḥammad was older than he was) and also called on the services of their two other brothers, whose *kunyas* were Abu'l-Qāsim and Abū 'Īsā. They were all favored by Aḥmad ibn Ṭūlūn, had great influence over him, and were greatly trusted by him. They were among the strongest and most pronounced opponents of the house of Hāshim.

Yūsuf ibn Ibrāhīm, the friend of Ibrāhīm ibn al-Mahdī, said: When 'Alī ibn Muḥammad ibn Abi'l-Muhājir was boasting of his ancestor, his preeminence in his craft, his merit, his culture, and his eloquence, I heard Ibrāhīm ibn al-Mahdī say to him, "'Abd al-Ḥamīd was the most ill-omened secretary on earth, for when he became vizier to Marwān, his bad luck was not confined to his own death, but also led to the loss of the Caliphate by the whole house of Marwān and was not done until Marwān himself was killed."

Aḥmad ibn Muḥammad, called Abū Naṣr and known as Ibn al-A'jamī, said that al-Ḥasan ibn Muḥammad remained secretary to Aḥmad ibn Ṭūlūn until he died and that Khumārawayh[9] turned against him and imprisoned him. A slave-girl called Banāt [or Nabāt], who had belonged to al-Ḥasan ibn Muḥammad, told me that Khumārawayh gave orders that she and all al-Ḥasan's slave-girls should be brought to him. "Among them was a slave-girl of his called Bid'a, who had been his favorite. Khumārawayh asked her to sing, and she refused. He summoned a eunuch called Siwār and whispered something to him. Siwār was absent for a while, and then returned bringing the head of al-Ḥasan ibn Muḥammad, which he placed in her lap. When she saw it she screamed, and we all screamed, and he gave orders for us to be removed from his presence."

Bakr ibn Māhān, called Abū Hāshim, served Ibrāhīm al-Imām[10]

[9] The son and successor of Aḥmad ibn Ṭūlūn.

[10] Ibrāhīm ibn Muḥammad ibn 'Alī, leader of the 'Abbasid faction and brother of the first two 'Abbasid Caliphs. He was arrested after the outbreak of the 'Abbasid revolution and died in prison in 749.

as secretary and wrote letters for him to the missionaries [*dāʿī*]. He gave his daughter in marriage to Abū Salama Ḥafṣ ibn Sulaymān,[11] a *mawlā* of the Banu'l-Ḥārith ibn Kaʿb and known as Abū Salama al-Khallāl. It is said of his byname that it comes from *Khall*, vinegar, but Thaʿlab quotes Ibn al-Aʿrābī as saying that it comes from *khilal al-suyūf*, sword scabbards [?], and that the Bedouin call those who make them *khallāl*. He quoted this verse as evidence:

> *Time wears away the ruins with weather as a sword wears away the scabbard.*

When Abū Hāshim was about to die, he wrote to Ibrāhīm al-Imām, saying that he was writing on the first day of the next world and the last day of this world and informing him that he had appointed Ḥafṣ ibn Sulaymān as his successor. Ibrāhīm wrote to Abū Salama ordering him to look after the affairs of his colleagues, and he wrote to the people of Khurāsān, saying that he had entrusted their cause to Abū Salama. So Abū Salama went to Khurāsān, where they accepted his authority and paid him one-fifth of their property and the expenses of the party.

The man in charge of correspondence to the Imam from the missionaries and of the reading of his letters to them at their meetings was Ṭalḥa ibn Zurayq, the brother of Muṣʿab ibn Zurayq, the grandfather of Ṭāhir ibn al-Ḥusayn; he was called Abu'l-Manṣūr.

Muhalhil ibn Ṣafwān was the *mawlā* of a woman who belonged to ʿAlī ibn ʿAbdallāh ibn al-ʿAbbās; she served Ibrāhīm al-Imām in prison and wrote letters for him and remained with him until Marwān killed Ibrāhīm.

When Ibn Hubayra was defeated and made for Wāsiṭ, and Ḥumayd and al-Ḥasan, the sons of Qaḥtaba, entered Kūfa, on 11 Muḥarram 132 [August 30, 749], they brought Abū Salama into the open and gave him the headship and named him vizier of the house of Muḥammad. He took charge of affairs and proclaimed the Hashimite Imamate but did not name the Caliph. When Abū

[11] A freed slave from Kūfa who served the ʿAbbasid cause, first as rebel and then as vizier. He was murdered in 750.

Muslim[12] wrote to him, he headed his letter, "To the amir Ḥafṣ ibn Sulaymān, vizier of the house of Muḥammad, from 'Abd al-Rahmān ibn Muslim, amir of the house of Muḥammad." When Abū Muslim proclaimed the *da'wa* in Khurāsān and conquered certain territories, he entrusted the secretaryship of the *dīwāns* in his presence [?] and the treasury to Abū Ṣāliḥ Kāmil ibn Muẓaffar, and he entrusted the secretaryship of the chancellery to Aslam ibn Ṣubayḥ.

When Ibrāhīm was imprisoned by Marwān, he feared for his family; he appointed Abu'l-'Abbās as his heir and as his successor in the Caliphate and commanded him to go to Kūfa, to Abū Salama. He also commanded his family to go with Abu'l-'Abbās, to listen to him, and to obey him, and announced his own death to them. Abu'l-'Abbās 'Abdallāh ibn Muḥammad set out, accompanied by his brother Abū Ja'far, his uncles Dā'ūd and 'Abdallāh, and also 'Īsā ibn Mūsā ibn Muḥammad ibn 'Alī, Mūsā ibn Dā'ūd ibn 'Alī, Yaḥyā ibn Ja'far ibn Tammām ibn al-'Abbās, together with a number of their *mawālī*. When they were within sight of Kūfa, Abu'l-'Abbās sent Ibrāhīm ibn Salama to Abū Salama to inform him of the arrival. Abū Salama disapproved of their coming and said, "They have risked their lives and been overhasty. Let them stay at Qaṣr Muqātil, which is two stages from Kūfa, until we can look into our situation." Ibrāhīm returned to them with this message, whereupon they wrote to him saying, "We are in open country, and we are not safe from discovery by the Syrian troops who are at Hīt, three stages from us." They asked him for permission to enter Kūfa and seek concealment there. He agreed unwillingly and lodged them among the Banū Awa, in the house of al-Walīd ibn Sa'd al-Jammāl, a *mawlā* of the Banū Hāshim; he hid them and their purpose for about two months from all the commanders and from the Shī'a.

Abū Salama's camp was at Hammām A'yan. He stayed there and sent his emissaries to the plains and the hills. The *dīwāns* were in his presence, and correspondence was dispatched and received by him. Abū Salama used to feed his companions in the morning and evening; he was fastidious with weapons and horses,

[12] The leader of the 'Abbasid rising in Khurāsān and the main organizer of their victory. He was murdered by order of the Caliph in 755.

but not with clothes. He used to speak clear and elegant Arabic, was learned in history, poetry, controversy, and Qur'ān-commentary, and was ready in argument and very serious.

Al-Jahshiyārī, pp. 38–41, 42–44, 53, 60, 79–81, 82–86.

50. Some Sayings of the Vizier Ibn al-Furāt (d. 924)

The basis of government is trickery; if it succeeds and endures, it becomes policy.

It is better to keep the affairs of government moving on the wrong path than to stand still on the right one.

If you have business with the vizier and can settle it with the archivist of the *dīwān* or with the privy secretary, do so and do not bring it to the vizier himself.

Hilāl al-Ṣābi', *Wuzarā'*, pp. 63–64, 119.

51. The Officers of the Fatimid Caliphate in Egypt (Tenth–Twelfth Centuries)

Group 3. The Enumeration of the Armies of the Fatimid Dynasty and the Explanation of the Ranks of the Men of the Sword, in Three Classes

The first class are the amirs, and they were of three ranks. The first rank is that of the amirs with the collar. They are the ones who were given golden collars round their necks; they correspond to the amirs of a thousand in our time.

The second rank is that of the bearers of rods. They are the ones who rode in ceremonial parades carrying silver rods which the Caliph brought out of the treasury of adornments for them to hold in their hands; they correspond to the amirs of the drum in our times.

The third rank is that of the lowest of the amirs, who were not yet entitled to rods; they correspond to the amirs of ten and of five in our time.

The second class are those in personal attendance on the Caliph [*khāṣṣa*], and they are of three kinds.

The first kind is the eunuchs, who are known today as *khādim* and *ṭawāshī*. Under the Fatimids they had a very exalted position. From among them came many holders of the offices personally attached to the Caliph. The highest among them were "the chin-strapped," who wrapped their turbans round their chins as do the bedouin and the North Africans at the present time. These were the nearest and most closely attached to the Caliph. Their number was more than 1000. . . .

The second kind are the young men of the personal service. These were a group of young men in personal attendance on the Caliph, numbering some 500 persons, among them amirs and others. Their status was the same as that of the pages [*khāṣṣakiyya*] in our time.

The third kind are the young men of the chambers. They were a group of young men, nearly 5000 in number, who were lodged in various separate quarters, each of which had a special name. They correspond to the royal mamlūks in barracks at the present time; they were known as the *kuttābiyya,* except that their numbers were complete and their deficiencies made good, and when they were summoned for duty they did not make difficulties. The young ones among them had separate quarters in charge of eunuchs, and their quarters were detached from the palace, inside the Gate of Victory, at the place where the Khānqāh of Baybars is now situated.

The third class consisted of the corps of the army. These were very numerous, each corps bearing the name of a group surviving from the time of a previous Caliph, such as the Ḥāfiẓiyya and the Āmiriyya, after those left behind by the Caliphs al-Ḥāfiẓ and al-Āmir;[1] or of a previous vizier, such as the Juyūshiyya and the Afḍaliyya, after those left by the Amīr al-Juyūsh Badr al-Jamālī and his son al-Afḍal;[2] or bearing the name of the officer to whom they were attached at that time, such as the Wazīriyya or such like; or of tribes and races, such as the Turks, the Kurds, the

[1] Two Fatimid Caliphs. Al-Āmir reigned from 1101 to 1130; al-Ḥāfiẓ, from 1132 to 1146.

[2] The title Amīr al-Juyūsh (Commander of Armies) was first adopted by the Fatimid vizier Badr al-Jamālī (d. 1094) and then held by his son and successor al-Afḍal (d. 1121).

Ghuzz, the Daylām, and the Maṣmūdīs; or of captives taken into the service, such as the Greeks, the Franks, the Slavs, or the black slaves acquired by purchase; or the manumitted slaves and other similar groups. Each corps had its own commanders and officers in authority over it.

Group 4. The Holders of High Office in the Fatimid State, in Two Sections

The first section consisted of those in personal attendance on the Caliph, in four classes:

The first class, the holders of offices from among the men of the sword, and they are of two kinds. The first kind, general offices of the army, is nine in number:

1. The vizierate. This is the most exalted office and the highest in rank. Know that the vizierate in the Fatimid state sometimes belonged to the men of the sword and sometimes to the men of the pen. In both cases, it was sometimes a vizierate with full delegated powers, resembling the Sultanate today or not far short of it, and was then called vizierate; at other times it was reduced below that and was then called *wasāṭa.*

   Nuwayrī said in *Nihāyat al-Arab:* The first who was addressed as vizier under the Fatimids was Ya'qūb ibn Killis, the vizier of the Caliph al-'Aziz; the first of the great viziers from among the men of the sword was Badr al-Jamālī, the vizier of al-Mustanṣir; the last of them was Ṣalāḥ al-Dīn Yūsuf ibn Ayyūb [Saladin], who rose from that office to become a Sultan in his own right. . . .
2. The office of the master of the gate. This is second in rank after the vizierate. Ibn al-Ṭuwayr said: It used to be called the lesser vizierate, and its holder was almost of the status of the present-day deputy of the Sultan. He took charge of the inspection of grievances when there was no vizier of the men of the sword. If, however, there was a vizier of the sword, then he himself presided at the inspection of grievances, and the master of the gate was among those who stood at his service.
3. The office of the commander-in-chief. Ibn al-Ṭuwayr said: Its holder was the chief intendant, responsible for the armies and their care. In his service and the service of the master of the gate were the chamberlains, according to their various grades.
4. The bearing of the parasol at great ceremonies, such as the

procession at the new year and the like. This was one of the great offices, and its holder was called the parasol-bearer. He was a great amir, and he had precedence and high rank among them because he carried something which was over the head of the Caliph.

5. The bearing of the Caliph's sword in ceremonial processions in which the parasol was carried. Its holder was called the sword-bearer.
6. The sixth office was the bearing of the Caliph's lance in ceremonial processions in which the parasol was carried. It was a short lance which was carried next to the Caliph, and its holder was called the lance-bearer.
7. The bearing of weapons around the Caliph in ceremonial processions. The holders of this office were called, because of their dress, the stirrup-men and also "the youths of the privy stirrup." They are the ones who in our time are called the arms-bearers and the axe-bearers. Their number exceeded two thousand men and they had twelve commanders, and these were the "lords of the Caliph's stirrup." They had special chief officers appointed over them for their knowledge. The seniors among these stirrup-men were entrusted with special tasks for the government, and when they entered upon such a task they had a very high standing in it.
8. The governorship of Cairo. Its holder had a high rank, great honor among them, and an assigned place in processions.
9. The governorship of Fusṭāṭ. This was lower in rank than the governorship of Cairo, as it is today, though at that time Fusṭāṭ was thriving and populous and greater than at this present time.

The second kind. Offices in the personal service of the Caliph held by eunuchs. There were several of these offices, and they were of two sorts.

The first sort. These pertaining to the chin-strapped eunuchs, consisting of nine offices.

1. The binding of the Caliph's crown. This means that its holder used to take charge of the tying of the crown which the Caliph wore at great ceremonial processions, and thus corresponds to the winder [*laffāf*] in our time. It was his prerogative to handle the crown which went on the Caliph's head. The binding of the crown in Fatimid times was in a special arrangement,

which not everybody knew, in an elongated shape, with a kerchief of the same color as the Caliph's garment. This binding was known as the binding of veneration. . . .

2. The office of the master of the audience. He was in charge of the arrangements when the Caliph sat in general public audience at ceremonies, and he went out to inform the vizier and the amirs when the Caliph was seated on his kingly throne. He had the title of *Amīn al-Mulk* [the trustee of kingship] and corresponds to the *Amīr Khāzindār* in our time.
3. The office of the master of correspondence. It was he who took the writing of the Caliph to the vizier and to others.
4. The intendancy of the palaces. This office corresponds to the intendancy of the residences in our time.
5. The office of the master of the treasury. This office corresponds to the Khāzindār in our time.
6. The office of the master of the register, known as the Daftar al-Majlis. He was the one in charge of the general offices [*dīwān*] of the affairs of the Caliphate.
7. The office of the inkpot-bearer, that is to say, the inkpot of the Caliph. . . . The holder of this office carried the inkpot in front of him on a saddle and took part with it in ceremonial processions.
8. The intendancy of the kinsmen. The holder was in charge of the *Sharīfs* who were the kinsmen of the Caliph, and his word carried authority among them.
9. The intendancy of the table. He was in charge of the Caliph's food, like the master of the household at the present time.

The second sort of offices in the personal service of the caliph consisted of those held by persons other than the chin-strapped eunuchs, and there are two famous offices among them.

The first was the deanship of the Ṭālibīs,[3] which corresponds to the deanship of the *sharīfs* at the present time. This could only be held by the elders of this community and the most distinguished among them. He had jurisdiction in their affairs and was responsible for excluding false claimants from their ranks. If there was any doubt about any one of them, he called upon him to establish his pedigree. It was also his task to visit the sick among them, walk at their funerals, attend to their needs, restrain transgressors among them, and prevent them from trans-

[3] The descendants of Abū Ṭālib, the father of 'Alī.

gressing and not decide anything pertaining to their affairs, save with the consent of their elders, etc.

The second office was the intendancy of the men. Its holder was responsible for the corps of men and troops, such as the intendancy of the young men in barracks, the intendancy of the Āmirī corps and the Ḥāfiẓī corps, the intendancy of the black men, and others. He corresponds to the Commander of the Mamlūks in our time.

The second class of the holders of offices in the presence of the Caliph were the men of the pen, of three kinds.

The first kind, the holders of religious offices, of which six are famous:

1. The chief qāḍī. He was among the greatest dignitaries in their time and the highest in status and esteem. Ibn al-Ṭuwayr said: No one took precedence of him or could countermand him. He had jurisdiction over the administration of the holy law, the mints, and the verification of their standards. The jurisdictions of Egypt, Syria, and North Africa might be combined in a single chief qāḍī, who was given a single brevet of investiture. . . . If the vizier was a man of the sword, he invested the qāḍī as his representative; if not, the qāḍī was invested by the Caliph. He was assigned a gray mule from the Caliph's stables, which he always rode, and was distinguished by this color from the mules of other dignitaries; he was also supplied from the saddle store with a heavy harness and a saddle with two silver bands and collars for ceremonies and was awarded gold-braided robes of honor [*khil'a*]. According to their practice, he could only appoint a legal witness [*shāhid*] by order of the Caliph and could only attend a wedding or a funeral by permission. When a vizier was present he was not addressed as chief qāḍī, as this was a prerogative of the vizier. On Mondays and Thursdays he sat in the palace in the early morning to greet the Caliph, and on Saturdays and Tuesdays he sat in the old mosque in Fusṭāṭ. He had a headcloth and a cushion, when he sat, and a stand on which his inkpot was placed. When he sat in session, the legal witnesses sat around him, on his right and his left, ranked by seniority. Ibn al-Ṭuwayr said: . . . Before him were four signers [*muwaqqi'*], in facing pairs, and at his door five chamberlains, two before him, two by the door of the enclosure [*maqṣūra*], and one admitting the litigants.

When in session he would in no circumstances rise for anyone.

2. The chief missionary [*Dāʿīʾl-duʿāt*]. In their time he followed in rank after the chief qāḍī and wore the same dress and insignia as he. His duty was to teach the doctrines of the Kin of the Prophet in the house known as the House of Wisdom[4] and administer the oath to those who joined their sect.
3. The inspector of markets [*Muḥtasib*]. He was one of their leading legal functionaries and notables. One of his perquisites was that when a robe of honor was conferred on him, the decree was read from the pulpits in Fusṭāṭ and Cairo. He had discretionary authority in the maintenance of public morals as prescribed by the rules of *ḥisba,* and nothing interposed between him and any matter with which he concerned himself. Deputies acted, with effective authority, on his behalf in Cairo, Fusṭāṭ, and all the provinces. He sat on alternate days in the two cathedral mosques of Cairo and Fusṭāṭ. The rest of his attributes are as at the present time.

   I say: I saw in some of their documents that the *ḥisba* of Fusṭāṭ and Cairo was sometimes added to the duties of the chiefs of police in these two places.
4. The custodian of the state treasury. This custodianship used only to be entrusted to men of eminence among the senior legal witnesses. He was empowered by the Caliph to sell at his discretion any category of the articles in his care, transactions with which are lawful; to manumit slaves [*mamlūk*]; to marry off slave-women; to farm out revenues as required; to buy at his discretion; and to build buildings, ships, etc. at his discretion, as required, with full authority from the Caliph.
5. The deputy [*nāʾib*]. This means the deputy of the master of the gate, mentioned above, called in our time the *Mihmandār*. Ibn al-Ṭuwayr, said: This deputyship is called "the noble deputyship" and is a high rank, held by leading legal witnesses and men of the pen. Its incumbent acts as deputy for the master of the gate in receiving envoys who come to the Caliph. He goes a certain distance to meet them and escorts every one of them to the appropriate place and provides all their needs. He allows nobody to meet them, himself investigates them, reports on them to the master of the gate, and strives to settle their business. It is he who presents them to the Caliph or to the vizier, leads them in, and requests permission for them to with-

[4] See p. 51.

draw. When the envoy enters, the master of the gate holds his right hand and the deputy holds his left hand, and the latter memorizes what they say and what is said to them. He strives to arrange the completion of their missions in the most advantageous way. If he is absent, he appoints a deputy until he returns. It is one of the conditions of his appointment that he take no gift or present from the envoys without permission. . . .

6. The readers [*qurrā'*]. They had readers who used to read in the presence of the Caliph when he sat in audience, rode in processions, and so on. They were called "readers of the presence" and were more than ten in number. They used to come to audiences and processions and read Qur'ān verses appropriate to the occasion.

Al-Qalqashandī, *Ṣubḥ al-Aʿshā,* iii, pp. 480–488.

3 War and Conquest

12

Holy War

Three groups of excerpts illustrate this theme. The first consists of passages from the Qur'ān and the ḥadīth, *with a speech ascribed to Abū Bakr; these prescribe and regulate the waging and conduct of the* Jihād, *the Holy War for Islam, which is a collective obligation of the Islamic community. The second group is concerned with more technical matters—weapons, armor, communications, espionage, and military personnel. The third group contains documents and narratives cited by the chroniclers, relating to the period of the first Arab expansion. Though some of them may be of questionable authenticity, they illustrate the manner of conquest and the terms of peace.*

52. From the Qur'ān

Fight in the path of God against those who fight you, but do not transgress, for God does not love transgressors.

Kill them wherever you encounter them, and expel them from whence they have expelled you, for dissension[1] [*fitna*] is worse than killing. But do not fight them by the Sacred Mosque unless they fight you first, and if they do fight you, then kill them. Such is the recompense of the unbelievers.

But if they desist, then God is forgiving and merciful.

Fight them until there is no more dissension, and religion is God's. If they desist, there is no enmity, save against the unjust.

ii, 186–9/190–3.

[1] Or perhaps "persecution."

When you meet those who are infidels, strike their necks until you have overwhelmed them, tighten their bonds, and then release them, either freely or for ransom, when war lays down its burdens. Thus it is, and if God wished, He would crush them Himself, but He tests you against one another. Those who are killed in the path of God, He does not let their good deeds go for nothing.

xlvii, 4/4–5.

53. Sayings Ascribed to the Prophet

Jihād is incumbent upon you with every amir, whether he be godly or wicked and even if he commit major sins. Prayer is incumbent upon you behind every Muslim, be he godly or wicked and even if he commit major sins. Prayer is incumbent upon you for every Muslim who dies, be he godly or wicked and even if he commit major sins.

Paradise is under the shadow of swords.

Where the believer's heart shakes on the path of God, his sins fall away from him as the fruit falls off a date palm.

If anyone shoots an arrow at the enemy on the path of God and his arrow reaches his enemy, whether it hits him or misses, it is accounted equal in merit to liberating a slave.

He who draws his sword in the path of God has sworn allegiance to God.

If anyone ransoms a prisoner from the hands of the enemy, I am that prisoner.

He who fights so that the word of God may prevail is on the path of God.

He who dies fighting on the frontier in the path of God, God protects him from the testing of the tomb.

The unbeliever and the one who kills him will never meet in Hell.

God sent me as a mercy and a portent; He did not send me as a trader or as a cultivator. The worst of the community on the Day of Resurrection are the traders and the cultivators, except for those who are niggardly with their religion.

A day and a night of fighting on the frontier is better than a month of fasting and prayer.

The best thing a Muslim can earn is an arrow in the path of God.

He who equips a warrior in the Holy War for God has the same reward as he, while the warrior's reward is not diminished.

He who when he dies has never campaigned or even intended to campaign dies in a kind of hypocrisy.

Fight against the polytheists with your property, your persons, and your tongues.

Swords are the keys of Paradise.

A sword is sufficient witness.

God wonders at people who are led to Heaven in chains.

A campaign by sea is like ten campaigns by land, and he who loses his bearings at sea is like one who sheds his blood in the path of God.

Every prophet has his monasticism, and the monasticism of this community is the Holy War in the path of God.

If a campaigner by sea is seasick, he has the reward of a martyr; if drowned, of two martyrs.

In Islam there are three dwellings, the lower, the upper, and the uppermost. The lower is the Islam of the generality of Muslims. If you ask any one of them he will answer, "I am a Muslim." In the upper their merits differ, some of the Muslims being better than others. The uppermost is the *jihād* in the cause of God, which only the best of them attain.

Will you not ask me why I laugh? I have seen people of my community who are dragged to Paradise against their will. They asked, "O Prophet of God, who are they?" He said, "They are non-Arab people whom the warriors in the Holy War have captured and made to enter Islam."

Shoot and ride! Of the two, I would rather have you shoot than ride. Anything in which a man passes his time is vain except for shooting with his bow, training his horse, or dallying with his wife. These three things are right. He who abandons archery after having learned it is ungrateful to the one who taught him.

Accursed be he who carries the Persian bow. Keep to the Arab bow and to the lances by which God gives you power in these lands and gives you victory over your enemy.

Learn to shoot, for what lies between the two marks is one of the gardens of Paradise.

Warfare is deception.

The Muslims are bound by their stipulations.

The Muslims are bound by their stipulations as long as these are lawful.

Of any village that you come to and stay in, you have a share, but of any village that is disobedient to God and His Prophet, one-fifth of it belongs to God and His Prophet and the rest is yours.

Treat an Arab as an Arab and a half-breed as a half-breed. The Arab has two shares and the half-breed one.

Kill the old polytheists but spare the young ones.

If you find a tithe collector, kill him.

Go in the name of God and in God and in the religion of the Prophet of God! Do not kill the very old, the infant, the child, or the woman. Bring all the booty, holding back no part of it. Maintain order and do good, for God loves those who do good.

Why are some people so bent on killing today that they even kill children? Are not the best of you the sons of idolators? Do not kill children! Do not kill children! Every soul is born with a natural disposition [to the true religion] and remains so until their tongue gives them powers of expression. Then their parents make Jews or Christians of them.

Expel the Jews and the Christians from the Arabian peninsula.

Accept advice to treat prisoners well.

Looting is no more lawful than carrion.

He who loots is not one of us.

He has forbidden looting and mutilation.

He has forbidden the killing of women and children.

He who flees is not one of us.

The bite of an ant is more painful to the martyr than the thrust of a weapon, which is more desirable to him than sweet, cold water on a hot summer day.

Excerpted from Al-Muttaqī, *Kanz,* ii, pp. 252–286.

54. Abū Bakr on the Rules of War (632)

O people! I charge you with ten rules; learn them well!

Do not betray, or misappropriate any part of the booty; do not practice treachery or mutilation. Do not kill a young child, an old man, or a woman. Do not uproot or burn palms or cut down fruitful trees. Do not slaughter a sheep or a cow or a camel, except for food. You will meet people who have set themselves apart in hermitages; leave them to accomplish the purpose for which they have done this. You will come upon people who will bring you dishes with various kinds of foods. If you partake of them, pronounce God's name over what you eat. You will meet people who have shaved the crown of their heads, leaving a band of hair around it. Strike them with the sword.

Go, in God's name, and may God protect you from sword and pestilence.

Al-Ṭabarī, i, p. 1850

13
Warfare

55. On Weapons and Tactics (Early Ninth Century)

The Persians said to the Arabs . . . you had only cane lances, tipped with ox-horn, and you used to ride your horses bareback in battle. If the horse had any saddle, it was just a strip of skin, without stirrups. The stirrup is a most excellent device for the rider who thrusts with his lance or strikes with his sword because he can stand in his stirrups or lean on them. The Arab rider used to thrust with a solid shaft, but we know that a hollow one is lighter to carry and gives a more powerful thrust. They boast of the length of the shaft and know nothing about thrusting with hunting spears. But the long shafts [? pikes] are for foot soldiers, the short ones for cavalrymen, and the hunting spear for hunting wild animals. They boast of the length of the lance and the shortness of the sword. If he who is proud of the shortness of his sword is a foot soldier, not a horseman, the horseman will boast of the length of his sword, and if length in the lance is desirable because of its long reach, which the enemy cannot escape, and because it shows the vigor of the rider and the strength of his hand, the same is true of the long, broad sword.

You used to put tips and ferrels on the shafts, so that the rider did not grasp the actual shaft. In thrusting he would rest on his thighs and rely on the dash of his horse.

One of you would hold his shaft in the middle, leaving as much behind as in front.[1] All you knew of thrusting was how to jab, stab, transfix, or throw.

You used to make war in separate, unorganized bands, for it

[1] The butt was not weighted to bring the point of balance nearer to it.

was agreed that partnership is bad in three things, kingship, war, and marriage.

You used not to fight by night, and you knew nothing of the night attack or the ambush, of right wing and left wing, center and flank, rear guard and vanguard, scouts and pioneers. Nor did you know anything of the instruments of war, such as the *ratīla* [?], the onager [*'arrāda*], the mangonel, the testudo, the trench, or the palisade. Nor did you know about coats and trousers, the attachment of swords, about drums and flags, protective armor, coats of mail, helmets, armlets, and alarm bells, nor about the lasso, or shooting arrows in fives,[2] or throwing naphtha and fire.

You had no flagbearer in battle, to rally in retreat and to encourage in attack. Your fighting consisted either of a quick strike, a slow advance, an advance in successive stages, or a furtive foray for plunder and loot.

. . . .

As regards what they (the Persians) say about stirrups: it was agreed that stirrups were ancient, but that the Arabs did not have iron stirrups until the time of the Azāriqa.[3] It was not the custom of the Arabs, when they wished to mount, to put their feet in the stirrups; instead, they used to leap onto their seats.

'Umar ibn al-Khaṭṭāb, may God be pleased with him, said, "Strength is not exhausted as long as he who has it can leap and draw." That means, a man's strength is not broken as long as he can draw the bow and leap onto the saddle without the help of stirrups.

And 'Umar said, "Repose is a hindrance; beware of fatness, for it is a hindrance."

For this reason Khālid b. Sa'īd b. al-'Āsī was killed when the enemy surprised him, and he wanted to mount and found no one to lift him. That is why, when 'Umar saw that the Emigrants and the Helpers had grown soft and fat and that many of them were about to follow the way of life of the Persians, he said, "Make yourselves as lean as Ma'add and live hard. Cut your stirrups and leap onto your horses." And he also said, "Go on foot until your

2 Presumably with some kind of apparatus.

3 A branch of the Kharijites, who rose in revolt in the late seventh century. See *EI*[2], s.v.

feet are sore, but keep your sandals on, for you do not know when you will need to run."

The Arabs did not omit to use stirrups with camel saddles; how, then, could they have failed to use them with horse saddles? Although they adopted stirrups, they did not use them except when it was unavoidable, not wishing to form habits of dependence which would induce flabbiness and weakness and make them resemble the people of luxury and ease.

Al-Aṣmaʿī said: al-ʿUmarī said: ʿUmar ibn al-Khaṭṭāb used to take his horse's left ear in his right hand, gather his limbs, and jump, and it was as if he had been born on the back of his horse. Al-Walīd b. Yazīd b. ʿAbd al-Malik did the same when he was heir apparent to Hishām. Then he turned to Maslama b. Hishām and asked him, "Could your father do as well?" and Maslama replied, "My father has a hundred slaves who can do as well." And people said that his answer was not to the point. Some of our teachers claim that not a single ʿAbbasid held power who was not a master of horsemanship.

Regarding what they said about the Arabs' lances, this matter is not as they imagine. There are different types of lance, such as the *nayzak,*[4] the *marbūʿ*, the *makhmūs*,[5] the *tāmm,*[6] and the *khatil.* This last is the one that is unsteady in the hand because of its excessive length. It is mentioned when one wishes to describe the physical strength of its owner, as for example, when Mutammim b. Nuwayra spoke of his brother Mālik and said, "He used to go out on a cold night, wearing a short coat, between two bursting waterskins, on a heavy camel, carrying his *khatil* spear." They said to him: By your father, this is the sport of the strong, for only he whose hand is powerful can bear the *khatil* spear. What proves the quality of his strength is that if a horseman sees a man in this guise, he fears and avoids him, and if the man attacks him, the man is stronger because the horseman is overawed.

The other situation is when they go out in pursuit after a raid and someone might attack a fleeing horseman whose back is to

[4] A word of Persian origin, denoting a short spear or javelin for throwing.

[5] From the roots four and five. These were presumably lances of four and five cubits respectively.

[6] Complete, that is, full-length. The various types are apparently listed in ascending order of length.

him and miss him because his spear is *marbū'* or *makhmūs*. For this purpose they use the *nayzak*, which is the shortest of spears. If the fleeing horseman escapes the pursuing horseman, he throws a *nayzak* at him. Sometimes he fears to engage him hand-to-hand and resorts to throwing rather than thrusting for that reason.

Al-Jāḥiẓ, *Al-Bayān wa'l-tabyīn*, iii, pp. 16–18, 23–25.

56. The Army of the Fatimid Caliph (Mid-Eleventh Century)

Each corps has its own name and designation.

One group are called Kitāmis.[1] These came from Qayrawān in the service of al-Mu'izz li-Dīn Allāh. They are said to number 20,000 horsemen. Another group are called Bāṭilīs, said to be men from North Africa who came to Egypt before the arrival of al-Mu'izz. They are said to number 15,000 horsemen. Another group is called Maṣmūdīs.[2] They are blacks from the land of the Maṣmūdīs and are said to number 20,000 men. Another group are called the Easterners, consisting of Turks and Persians. They are so-called because they are not of Arab origin. Though most of them were born in Egypt, their name derives from their origin. They are said to number 10,000 powerfully built men. Another group are called the slaves by purchase [*'Abīd al-shirā*]. They are slaves bought for money and are said to number 30,000 men. Another group are called Bedouin. They are from the Ḥijāz and are all armed with spears. They are said to number 50,000 horsemen. Another group are called Ustāds.[3] These are servants [? eunuchs], black and white, bought for service. They number 30,000 horsemen. Another group are called palace men [*Sarāyī*]. They are foot soldiers coming from all countries. They have their own separate commander who looks after them. Each race fights with the weapons of its own country. They number 10,000 men. Another group are called Zanj. They all fight with the saber and are said to number 30,000 men.

[1] From the Berber tribe of Kitāma. See *EI*¹, "Ketāma."

[2] A Berber tribal group. See *EI*¹, "Maṣmūda."

[3] A title of Persian origin, later used for scholars, teachers, and other dignitaries. At this time it is used, euphemistically, for eunuchs.

All these troops are maintained by the Sultan, and each man is assigned fixed monthly pay, according to his rank. They never write assignments, even for a single dinar, neither on the officials nor on the subjects. The tax collectors remit the money collected in the country every year to the treasury, and from the treasury pay is given to the soldiers at fixed times. In this way neither the officials nor the people suffer any harm from the requisitions of the soldiers.

There was also a corps composed of the sons of kings and sovereigns from various parts of the world who had come to Egypt. They were not counted as soldiers of cavalry. They came from North Africa, the Yemen, Byzantium [Rūm], the lands of the Slavs, Nubia, and Ethiopia. The sons of the king of Delhi and their mother had gone there, as had the sons of the kings of Georgia, the princes of Daylam, and the sons of the Khāqān of Turkistān. There were also other kinds of people, as well as many men of letters, poets, and jurists in attendance, all receiving regular salaries.

None of these high-born young men had less than 500 dinars pay a month, and some had 2,000 North African dinars. Their only task was to attend and greet the vizier when he mounted his horse and then to return to their own quarters.

Nāṣir-i Khusraw, *Safar-nāma*, pp. 66–67.

57. Mangonels and Naphtha (Twelfth Century)

They are of different materials and types and varying assemblage and construction. Among them are the distinctive Arab mangonel, which is the surest and most reliable of these products; the Turkish mangonel, which requires the fewest appurtenances and the least attention; and the Frankish mangonel. We shall speak of all these in their proper place, please God.

Know . . . that the operation of the mangonel involves secrets which must be well kept and guarded and principles which he who wishes to know them must master so that they help him to achieve his purpose . . . as, for example, this: If the operator stands directly under the cup in a straight line, the stone is very high and the range is short, and it often falls on the crew; if the operator moves from the cup toward the end of the shaft by about a span, the range is far; the furthest one should move from the shaft is two spans, for if one goes beyond this the launch will not work. The longest range that the stone can reach is 60 fathoms [*bāʿ*]; the shortest, 40. The length or shortness of the range is also determined by the flexibility or dryness of the shaft. If the shaft is flexible, but not too much so, it has a longer range and greater force; if it is dry, less so. The operator should part his legs, adjust the cup with his hands, and sit down while pulling the cup with all his might. The best wood for the shaft is cherry. If none is available, a close-grained wood of intermediate quality should be used, cedar or the like.

Description of the Arab Mangonel

It is made of good quality wood, arranged in a triangle with two equal sides and a base inferior to the height by one-ninth, neither more nor less. It is put together with cords, wood, and iron rivets, precisely adjusted, and the axle is placed at the summit of the triangle. The axle should be made of holm oak, with a bearing underneath of the same wood. In the middle and under the axle there should be a roof to protect the men who are operating it from injury, as the men stand below it. The shaft which is made for it should be adjusted to it, and its proportion relative to the height should be one and one-third exactly. At the end of the cup one cord should be attached, a cubit long, and another cord tied, when the stone is put together in the cup, to a strong, iron hook placed at the end of the shaft so as to come out when the cup is released and the stone is thrown. The distance between the place where the shaft meets the axle and the hemp cord attachments should be one-seventh exactly. See the drawing [Figure 1].

Description of the Persian, that is, the Turkish, Mangonel

It is made with a pole of hard wood raised in a slanting position, supported by a strut at a point a quarter of its height from the top, and fixed in the ground at some distance from the main pole so as to support it. At the top of the pole is the emplacement

FIG. 1

for the axle to which the shaft is attached. The length of the shaft in relation to the height should be one and one-third. The cup and the hemp cords should be the same as for the Arab mangonel described above. See the drawing [Figure 2].

FIG. 2

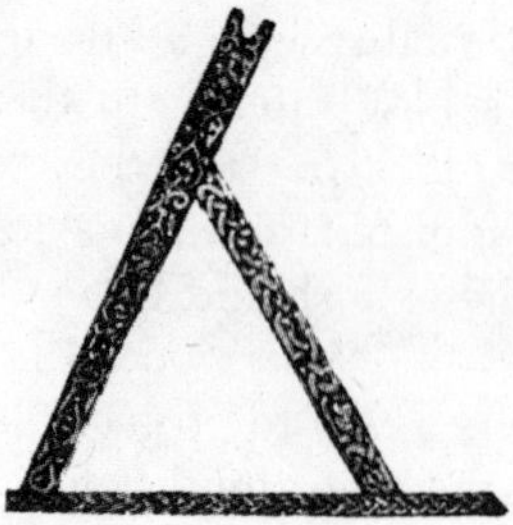

Description of the Roman, that is, the Frankish, Mangonel

It is made of hard wood in the shape of an isosceles triangle, with the tops of the two sides overlapping so as to make a small triangle. It is lined with holm oak into which the axle of the shaft is fixed. The base of this triangle should be longer than each of the sides by one ninth and no more. The height should be three-fifths of the shaft and the proportions of the hemp cords and the cup as above. At one-third of the length of the shaft, toward the end where the axle is placed, two other shafts should be attached, joining with the upper third and advancing toward its end with a strut to support them. At the end they should be separated by

4 fingers on every side. They should be about 2 cubits long and the axle should be connected with all three shafts at the same time. See the picture [Figure 3].

FIG. 3

Description of a Persian Mangonel, Made for Me by Shaykh Abu'l-Ḥasan ibn al-Abraqī al-Iskandarānī, with a Throwing Power of Fifty Pounds, More or Less

Its base is a crossbow [*jarkh*], and it is operated by a single man who makes the launch. When the man pulls the shafts, the hemp cords, which stretch the bowstring, reach its bolt; then the man catches the cup in a ring fixed to a strut which holds the shaft. Then he takes the bow and shoots and releases the shaft so that the stone is thrown.

Take a Persian mangonel and set it up to make a launch. Dig a hole by the side of the pole, to a depth equal to the length of the hemp cords on the shaft. Then take a close-meshed hemp net and place at its ends three strong hemp ropes, long enough to reach from the top of the shaft, where the axle is, to the bottom of the hole; at the end of the shaft there should be an iron ring, to which the ropes attached to the net are tied; and in the net stones should be placed in a quantity corresponding to the strength of the men who pull the shaft. At the end of the shaft, by the cup rope, there should be two nails placed on a windlass hanging from the shaft. When the man pulls this shaft, after having placed the stone in the cup and tied the cup rope to the hook placed at the top of the shaft, he . . . the cup with an iron hook placed at its end in a ring fixed to a strut which supports the action of the net . . . its cord with the ropes which raise the net in a hook fixed to these ropes, and when the ropes rise with the net . . . the arrow in its course. He shoots and then immediately returns to the cup and releases it according to his judgment. There are various ways of pulling it. Here is a picture of it [Figure 4]. One may pull the net by pulling the top of the shaft,

FIG. 4

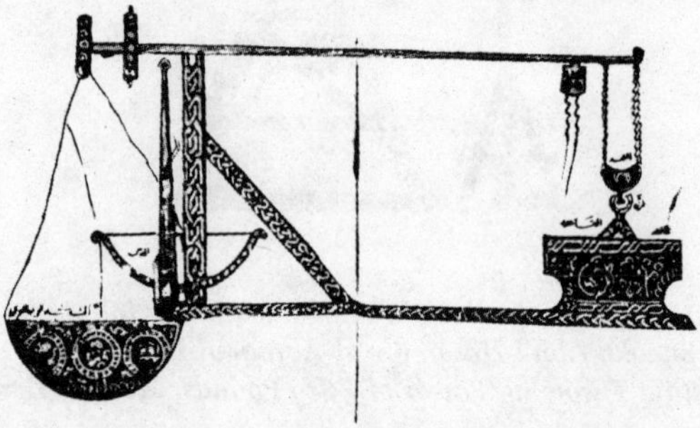

since it swings back like a steelyard and can be pulled and caught. The crossbow should be placed at the bottom of the strut of the mangonel, on two iron hooks which hold it. One draws the bow string and pulls it toward the bolt on its course. When the man catches the cup in the strut, he takes the bow and holds it so that the net pulls the shaft. He brings it back to its position. This traction is stronger than that of men, since the net draws according to its proportion.

. . . .

Description of an Incendiary Artificial Naphtha Which Will Serve for Whatever Naphtha Serves

Take a pitcher of olive oil and 1 maund of unslaked lime. Grind the lime to a fine powder, mix it thoroughly with the oil, and place the mixture immediately in a retort to which you attach an alembic. Take a pan and burn a strong flame under it until the whole is distilled. Then take the distilled oil, add about a twelfth of new unslaked lime, powdered as before, and distill again in the same way. To what is distilled add a sixteenth of powdered lime and distill a third time in the same way. Then take what is distilled and add about a fourth part of naphtha. It is ready for use and will burn with a power that has no equal.

How to Make an Excellent Naptha to be Thrown with the Mangonel

Take 10 pounds of tar, 3 pounds of resin, 1½ pounds each of sandarac and lac, 3 pounds of pure, good quality sulphur, free from all soil, 5 pounds of melted dolphin fat, the same quantity of liquefied, clarified fat from goats' kidneys. Melt the tar, add the fats, then throw in the resin after having melted it separately. Then grind the other ingredients, each one separately, add them to the mixture, put fire under it, and let it cook until all is thoroughly mixed. If you wish to use it in time of war, take one part, add about a tenth part of the mineral sulphur called naphtha, which is greenish and looks like old oil, place the whole in a skillet and boil until it is about to burn. Take the pot, which should be earthenware, and a piece of felt. Then throw it with a mangonel against whatever you wish to burn. It will never be extinguished.

Marḍī ibn ʿAlī al-Ṭarsūsī, *Tabṣirat arbāb al-albāb fī kayfiyyat al-najāt fi'l-ḥurūb*, pp. 16–18, 20–21.

58. On the Pigeon Post (1171–1172)

Ibn al-Athīr said: In the year 567 [1171–1172], al-Malik al ʿAdil Nūr al-Dīn[1] gave orders to use carrier pigeons. These are the messenger birds which fly back to their lofts from distant lands. They were adopted in all his territories.

The reason for this is that his territories had become so extensive and his realm so great that it reached from the border of Nubia to the gate of Hamadān, with only the land of the Franks intervening. The Franks, may God curse them, sometimes attacked some of the border areas, but by the time news of this reached him and he was able to set out against them, they had already in part achieved their purpose. He therefore issued orders concerning this matter and sent them in writing to all his territories. He

1 The Zangid ruler Nūr al-Dīn, reigned 1146–1174.

authorized rations for the pigeons and for their breeders. They gave him great satisfaction. News reached him at once in this way. On every border he had men on duty with pigeons from the neighboring city. When they saw or heard anything, they at once wrote it down, attached it to the bird, and sped it without delay to the city from which it came. There the message was transferred to another bird, which came from the next city on the way to Nūr al-Dīn, and so on until the report reached him. In this way the borders were protected, and when a band of Franks attacked one of them, news reached him on the same day. Then he wrote to the troops nearest to that border, ordering them to muster and march with dispatch and take the enemy by surprise. They did so and were victorious, while the Franks were lulled in the belief that Nūr al-Dīn was far away from them. May God have mercy on Nūr al-Dīn and be pleased with him. How great was his concern for his subjects and his realms!

Al-ʿImād said: Nūr al-Dīn did not stay in the city in spring and in summer but was occupied in guarding the borders and protecting them from harm, so as to defend his territories with the sword against the enemy. He waited anxiously for reports from Egypt about conditions there, concerning the maintenance of order and the suppression of disorder. So he decided to make use of carrier pigeons and set them in flight to bring him news of his lands. He instructed me to send orders to the pigeon breeders and to encourage them. He was then outside Damascus, encamped in the Lawān valley. At that time we had the upper hand and were pressing the enemy hard. It was on the 17th Dhu'l-Qaʿda of the same year [July 11, 1172].

Abū Shāma, *Kitāb al-Rawḍatayn,* i/2, pp. 520–521.

59. Enemy Spies (Eighth Century)

If the Muslims find a man claiming to be a Muslim acting as a spy for the polytheists against the Muslims and writing reports on their weak points to them, and he confesses this voluntarily, he shall not be killed, but the Caliph shall punish him suitably.

Likewise, if a *dhimmī* does this, he shall be punished and put in prison, but this shall not invalidate the pact [*'ahd*]. The same shall apply if a *musta'min* among us commits this offense, but he shall be punished for everything.

But if, when he asked for the *Amān,* the Muslims said to him, "We give you *Amān* on condition that you do not spy on the Muslims for the polytheists," or "We give you *Amān,* on condition that it ceases to be valid if you report on the weak points of the Muslims to the people of war," then the case is dealt with accordingly, and there is no objection to killing him. And if the Imam decides to crucify him as an example to others, there is no objection to that. If he decides to treat him as booty, that also is permissible, as with other prisoners. But it is preferable to kill him as an example to others.

If it is a woman instead of a man, there is no objection to killing her either, but it would be reprehensible to crucify her.

If they catch a youth under age in these circumstances, he shall be made booty and shall not be killed.

An old man who cannot fight but is of sound mind is in the same position as a woman.

If the *musta'min* denies that he has done this, and says, "The letter that they found on me was one I found on the way and picked up," then the Muslims should not kill him without proof. If they threaten him with shackles or flogging or imprisonment until he confesses that he is a spy, then this confession is of no account. He can only be convicted as a spy by his own voluntary confession or by the testimony of two public witnesses. In this matter the testimony of *dhimmīs* or enemy subjects may be accepted against him.

If the Imam finds on a Muslim or a *dhimmī* or a *musta'min* a letter in his handwriting, and known as such, addressed to the king of the people of war, informing him of the secrets of the Muslims, the Imam shall imprison him, but shall not flog him in this case; he shall imprison him for the protection of the Muslims until his affair is made clear. If it is not made clear, he shall be released and deported to the house of war, and the Imam shall not allow him to reside after this in the House of Islam for a single day.

Al-Shaybānī, *Kitāb al-Siyar al-Kabīr*, iv, pp. 225–228.

60. Spies (Eleventh Century)

Spies must always go to all parts, disguised as merchants, travelers, Sufis, medicine-sellers, or beggars and report on all that they hear, so that nothing may remain hidden and so that if anything happens it may be dealt with in time. For it has often happened that governors, fief holders, officers, and commanders have plotted mutiny and rebellion and intended mischief against the king, but a spy came and informed the king, who at once mounted his horse and set out, took them by surprise, captured them, and brought their plans to nothing. Likewise if a foreign king and army was preparing to invade the country, he did his work and they were repelled. Spies also reported news, good and bad, about the subjects, and kings attended to them.

Niẓām al-Mulk, *Siyāsat-nāma,* pp. 68–69.

61. The Origin of the Janissaries (Fourteenth Century)

One day a scholar called Kara Rüstem came from the land of Karaman. This Kara Rüstem went to Čandarli̊ Halīl, who was military judge [*qāḍī'asker*], and said, "Why do you let so much state income go waste?" The military judge Kara Halīl asked, "What income is this that is going waste? Tell me at once." Kara Rüstem said, "Of these prisoners that the warriors in the holy war bring back, one-fifth, according to God's command, belongs to the Pādishāh. Why do you not take this share?" The military judge Kara Halīl said, "I will submit the matter to the Pādishāh!" He submitted it to Gāzī Murād,[1] who said, "If it is God's command, then take it." They called Kara Rüstem and said, "Master, carry out God's command." Kara Rüstem went away and stayed in Gallipoli and collected twenty-five aspers from each prisoner. This innovation dates

[1] Murād I (1362–1389).

from the time of these two men. To collect a tax from the prisoners in Gallipoli has become the practice since Čandarlî Kara Halīl and Kara Rüstem. After that he also instructed Gāzī Evrenos to take one out of every five prisoners captured in the raids and, if anyone had only four prisoners, to take twenty-five aspers from him. They acted according to this rule. They collected [*devshirme*][2] the young men. They took one in every five prisoners captured in the raids and delivered them to the Porte. Then they gave these young men to the Turks in the provinces so that they should learn Turkish, and then they sent them to Anatolia. The Turks let these young men work in the fields for a while and made use of them until they learned Turkish. After a few years they brought them to the Porte and made them janissaries, giving them the name *Yenī Čeri* [new troops]. Their origin goes back to this time.

Anonymous Ottoman Chronicle, pp. 21–22.

[2] See *EI*², s.v.

14

Conquest

62. Letter to the Persians (633)

In the name of God, the Merciful and the Compassionate.

From Khālid ibn al-Walīd to the kings [*mulūk*] of Persia.

Praise be to God who has dissolved your order, frustrated your plans, and split your unanimity. Had He not done this to you, it would have been worse for you. Submit to our authority, and we shall leave you and your land and go by you against others. If not, you will be conquered against your will by men who love death as you love life.

In the name of God, the Merciful and the Compassionate.

From Khālid ibn al-Walīd to the border-chiefs [*marzubān*] of Persia.

Become Muslim and be saved. If not, accept protection from us and pay the *jizya*. If not, I shall come against you with men who love death as you love to drink wine.

Al-Ṭabarī, p. 2053
(variants in al-Ṭabarī, i, p. 2020; Abū Yūsuf, p. 85; and Abū 'Ubayd p. 34).

63. The Conquest of Mesopotamia (637–641)

As regards the question which you put to me, O Commander of the Faithful, concerning the conquest of Syria and Mesopotamia and the conditions on which peace was concluded with their inhabitants, I wrote to inquire of an old man in Ḥīra who is well-informed about the conquest of these two countries, and he wrote to me as follows:

May God preserve you and keep you in good health. I have assembled for you all that I know about Syria and Mesopotamia, but without including anything which I learned from the jurists or from anyone else citing the authority of the jurists. I report only statements from persons considered competent in this matter, and I did not ask any of them what were their authorities.

Before Islam, Mesoptamia belonged in part to the Romans and in part to the Persians, each with troops and officials in the parts they held. Ra's al-'Ayn and the country on this side of it, as far as the Euphrates, belonged to the Romans; Niṣībīn and the country beyond it, as far as the Tigris, belonged to the Persians. The plain of Mārdīn and Dārā, as far as Sinjār and the desert, was Persian; the mountains of Mārdīn, Dārā, and Ṭūr 'Abdīn were Roman. The watch-tower between the Romans and Persians was a fortress called Sarja between Dārā and Niṣībīn. When Abū 'Ubayda ibn al-Jarrāḥ, may God be pleased with him, marched with his troops against Syria, Abū Bakr, may God be pleased with him, sent Shuraḥbīl ibn Ḥasana with him to be governor of the district of Jordan, Yazīd ibn Abī Sufyān to be governor of Damascus, and Khālid ibn al-Walīd, whom he had transferred from Yamāma to help him, to be governor of Ḥimṣ. After entering Syria he also sent 'Amr ibn al-'Āṣ to help him. When God had given them conquest, Abū 'Ubayda established himself on the borders of Syria, while Shuraḥbīl went to Jordan, Yazīd b. Abī Sufyān to Damascus, and Khālid b. al-Walīd to Ḥimṣ. When they were fully in control, Abū 'Ubayda sent Shuraḥbīl toward Qinnasrīn, which he conquered, and sent 'Iyāḍ ibn Ghanam al-Fihrī to Mesopotamia. The seat of the Roman governor was then at Al-Ruhā.[1] 'Iyāḍ b. Ghanam advanced against it and did not interfere with any of the towns or districts through which he passed, meeting neither troops nor ambush until he reached Al-Ruhā. Its defenders closed the gates, and 'Iyāḍ besieged it for a period of time which was not stated to me. When the governor saw the siege and despaired of help, one night he opened a gate leading to the mountain and fled with the greater part of his

[1] Also known, in other periods, as Edessa and as Urfa.

troops. There remained in the city the Nabataean[2] inhabitants, who were numerous, and those Romans who did not wish to flee, who were few. They sent to 'Iyāḍ b. Ghanam asking for peace, for a sum which they specified. 'Iyāḍ write, referring this to Abū 'Ubayda b. al-Jarrāḥ, who sent the letter on to Mu'ādh ibn Jabal to read. Mu'ādh said to him, "If you grant them peace for a fixed sum which they are then unable to pay, you will not be able to put them to death and you will have to release them from their obligations. If they are able to pay easily, they will do so anyway but without being humbled as God commanded.[3] Therefore, respond to their offer by granting them peace on condition that they pay what they can. Whether they do it easily or not, you will only claim what is within their capacity; your terms will be valid and not annulled." Abū 'Ubayda accepted this and wrote accordingly to 'Iyāḍ ibn Ghanam. When the letter reached 'Iyāḍ b. Ghanam, he informed the townspeople of its contents. They disagreed on the matter. Some said, "Agree to peace on the basis of payment according to capacity." Others said, "Refuse it!" The townspeople knew that they had in their possession property and income which would disappear if they agreed to pay according to capacity. They therefore refused anything but a fixed sum. When 'Iyāḍ saw their stubborness and the strength of their defenses, he despaired of taking the city by storm and granted them peace on the terms which they offered. God knows what these were, but the peace was signed and the city submitted; of this there is no doubt.

After this 'Iyāḍ ibn Ghanam marched or possibly sent an army against Ḥarrān, which was the nearest town. The inhabitants, Nabataeans and a few Romans, closed the gates, but when 'Iyāḍ told them what terms the people of al-Ruhā had agreed upon and when they realized that their capital had been conquered, they all agreed to submit on the same terms. As to the villages and rural areas, no claim was made and no resistance attempted. In every district, once the seat of government had been conquered, the country people said, "We are the same as the

[2] A term used by the Arabs for the Aramaic-speaking native population.
[3] Cf. Qur'ān, ix, 29, and vol. II, p. 195.

people of our town and our chiefs." I have not heard that 'Iyāḍ accorded them the same treatment or declined to do so, but the governors appointed after the conquest by the Caliphs treated the inhabitants of the country districts in the same way as those of the cities, except for the burden of supplying the army which they alone [and not the townspeople] bore. Certain scholars who claim to have knowledge on this point say, "They did this because the country people have lands and tillage, while the townspeople do not." Those who know and who argue about the evidence reply, "We are in possession of rights established by your predecessors and confirmed in your registers. You do not know any more than we do how it was in the beginning. How, therefore, can you lawfully impose a new burden on us which did not exist before and for which you have no proof and thus violate your own established order of things which still stands?"

As for that part of Mesopotamia which was in the hands of the Persians, I heard nothing that I can recall except that the Persians, when their defeat at Qādisiyya became known to their troops in this region, withdrew altogether and abandoned the places where they had been. Only the inhabitants of Sinjār established a watchtower in their city to protect their plain and the plains of Mārdīn and Dārā, and they remained in their city. When Persia perished and men came to summon them to Islam, they accepted and still remained in their city.

'Iyāḍ ibn Ghanam al-Fihrī levied poll taxes in Mesopotamia at the rate of 1 dinar, 2 *mudd* of wheat, 2 *qisṭ* of oil, and 2 *qisṭ* of vinegar per head, treating them all the same. I have not heard whether this was in accordance with terms of peace or a confirmed order or a report on the authority of the jurists or reliable tradition. When 'Abd al-Malik ibn Marwān succeeded, he sent al-Ḍaḥḥāk ibn 'Abd al-Raḥmān al-Ash'arī. Finding the taxes taken from them insufficient, he counted the heads of the population. Assuming that everyone worked with his hands, he made an estimate of his annual earnings, deducted what he spent on food, condiments and clothing, and deducted feast days throughout the year. He then found that what everyone had left was 4 dinars a year. He therefore fixed this as poll tax for all of them, treating them all the same. He then taxed the lands in proportion to their nearness or farness. He levied 1 dinar on 100 *jarībs* of cultivated land, if it was near, and the same amount on 200 *jarībs* if it was far. He also levied 1 dinar on 1000 shoots of vine if near, or on 2000 shoots if far, on 100 olive trees if near, or on 200 olive trees if far. He called far that which was at a day's journey or more, and near, that which was less than a day's journey.

Syria and Mosul were taxed in the same way.

Abu Yūsuf, *Kitāb al-Kharāj*, pp. 39–41.

64. The Conquest of Nubia (651–ca. 720)

He said: Then 'Abdallāh ibn Sa'd raided the blacks, that is, the Nubians; according to Yaḥya ibn 'Abdallāh ibn Bukayr this was in the year 31 [651–652]. 'Abdallāh ibn Maslama said: Ibn Lahī'a said, on the authority of Yazīd ibn Abī Ḥabīb: 'Abdallāh ibn Sa'd ibn Abī Sarḥ was 'Uthmān's governor in Egypt in the year 31, and the Nubians fought against him.

Ibn Lahī'a said: Al-Ḥārith ibn Yazīd said: there was hard fighting between them, and on that day Mu'āwiya ibn Ḥudayj, Abū Shamir ibn Abraha, and Ḥaywīl ibn Nāshira were hit [by arrows] in the eye. The Nubians were then nicknamed *Rumāt al-hadaq,* those who hit the pupil of the eye. 'Abdallāh ibn Sa'd made an armistice with them, since he could not cope with them. The poet said:

My eye has not seen anything like the day of Dumqula,
when the horses galloped, though weighed down with mail.

Ibn Abī Ḥabīb said in his version: 'Abdallāh made terms with the Nubians for an armistice between them and the Muslims, to the effect that the Muslims would not raid the Nubians and the Nubians would not raid the Muslims, that the Nubians would pay a certain number of slaves every year to the Muslims, and that the Muslims would pay certain quantities of wheat and lentils every year to the Nubians.[1]

[1] On the pact with the Nubians, see *EI*², "Baḳṭ."

Ibn Abī Ḥabīb said: there was no bond or covenant between them and the people of Egypt, but only an armistice with mutual safe-conduct [*amān*].

Ibn Lahī'a said: there is no objection if their slaves are bought from them or from others. Abū Ḥabīb, the father of Yazīd ibn Abī Ḥabīb (his personal name was Suwayd [roughly, Blackie]) was one of them.

Sa'īd ibn 'Ufayr said, on the authority of Ibn Lahī'a: I heard Yazīd ibn Abī Ḥabīb say: my father was a captive from Dumqula, the freedman of a man from Medina of the Banū 'Āmir tribe; his name was Shurayk ibn Ṭufayl.

He said: According to certain shaykhs in Egypt, the peace agreed with the Nubians provided for 360 slaves a year, but others say 400 slaves a year, of which 360 slaves for the common booty [*fay'*] of the Muslims and 40 slaves for the governor. He said: Some old men claimed that there were to be 17 wet nurses.

Then 'Abdallāh ibn Sa'd went away from them, and it is said, according to what was related by some of the early shaykhs, that he looked in one of the registers in Fusṭāṭ and read it before it was torn up and memorized the following: we make a bond and compact with you that you should supply us with 360 slaves every year; that you should enter our country as temporary visitors, not permanent residents, and we shall enter your country in the same way; that if you kill any Muslim your armistice is void, and likewise if you harbor any slave belonging to the Muslims. You must return runaway slaves belonging to the Muslims and fugitive *dhimmīs* who seek asylum with you.

He said: Another shaykh maintained that there was no commitment from the Muslims to the Nubians. According to this version, when the Nubians made their first delivery in the first year of the pact, they presented forty slaves to 'Amr ibn al-'Āṣ. He did not wish to accept this gift from them and therefore turned it over to a very eminent Copt called Nastaqūs, who acted for them in this matter. He sold the slaves and bought supplies for the Nubians, who then adduced this as an argument to show that 'Amr had sent them wheat and horses because they were deprived of wheat and horses. They produced this story at an early date and achieved their aim. This is their story.

To continue the narrative: When 'Abdallāh was returning along the bank of the Nile, the Bujja[2] gathered about him. He made inquiries about them and was informed of their position. He found them unimportant and went his way, leaving them behind, and they had no agreement or peace terms. The first who made peace terms with them was 'Ubaydallāh ibn al-Ḥabḥāb.[3] A certain shaykh claims that he read Ibn al-Ḥabḥāb's letter, and it provided that they would send 300 young camels[4] every year; that they would come to the Egyptian countryside as traveling merchants but not as residents; that they would not kill any Muslim or *dhimmī,* and if they did, their covenant was void; and that they would not harbor Muslim slaves and would return any runaways to the Muslims. . . . For every sheep which a Bujja took he would pay four dinars, and for every cow ten dinars. They had an agent resident in Egypt as a hostage in the hands of the Muslims.

Ibn 'Abd al-Ḥakam, pp. 188–189.

65. Peace Terms (633–643)

Bānqiyā and Basmā (633)

In the name of God, the Merciful and the Compassionate.

This is a letter from Khālid ibn al-Walīd to Ṣalūba ibn Nasṭūnā and his people.

I have made a pact with you for *jizya* and defense for every fit man, for both Bānqiyā and Basmā, for 10,000 dinars, excluding coins with holes punched in them, the wealthy according to the measure of his wealth, the poor according to the measure of his poverty, payable annually. You have been made head of your people and your people are content with you. I, therefore, and the Muslims who are with me, accept you, and I [? you] and your people are content. You have protection

[2] A nomadic Sudanese tribe in the area between the Nile and the Red Sea. See *EI*[2], "Bedja."

[3] Administrator of finances in Egypt, under the Caliph Hishām.

[4] The printed text is vocalized to read *bikr*—virgin; *bakr*—young camel, is a more likely reading. The consonants in the two words are the same.

[*dhimma*] and defense. If we defend you, the *jizya* is due to us; if we do not, it is not, until we do defend you.

Witnessed by Hishām ibn al-Walīd, al-Qa'qā' ibn 'Amr, Jarīr ibn 'Abdallāh al-Ḥimyarī and Ḥanẓala ibn al-Rabī'.

Written in the year 12, in Ṣafar [April–May 633].

Al-Ṭabarī, i, p. 2050.

Jerusalem (*636*)

In the name of God the Merciful and the Compassionate.

This is the safe-conduct accorded by the servant of God 'Umar, the Commander of the Faithful, to the people of Aelia [Jerusalem].

He accords them safe-conduct for their persons, their property, their churches, their crosses, their sound and their sick, and the rest of their worship.

Their churches shall neither be used as dwellings nor destroyed. They shall not suffer any impairment, nor shall their dependencies, their crosses, nor any of their property.

No constraint shall be exercised against them in religion nor shall any harm be done to any among them.

No Jew shall live with them in Aelia.

The people of Aelia must pay the *jizya* in the same way as the people of other cities.

They must expel the Romans and the brigands [?] from the city. Those who leave shall have safe-conduct for their persons and property until they reach safety. Those who stay shall have safe-conduct and must pay the *jizya* like the people of Aelia.

Those of the people of Aelia who wish to remove their persons and effects and depart with the Romans and abandon their churches and their crosses shall have safe-conduct for their persons, their churches, and their crosses, until they reach safety.

The country people who were already in the city before the killing of so-and-so may, as they wish, remain and pay the *jizya* the same way as the people of Aelia or leave with the Romans or return to their families. Nothing shall be taken from them until they have gathered their harvest.

This document is placed under the surety of God and the

protection [*dhimma*] of the Prophet, the Caliphs and the believers, on condition that the inhabitants of Aelia pay the *jizya* that is due from them.

Witnessed by Khālid ibn al-Walīd, 'Amr ibn al-'Āṣ, 'Abd al-Raḥmān ibn 'Awf, Mu'āwiya ibn Abī Sufyān, the last of whom wrote this document in the year 15 [636].

Al-Ṭabarī, i, pp. 2405–2406.

Jurjān (639)

In the name of God, the Merciful and the Compassionate.

This is a letter from Suwayd ibn Muqarrin to Ruzbān Ṣūl ibn Ruzbān, the inhabitants of Dihistān, and the rest of the inhabitants of Jurjān.

You have protection and we must enforce it on the condition that you pay the *jizya* every year, according to your capacity, for every adult male. If we seek help from any of you, the help counts as his *jizya* in place of the payment. They have safe-conduct for themselves, their property, their religions, and their laws. There will be no change in what is due to them as long as they pay and guide the wayfarer and show good will and lodge the Muslims and do not spy or betray. Whoever stays with them shall have the same terms as they have, and whoever goes forth has safe-conduct until he reaches a place of safety, provided that if anyone insults a Muslim he is severely punished, and if he strikes a Muslim, his blood is lawful.

Witnessed by Sawād ibn Quṭba, Hind ibn 'Amr, Simāk ibn Makhrama, and 'Utayba ibn al-Naḥḥās.

Written in the year 18 [639].

Al-Ṭabarī i, pp. 2658–2659.

Ṭabaristān and Jīl Jīlān (639)

In the name of God, the Merciful and the Compassionate.

This is a letter from Suwayd ibn Muqarrin to Farrukhān, the Isfahbadh of Khurāsān, regarding Ṭabaristān and Jīl Jīlān, of the people of the enemy.

You are safe, by the safe-conduct of Almighty God, on the

condition that you prevent your brigands and your border people from fighting us, that you do not harbor rebels against us, that you seek protection from the governor on the border of your land for 500,000 dirhams of the coin of your country. If you do this, none of us will attack you or enter your territory or come to you without your permission. Our communications through your territory, with permission, are under safe-conduct; so too, are your communications. You will not harbor rebels against us nor spy on us for an enemy nor betray us. If you do this, there is no bond [*'ahd*] between you and us.

Witnessed by Sawād ibn Quṭba al-Tamīmī, Hind ibn 'Amr al-Murādī, Simāk ibn Makhrama al-Asadī, Simāk ibn 'Ubayd al-'Absī, and 'Utayba ibn al-Naḥḥās al-Bakrī.

Written in the year 18 [639].

Al-Ṭabarī, i, pp. 2659–2660.

Ādharbayjān (*639*)

In the name of God, the Merciful and the Compassionate.

This is what 'Utba ibn Farqad, governor for 'Umar ibn al-Khaṭṭāb, Commander of the Faithful, gave to the inhabitants of Ādharbayjān, its plains and hills and dependencies and borderlands and all the people of its communities: Safe-conduct for themselves, their property, their religions, and their laws, on the condition that they pay the *jizya* according to their capacity, but not for the child or the woman or for the sick or the pious hermit, who owns nothing of the goods of this world. This is for them and for whoever dwells with them. Their obligation is to lodge any Muslim from the Muslim armies for a day and a night and to guide him. If anyone of them dies in a year, he is relieved of the *jizya* for that year. If anyone stays [with them] he is in the same position as they are [that is, as regards obligations and rights]; if anyone goes forth, he has safe-conduct until he reaches safety.

Written by Jundub and witnessed by Bukayr ibn 'Abdallāh al-Laythī and Simāk ibn Kharsha al-Anṣārī.

Written in 18 [639].

Al-Ṭabarī, i, p. 2662.

Iṣfahān (642)

In the name of God, the Merciful and the Compassionate.

A letter from 'Abdallāh to the Fādhūsafān and the inhabitants of Iṣfahān and its surroundings.

You are safe as long as you discharge your obligations, which are: to pay the *jizya,* which you must pay according to your capacity every year, paying it to whoever is the governor of your country, for every adult male; you must also guide the Muslim [traveler], keep his road in repair, lodge him for a day and a night, and provide the walker with a mount for one stage.

Do not assert your authority over any Muslim. What you owe to the Muslims is your goodwill and the payment of your dues; you have safe-conduct (*amān*) as long as you comply. But if you change anything, or if anyone among you changes anything and you do not hand him over, then you have no safe-conduct. If anyone insults a Muslim, he will be severely punished for it. If he strikes a Muslim, we shall kill him.

Written and witnessed by 'Abdallāh ibn Qays, 'Abdallāh ibn Warqā', and 'Iṣma ibn 'Abdallāh.

Al-Ṭabarī, i, p. 2641.

Rayy (642–643)

In the name of God, the Merciful and the Compassionate.

This is what Nu'aym ibn Muqarrin gave to al-Zaynabī ibn Qūla. He gave him safe-conduct (*amān*) for the inhabitants of Rayy and others who were with them, on condition of the annual payment of the *jizya,* according to capacity, for every adult male and on condition that they show goodwill and guide travelers, that they neither spy nor betray, that they lodge the Muslims for a day and a night, that they show deference to the Muslims. Anyone who insults or belittles a Muslim will receive crushing punishment; anyone who strikes a Muslim will be killed. If anyone changes this and his dead body is not handed over, then he will have changed the status of your whole community.

Written and witnessed.

Al-Ṭabarī, i, p. 2655.

Dunbāwand (642–3)

In the name of God, the Merciful and the Compassionate.

This is a letter from Nu'aym ibn Muqarrin to Mardān-shāh Maṣmughān of Dunbāwand and the inhabitants of Dunbāwand, Khuwār, Lāriz, and Shīrrīz.

You have safe-conduct, together with those who join with you in refraining from fighting. You should keep the inhabitants of your country from fighting and obtain the protection of the governor on your frontier for 200,000 dirhams, weight 7, every year. No one will attack you and no one will enter your lands without permission as long as you observe this and until you change it. If anyone changes it, there is no bond for him or for whoever refuses to hand him over.

Written and witnessed.

Al-Ṭabarī, i, p. 2656.

Qūmis (642–643)

In the name of God, the Merciful and the Compassionate.

This is what Suwayd ibn Muqarrin gave to the inhabitants of Qūmis and those who are dependent on them, concerning safe-conduct for themselves, their religions, and their property, on condition that they pay the *jizya* from the hand for every adult male, according to his capacity, that they show goodwill and do not deceive, that they guide [the Muslim traveler], and that they accommodate Muslims who make a halt with them for a day and a night with their average food. If they change this or make light of their obligations, the pact [*dhimma*] with them is void.

Written and witnessed.

Al-Ṭabarī, i, p. 2657.

Tiflīs (642–643)

In the name of God, the Merciful and the Compassionate.

This is a letter from Ḥabīb ibn Maslama for the inhabitants of Tiflīs, in the land of Hurmuz, giving safe-conduct to you, your children, your families, your convents, your churches, your religions, and your prayers, on condition that you accept the humiliation [?] of the *jizya* at the rate of a full dinar for every household. You must not join separate households together in order to reduce the *jizya* which you pay, nor may we separate what is joined in order to increase the *jizya* which we receive.

You owe us your goodwill and your help, as far as you can, against the enemies of God and His Prophet and of those who believe; lodging for the Muslim wayfarer for a night, with food and drink such as are lawful for the people of the book; and guidance on the road, as far as this causes no harm to you. If one of the Muslims is stranded among you, you must deliver him to the nearest group of believers and Muslims, unless some obstacle intervenes. If you repent, perform the prayer, and pay the *zakāt,* then you are our brothers in religion [and our *mawālī*].[1] But he who turns away from the faith, Islam, and the *jizya* is the enemy of God and His Prophet and of those who believe. We seek help from God against him.

If something happens which distracts the Muslims from helping you and your enemy overcomes you, this is not held against them [? you] and does not invalidate the pact with you after you return to the side of the believers and Muslims. This is what is due from you and what is due to you.

Witnessed by God and His Angels and His Prophets and those who believe, and God is sufficient witness.

Abū 'Ubayd, pp. 208–209
(variants in al-Ṭabarī, i, p. 2675; al-Balādhurī, *Futūḥ*, pp. 201–202).

Tiflīs (variant)

In the name of God, the Merciful and the Compassionate.

This is a letter from Ḥabīb ibn Maslama for the inhabitants of Tiflīs of the Georgians, in the land of Hurmuz, giving you safe-conduct for yourselves, your property, your convents, your churches, and your prayers, on the condition that you submit to the humiliation [?] of the *jizya* at the rate of a full dinar per household.

[1] Not in Abū 'Ubayd.

You owe us your goodwill and your help against the enemies of God and our enemies; lodging for the wayfarer for the night, with the food and drink permitted for the people of the book; and guidance on the road, as far as this causes no harm to any of you. If you become Muslims and perform the prayer and pay the *zakāt,* then you are our brothers in religion and our *mawālī.* But if anyone turns away from God and His Prophets and His books and His party, then we declare war against you without limit, for God does not love traitors.

Witnessed by 'Abd al-Raḥmān ibn Khālid, al-Ḥajjāj and 'Iyāḍ.

Written by Rabāḥ, who called on God and His angels and those who believe as witnesses. And God is sufficient witness.

Al-Ṭabarī, i, p. 2675.

Tiflīs 2

In the name of God, the Merciful and the Compassionate.

This is a letter issued by al-Jarrāḥ ibn 'Abdallāh for the inhabitants of Tiflīs, in the district of Manjalīs, in the realm of Georgia (Jurzān).

They came to me with a letter of safe-conduct given to them by Ḥabīb ibn Maslama, on condition of their accepting the humiliation of the *jizya* and stipulating a truce with them covering their lands, their vineyards, and their mills, which are called Awārī and Sābīnā in the district of Manjalīs, and covering Ṭa'ām and Daydūnā in the district of Quhuwit [Cogovit], of the realm of Georgia, on condition that for these mills and vineyards they pay, every year, 100 dirhams, once only and without repetition. I have therefore given effect to their safe-conduct and truce and have given orders that their dues be not increased. Whoever has my letter read to him, let him not overstep it in his dealings with them, please God.

Al-Balādhurī, *Futūḥ,* p. 202.

Glossary

Abbreviations

Dozy R. Dozy, *Dictionnaire détaillé des noms des vêtements chez les arabes,* Amsterdam (Müller), 1845.

EI[1] *Encyclopaedia of Islam,* first edition, Leiden (Brill), 1908–1938.

EI[2] *Encyclopaedia of Islam,* second edition, Leiden (Brill), 1954– in progress.

IMG W. Hinz, *Islamische Masse und Gewichte,* Leiden (Brill), 1955.

Schacht J. Schacht, *An Introduction to Islamic Law,* Oxford (Clarendon), 1964.

'Abd: the commonest Arabic term for slave, often combined with one or another of the divine names or attributes to form personal names, for example, 'Abd Allāh, slave of God; 'Abd al-Raḥmān, slave of the Merciful; 'Abd al-Karīm, slave of the Generous. In most Arabic-speaking countries the word *'abd* was in time specialized to mean "black slave," later simply "black." Male white slaves, usually military, were called *mamlūk,* a passive participle meaning "owned." Other terms for slaves included *ghulām* and *khādim* [q.v.] (*EI*[2], s.v.).

'Adāla: rectitude, good morals. A legal term denoting certain qualities, possession of which is a condition for public and juridical functions and offices. The possessor of *'adāla* is called *'adl.* A witness in proceedings before a qāḍī must be an *'adl.* In time groups of recognized, irreproachable witnesses, called *shāhid* or *'adl,* came to form a branch of the legal profession and acted as notaries or scriveners (*EI*[2], " 'Adl").

'Adl: see *'Adāla.*

'Ahd: covenant or pact, usually used for political treaties and arrangements such as the appointment of an heir apparent, the

safeguards conceded in a surrender on terms, and the limited rights granted to non-Muslims, whether inside the Islamic state (see *dhimma*); or outside it (see *amān*). The person or group granted *'ahd* is called *mu'āhad* (*EI*², "'Ahd").

Ahl: people, family, or kin (Arabic–cf. Hebrew *ohel,* tent). *Ahl al-Bayt,* people of the house, normally refers to the family and descendants of the Prophet. *Ahl al-dhimma,* people of the pact, is a common term for the protected non-Muslim subjects (see *dhimma*); *ahl al-ḥarb,* people of war, denotes non-Muslims beyond the Islamic frontier (see *Dār al-Ḥarb*).

Amān: safety, protection, or, in battle, quarter; sometimes also the pardon given to a rebel or similar offender. It is used technically for the safe-conduct or pledge of security given to a non-Muslim from outside the Islamic state (see *ḥarbī*). It may be given at the termination of hostilities or, more commonly, to an outsider visiting the Muslim lands for a limited period. The recipient of *amān* is called *musta'min* (*EI*², s.v.).

Amīr: an Arabic title literally meaning "commander," often translated "prince." *Amīr al-Mu'minīn,* Commander or Prince of the Believers, was one of the earliest and most distinctive titles of the Caliphs. The title "amir" was variously used of high military officers, governors of provinces, and increasingly, of the virtually independent rulers who emerged in many parts of the Islamic Empire under the nominal suzerainty of the Caliph. In the tenth century the title *Amīr al-Umarā',* amir of amirs, was adopted by the military rulers of the capital to indicate their primacy over the other amirs in the provinces (*EI*², s.v.).

Amṣār: plural of *miṣr,* the term applied to the fortress cities established or maintained by the Arabs in the early days of their empire. The most important *amṣār* were Kūfa and Basra in Iraq, Qumm in Persia, Fusṭāṭ in Egypt, and Qayrawān in North Africa. As a proper name Miṣr means Egypt or its capital city.

Anṣār: literally helpers, the designation applied to the Medinans who joined the Prophet Muḥammad after his migration to Medina from Mecca (*EI*², s.v.).

Ardabb or *Irdabb:* a measure of capacity of varying value, in medieval times usually about 90 liters (*IMG,* pp. 39–40).

'Arrāda: a medieval siege weapon, in which a projectile is propelled by a shaft driven forward by the release of a rope (*EI*², s.v.).
Atabeg, Atabek: a Turkish title, meaning literally "father-prince," given to the tutors or guardians of Seljuq and other Turkish princes. In time the *atabegs* became powerful officers of state, even governors and founders of dynasties. In Mamlūk Egypt the Atabeg was the commander-in-chief of the army (*EI*², s.v.).
Banū: sons of; commonly used in the names of Arab tribes.
Barīd: from the Latin *veredus,* Greek *beredos,* a post-horse (cf. German *Pferd*), the term commonly applied to the post and intelligence services of Islamic states and also to the couriers, mounts, and stages. The head of the organization was called *Ṣāḥib al-Barīd*—postmaster (*EI*², s.v.).
Bay'a: recognition of authority, especially the act by which a new Caliph or heir apparent is proclaimed and recognized (*EI*², s.v.).
Beg, Bey: a Turkish title, roughtly "lord" or "prince," often used as equivalent of the Arabic "amir" (*EI*², s.v.).
Bid'a: innovation; a belief or practice for which there is no authority in the *Sunna.* In Islamic usage it is used in a sense approximate to heresy (*EI*², s.v.).
Caliph: see *Khalīfa.*
Dā'ī: summoner; a religious propagandist or missionary, especially among the Ismā'īlīs and similar dissenting groups. The mission is called *da'wa* (*EI*², s.vv.).
Dāniq: a coin or weight, one-sixth of a dirham or, more frequently, of a dinar.
Dār al-Ḥarb: House of War; the non-Muslim world beyond the Islamic frontier. Between the House of War and the House of Islam (*Dār al-Islām*) there must be, according to legal theory, a perpetual state of war until all the world accepts the rule of Islam (see *jihād*). Until then the state of war may be suspended by truces but cannot be ended by a peace. A person coming from the House of War is called *ḥarbī* (*EI*², s.v.).
Da'wa: see *dā'ī*
Devshirme: the Ottoman Turkish term for the periodic levy of

Christian boys, collected for training and recruitment into the Janissaries, the Imperial Household, and the administration (*EI*,[2] s.v.).

Dhimma: the pact or covenant accorded by the Muslim state and community to the followers of other revealed religions living under their rule, according them protection and certain limited rights on the condition of their recognition of the supremacy of Islam. Members of religious communities benefiting from the *dhimma* are called *dhimmī* (*EI*[2], s.v.).

Dhirā': the cubit, or arm's length, subdivided into 24 digits (*aṣba'*). The length of the cubit varies in different regions and for different purposes. It is usually in the neighborhood of 50 to 60 centimeters (*EI*[2], s.v.; *IMG,* pp. 55–62).

Dihqān: the country gentry of pre-Islamic Persia. Under the early Caliphate they retained for a while their fiscal functions and social privileges but later sank gradually to the level of the peasantry (*EI*[2], "Dihḳān").

Dīnār: from the Greek *dênarion,* Latin *denarius,* the unit of gold currency under the Caliphate. The term went out of use between the twelfth and fourteenth centuries but has been revived in modern times (*EI*[2], s.v.).

Dirham: from the Greek *drakhmê,* the unit of silver currency used in the Islamic states from the beginning to the Mongol conquests. The term is also used to designate a weight, which varied greatly at different times and places and for different commodities (*EI*[2], s.v.; *IMG,* pp. 1–2).

Dīwān: an Arabic word of Persian origin, probably from a root meaning "to write." In early Islamic times the term was used of the central register of Muslim warriors and pensioners; later it denoted government departments in general. In the Ottoman Empire the *dīwān* was a kind of state council, presided over by the Sultan and later by the Grand Vizier. The collected poems of a poet are known as his *dīwān* (*EI*[2], s.v.).

Emir: see amir.

Faqīh: see *fiqh.*

Farsakh: a measure of distance, based on the ancient Persian parasang and used in the eastern provinces of the Caliphate. It was regarded as the equivalent of three miles, as used in the western (ex-Byzantine) provinces. The mile, of 4000 cubits (*dhirā'*), is estimated at about 2 kilometers (*EI*², s.v.; *IMG*, pp. 62–63).

Fatwā: a ruling or opinion on a point of holy law issued by a muftī (*q.v.*) and corresponding to the Roman *Responsa prudentium.* The Turkish form is *fetva* (*EI*², s.v.).

Fetva: see *Fatwā.*

Fiqh: the technical term for the science of Islamic law. The doctors of the law are called *faqīh.* Of the various schools of *fiqh* that arose among Sunnī Muslims, four are regarded as orthodox. They are named after the jurists whose teachings they follow: Ḥanafī (after Abū Ḥanīfa, d. 767); Mālikī (after Mālik ibn Anas, d. 795); Shāfi'ī (after al-Shāfi'ī, d. 820); and Ḥanbalī (after Aḥmad ibn Ḥanbal, d. 855). The Shī'a, Khārijites, and other sects have their own schools of jurisprudence, differing in some particulars from those of the Sunnīs (*EI*², "Fiḳh").

Fitna: a word originally meaning "testing" or "temptation," commonly used in the sense of sedition and upheaval (*EI*², s.v.).

Ghāzī: an Arabic term originally meaning "one who took part in a *ghazwa,*" razzia; later used to designate those who took part in the Holy War against the unbelievers. The name was also adopted by associations of march warriors, notably in Anatolia (*EI*², s.v.).

Ghiyār: the compulsory mark or sign worn by the *dhimmīs* (see *dhimma*) to distinguish them from Muslims. It usually consisted of a patch of cloth of a prescribed color and sometimes also of other items of clothing (*EI*², s.v.).

Ghulām: a young, male slave. The term is variously used of a servant or bodyguard, a palace guard or attendant, a young mamlūk (q.v.), or an artisan bound to a master. The term, the root meaning of which is "young man," is sometimes also used of freedmen bound by certain ties to their former masters (see *mawlā*) and even of free servants and attendants (*EI*², s.v.).

Ḥadd (plural *Ḥudūd*): impediment, limit, frontier, and hence the restrictive commandments contained in the Qur'ān. In the technical vocabulary of Islamic law, *ḥadd* denotes the punishments for certain offenses specified in the Qur'ān. The offenses are fornication, false accusation of fornication, drinking wine, theft, and highway robbery. The punishments are execution, amputation of the hand and/or foot, and flogging (*EI*², s.v.).

Ḥadīth: a tradition relating an action, utterance, or decision of the Prophet. The corpus of *ḥadīth* constitutes one of the major sources of Islamic law (*EI*², s.v.).

Ḥajj: the pilgrimage to Mecca, 'Arafāt and Minā, required of a Muslim at least once in his lifetime. One who has performed the pilgrimage is called *Ḥājj* in Arabic and *Ḥajjī* in Persian and Turkish (*EI*², s.v.).

Ḥanafī: see *fiqh*.

Ḥanbalī: see *fiqh*.

Ḥaram: an Arabic term conveying the meaning of forbidden, sacrosanct, or taboo. It is used especially for the holy places in Mecca and Medina and for sanctuaries in Jerusalem, Karbalā', Meshed, and elsewhere. The word is also used at times to designate the women's quarters of a house.

Hijra: often misspelled *Hegira;* the migration of the Prophet Muḥammad from Mecca to Medina in 622 A.D., according to most accounts on September 20. The Muslim calendar dates, not, as is commonly supposed, from the *Hijra,* but from the beginning of the Arab year in which the *Hijra* took place, that is, from July 16, 622. The Muslim year is purely lunar and has 354 days. The months do not therefore correspond to seasons, and there are approximately 103 Hijrī years to one hundred solar years according to the Gregorian calendar (*EI*², s.v.).

Ḥisba: see *muḥtasib*.

Ichoghlanï: a Turkish term, literally "inside boy," meaning "page of the inner (palace) service." It was applied in Ottoman usage to the boys recruited through the *devshirme* (*q.v.*) and also to other recruits—slaves, hostages, and later even free-born Muslims—selected and trained for the palace and imperial services (*EI*², "'Ič-oghlanï").

'Īd: festival. There are two major religious festivals in the Muslim year: the festival of sacrifices (*'Īd al-aḍḥā*), which is connected with the Pilgrimage to Mecca, and the festival of breaking the fast (*'Īd al-fiṭr*) after the end of Ramaḍān (*EI*², s.v.).

Ijāza: license, that is, to teach; the document given by a Muslim teacher to a disciple certifying that he has satisfactorily attended a course and is therefore able to teach it. The certificate is often appended to the disciple's transcript of his master's lectures (*EI*², s.v.).

Ijmā': consensus (that is, of the *'ulema'*), one of the major sources of Islamic law. Technically it is defined as "the unanimous doctrine and opinion of the recognized religious authorities at any given time." In the absence of any constituted ecclesiastical authority in medieval Islam, it comes to mean something like the climate of opinion among the learned and the powerful (*EI*², s.v.).

Ijtihād: literally, "exerting onself"; in the technical language of Islamic law, "the use of individual reasoning," later restricted to "reasoning by analogy." In the late ninth century it came to be accepted that only the great masters of early Islam had had the right to use individual reasoning and that, since all important questions had been considered and resolved by them, "the gate of *ijtihād* was closed." One who exercised *ijtihād* was called *mujtahid* (*EI*², s.v. " 'Idjtihād").

Il-Khan: see khan.

Imām: a leader, especially in prayer, and hence by extension the sovereign head of the universal Islamic state and community. *Imām* is one of the titles of the Caliph and that most commonly used by the jurists when discussing the laws relating to the Caliphate. The term is also used by the Shī'a for their own claimants to the headship of Islam and in this sense connotes an extensive spiritual authority absent from Sunnī usage. The office of Imam is called *Imāma* (*EI*², s.v. " 'Imāma' ").

Iqṭā': an administrative grant, often misleadingly translated "fief." The term is used generically for a number of different types of grant, each with its own designation. An early form was a cession, in practice irrevocable, of public lands to an individual who collected all taxes on these lands and paid only the tithe to the state (see *'ushr*). This was in time replaced by another type, the *iqṭā'* proper, whereby the state granted all its fiscal rights over lands that remained juridically the property of their previous owners. The grantee paid no tax to the state but held his grant in lieu of payment from the public treasury for service. His grant was thus in principle limited, functional, and revocable, and carried only fiscal rights over the land and its inhabitants. At times such *iqṭāʿ* became long-term or even hereditary. A third type was a form of fiscal autonomy whereby the taxes for a region or group were commuted for a fixed annual payment (*EI*², "Ḍayʿa," "Īghār," "Iḳṭāʿ").

Jāhiliyya: (the time of) ignorance, that is, pre-Islamic Arabia.

Jarīb: a measure of capacity, variously assessed at about 16, 26, 29.5 liters and in Mongol Persia at about 130 liters (*IMG,* p. 38). *Jarīb* was also used of a square measure, fixed for canonical purposes at 1592 square meters but with local variants (*IMG,* pp. 65–66).

Jihād: literally effort or striving; the name commonly given to the Holy War for Islam against the unbelievers. Jihād, in medieval times usually understood in a military sense, was a collective duty imposed on the Muslim community by the Holy Law. A fighter in *jihād* is called *mujāhid* (*EI*², "Djihād").

Jizya: the poll tax paid by protected non-Muslim subjects of the Muslim state (see *dhimma*). The rate was in time fixed by Holy Law at one, two, or four gold pieces per annum for each adult male, according to his wealth (*EI*², "Djizya").

Jund: an Arabic word of Iranian origin denoting troops or an army. In the early Caliphate it was used especially for the army corps quartered in the various districts of Syria and Palestine and hence to the districts themselves. The term was not used in this sense for the military districts of Iraq or Egypt, but it reappeared in Spain with the settlement of the eastern *junds* from 742 A.D. (*EI*², "Djund").

Kaʿba: a cubelike building, almost in the center of the great mosque in Mecca. The Black Stone, venerated as a sacred object, is inside the building, built into the wall at the eastern corner. The four inside walls are covered with black curtains (*kiswa*), fastened to the ground with copper rings. The Kaʿba is regarded as the palladium of Islam and forms the focal point of the ceremonies of pilgrimage (*EI*¹, s.v.).

Kāfir: an unbeliever, that is, one who does not accept Islam. Sometimes this term is applied to a heretical Muslim whose beliefs or practices go beyond the limits of permitted variation. The condition or doctrines of the *kāfir* are called *kufr.* To denounce a person or group as *kāfirs,* or a doctrine as *kufr,* is called *takfīr* (*EI*[1], s.v.).

Khādim: a servant or attendant, whether slave or free, male or female. At certain times and places the term connoted a eunuch; at others, a black slave or slavewoman (*EI*[2], "'Abd"; *EI*[1], s.v.).

Khalīfa: an Arabic term combining the notions of deputy and successor; adopted as title by the successors of Muḥammad in the headship of the Islamic state and community. With the rapid growth of that state into a vast empire, the term came to connote imperial sovereignty, combining both religious and political authority. With the rise of the military power of the amirs and the Sultans, the status of the Caliphs declined, and they became little more than figureheads with some religious prestige as titular heads of Sunnī Islam but no real power. In the forty years after the death of the Prophet, the period known as the patriarchal Caliphate, four Caliphs held office by a form of election. Thereafter the Caliphate became in practice, though not in theory, dynastic and was held by two successive dynasties, the Umayyads based on Syria and the 'Abbasids based on Iraq. The 'Abbasid Caliphate was extinguished by the Mongol conquest in 1258, but a line of puppet Caliphs, sired by a refugee from Baghdad, survived at the Court of the Mamlūk Sultans in Cairo until 1517. Rival Caliphates were maintained for a while by the Umayyads in Cordova and, with an Ismā'īlī religious basis, by the Fatimids in Tunisia and then in Egypt.

Khan: (a) a large building for the accommodation of travelers, merchants, and their wares. In Persia the usual term was *karvānsarāy.* (b) a Turkish title, originally a contraction of *khāqān* which, as a title of sovereignty, usually denoted supremacy over a group of tribes or territories. The title *khan* was used by Turkish Muslim rulers in central Asia from the tenth century onward; in the Mongol period it was at first used exclusively by members of the house of Jenghiz and later, by abuse, by other rulers. The Mongols at first distinguished between *khān* and *khāqān,* reserving the latter for their supreme ruler in East Asia.

The Mongol rulers of Persia were known as *Il-Khāns,* a term indicating subordination to a superior authority (*EI*[2], "Il;" *EI*[1], "Khāḳān," "Khān").

Kharāj: at first a generic term for taxes and tribute, then specialized to mean land tax as opposed to poll tax (*EI*[2], "Ḍarība," "Djizya;" *EI*[1], "Kharadj").

Kharijites: from Arabic *Khārijī,* plural *Khawārij;* the name of the earliest body of sectaries to secede from the main body of Muslims. They differed from others on two main points: in their theory of the Caliphate, which was strictly elective and consensual, and in their rejection of the doctrine of justification by faith without works (*EI*[1], "Kharidjites").

Khāṣṣ, Khāṣṣa: special, particular, as opposed to *'āmm, 'āmma,* general. This pair of words is used in various contexts, especially to denote the contrast between the common people (*'āmma*) and the privileged (*khāṣṣa*), that is, those who have power, wealth, position, descent, and education. The term *khāṣṣ* is also applied to military and other personnel attached to the person of the sovereign, and, later, to crown lands and revenues.

Khaṭīb: see *khuṭba.*

Khil'a: a robe bestowed by a sovereign as a mark of favor or honor (*EI*[1], s.v.).

Khuṭba: an address or sermon given during the public prayers in the mosque on Friday. In early times this was often a pronouncement by the sovereign or governor, dealing with political, military, and similar matters. Later it came to be a kind of sermon delivered by a preacher known as the *khaṭīb* and normally included the bidding-prayer for the sovereign. Mention in the *khuṭba* was one of the recognized tokens of sovereignty or suzerainty in Islam; omission from it was a signal of revolt (*EI*[1], s.v. and "Masdjid," pp. 346–349.

Kunya: part of the Arab personal name. The *kunya* was an appellation consisting of *Abū* (father of) or *Umm* (mother of) and followed by a name, usually that of the bearer's eldest son (*EI*[1], "Ism").

Madhhab: school of religious doctrine or law; usually applied to the four main schools of Sunnī jurisprudence (see *fiqh*).

Madrasa: a college or seminary for Muslim learning, frequently but not necessarily attached to a mosque. The Turkish form is *medrese* (*EI*[1], "Masdjid," pp. 350 ff.).

Mahdī: divinely guided; a messianic figure of the kin of the Prophet who according to popular belief, will return to earth and inaugurate an era of justice and plenty. His coming will be preceded and accompanied by various signs and portents. Many pretenders to this office have appeared in the course of the centuries. For the Twelver Shī'a (q.v.), the Mahdī is the twelfth Imam in the line of 'Alī ibn Abī Ṭālib, the cousin and son-in-law of the Prophet (*EI*[1], s.v.).

Makrūh: disapproved, deplored. Islamic law classifies actions in five categories: mandatory, recommended, permitted, disapproved, and forbidden (*EI*[1], "Sharī'a," p. 322).

Mālikī: see *Fiqh*.

Mamlūk: owned, hence a slave. The term mamlūk was in practice restricted to male white slaves, in particular those serving in the army and in government. This form of slavery came to be the usual path to military and political preferment and power. Many dynasties were founded by mamlūks, the most notable being the Egyptian regime known to scholarship but not to contemporaries as the Mamlūk Sultanate, which lasted from about 1250 to 1517.

Maqṣūra: a box or compartment erected in the mosque for the ruler, usually near the prayer niche (*EI*[1], "Masdjid," p. 336).

Mawālī: see *mawlā*.

Mawlā (plural *mawālī*): an Arabic term, the commonest meaning of which is "freed slave," "freedman," or "client." After liberation, the *mawlā* retains certain ties with his former master and becomes a client member of his master's tribe. The same term was used by adoptive or client members of a tribe who were not necessarily former slaves. In the early Islamic centuries the term *mawālī* was applied generally to the non-Arab converts to Islam.

Maẓālim: plural of *maẓlama* (grievance). *Al-Naẓar fi'l-maẓālim* (the investigation of grievances) was a court of inquiry, conducted at first by the Caliph in person and later by an official appointed for the purpose, to examine complaints of miscarriage or denial of justice brought against agents of the government, powerful individuals, or the qāḍīs themselves. It became a regular judicial institution with its own rules and procedure (*EI*[2], "Nāẓir al-Maẓālim"; Schacht, p. 51).

Milk (in Ottoman usage *mülk*): a form of ownership in Islamic law, corresponding approximately to the modern freehold. A grant of *milk* was called *tamlīk* (*EI*[2], s.v.; Schacht, p. 136).

Mithqāl: a unit of weight, particularly for precious metals, based on the Byzantine *solidus*. The dinar weighed one *mithqāl* of an average standard weight of 4.231 grams (*EI*[1], "Mithḳāl"; *IMG*, pp. 1–2).

Mu'āhad: see *'ahd.*

Mudd: a canonical measure of capacity in early Islam, probably a little over a liter (*IMG*, pp. 45–46).

Muftī: an authoritative specialist in Islamic law, competent to issue a *fatwā* (*q.v.*). Unlike the qāḍī (q.v.), the muftī was not at first an official appointee. His status was private, his function advisory and voluntary, and his authority derived from his personal scholarly reputation. Later some rulers appointed official muftīs from among recognized scholars, without thereby increasing their authority or eliminating the private practitioners (Schacht, pp. 73–75).

Muḥtasib: an officer entrusted with the maintenance of public morals and standards in the city, especially in the markets. His task is defined as "to promote good and prevent evil," that is, detect and punish immorality, the use of false weights and measures, the adulteration of wares and similar offenses, and generally to enforce the rules of honesty, propriety, and hygiene. He was appointed by the state but was usually a jurist (*faqīh*) by training. The function of the *Muḥtasib* is called *ḥisba* (*EI*[1], s.v.; *EI*[2], "Ḥisba").

Mujāwir: a sojourner, especially in or near a mosque or holy place, whose purpose was study or religious meditation.

Mujāhid: see *jihād.*

Mujtahid: see *ijtihād.*

Muqāṭa'a: a term used in a variety of technical senses, mostly connected with the collection of taxes in the form of a global, agreed sum instead of by variable, separate assessment. It often, but not always, connotes some form of tax farming.

Murābiṭ: see *ribāṭ.*
Musta'min: see *amān.*
Muwallad: literally begotten, born; originally a person, usually a slave, of non-Arab origin brought up among the Arabs. The term was later applied to the children of non-Arab converts to Islam to distinguish them from first-generation converts (see *mawlā*). Later the term was applied to the children of mixed marriages, Arab and non-Arab, slave and free, black and white. At some stage it seems to have acquired the meaning of mulatto (*EI*[1], s.v.).
Nā'ib: a deputy or substitute, especially of a qāḍī. In the Mamlūk Sultanate the *Nā'ib al-Salṭana* was a sort of deputy Sultan (*EI*[1], s.v.).
Pādishāh: a Persian title of sovereignty, often understood to connote imperial supremacy. It was used chiefly by Persian and Turkish-speaking dynasties.
Qāḍī: a judge administering the Holy Law of Islam (*EI*[2], "Ḳāḍī;" Schacht, pp. 34 ff; 50 ff; 188 ff).
Qā'id: leader, especially a military leader or senior officer. In Muslim Spain it connoted a general, an admiral, or even a commander-in-chief. In North Africa it was also used for tribal or regional chiefs recognized or appointed by the government (*EI*[2], "Ḳā'id").
Qalansuwa: a high, often conical cap worn by men, either under the turban or by itself (Dozy, pp. 365–371; *EI*[1], "Ḳalansuwa").
Qayṣariyya: From Greek *kaisareia,* imperial, belonging to Caesar; a public building or group of buildings with markets, shops, workshops, warehouses, and sometimes living quarters (*EI*[1], "Ḳaiṣarīya").
Qibla: The direction of Mecca, toward which Muslims turn in prayer. In mosques it is indicated by the prayer niche (*miḥrāb*) (*EI*[1], "Ḳibla").
Qīrāṭ: from the Greek *keration,* a grain or seed; one twenty-fourth part of a *mithqāl* and, by extension, one twenty-fourth part of any whole. As a unit of weight for commodities, the *qīrāṭ* shows some variation (*EI*[1], "Ḳīrāṭ"; *IMG,* p. 27).
Qisṭ: a measure of capacity, variously assessed at from 1.2 to 2.5 liters (*IMG,* p. 50).

Qurrā': readers, especially of the Qur'ān.
Raṭl: a unit of weight, varying greatly with time, place, and the material weighed and ranging from under a pound to more than 4 pounds (*EI*[1], s.v.; *IMG*, pp. 27–33).
Ra'īs: head or chief; a title given to certain functionaries in medieval Islamic administration. The *ra'īs* might be the head of a government department (see *dīwān*). Under the Seljuqs and their successors the term was most commonly used for the officer in charge of civil affairs in a city, whose duties included police duties. He might be either a notable of the city, recognized and appointed by the royal authority, or a royal officer.
Ribāṭ: a fortified Muslim monastery, usually in the border areas between the Islamic world and its non-Muslim neighbors. Its inhabitants, called *Murābiṭ* (plural *Murābiṭūn*), were pious volunteers, dedicated to the Holy War for Islam (*EI*[1], s.v.).
Rūm: the Arabic word for Rome. In medieval times this was the normal Islamic term for the Byzantine Empire and was sometimes extended to European Christians in general. After the Turkish invasion of Anatolia, the term was commonly used for the former Byzantine territories under Turkish rule and sometimes even for the Turks themselves.
Ṣadaqa: alms, probably from the Hebrew *ṣedāqā;* sometimes used in the general sense of almsgiving and sometimes, more technically, as a synonym of *zakāt* (q.v.) (*EI*[1], "Ṣadaḳa").
Sayyid: lord, master. At first this title was applied to the chief of an Arabian tribe; later it was used as an honorific appellation for other men of authority, including Sufi saints and teachers. *Sayyidī* or *Sīdī* ("my master"), was a usual form of respectful address to such persons. The term *Sayyid* was also used extensively, but not exclusively, for the descendants of the Prophet (*EI*[1], "Sharīf," pp. 325–326).
Shāfi'ī: see *fiqh*.
Shāhid: a witness, more specifically one whose name appears on the list of trustworthy witnesses drawn up under the qāḍī's authority (see *'adāla*).
Sharī'a: the Holy Law of Islam (*EI*[1], s.v.).
Sharīf (plural *Ashrāf*): noble, well-born; at first used generally

of the leading families, then more particularly of the descendants of the Prophet (*EI*[1], s.v.).

Shaykh: an Arabic word meaning "old man," "elder"; used in a wide variety of contexts: for the chiefs of tribes, religious dignitaries, for the heads of religious fraternities or of craft guilds and generally as a term of respect for men of position, authority, or advancing years.

Shīʿa: party or faction, hence specifically the party of ʿAlī, the kinsman and son-in-law of the Prophet. The *Shīʿa* began as a group of Muslims who advocated the claims of ʿAlī, and later of his descendants, to the Caliphate. It developed rapidly into a religious movement differing on a number of points of doctrine and law from Sunnī Islam. The Shīʿa split into many subsects the most important of which are the *Ithnāʿasharī* (Twelver) Shīʿa (so called because of their acceptance of twelve Imams), the Ismāʿīlīs, and the Zaydīs (*EI*[1], s.v.).

Sipāhī: a Persian word meaning "soldier" and later specialized to mean a horse soldier. In the Ottoman Empire the *sipāhī* was a quasi-feudal cavalryman who received a grant known as *timar* (*EI*[1], "Timar"; *EI*[2], " ʿAskarī").

Sulṭān: an abstract noun meaning ruler or power, particularly that of the government. At first informally, then, from the eleventh century, officially, it was applied to the person of the ruler and came to designate the supreme political and military authority, as contrasted with the religious authority to which the Caliphs were increasingly restricted (*EI*[1], s.v.).

Sunna: see Sunnī.

Sunnī: a Muslim belonging to the dominant majority group in Islam, sometimes loosely translated "orthodox." A Sunnī is a follower of the *Sunna,* the accepted practice and beliefs of the Islamic community, based on the precedents of the Prophet, his Companions, and his accredited successors, as established and interpreted by the consensus (see *ijmāʿ*) of the learned (*EI*[1], s.v.).

Tamlīk: see *milk.*

Takbīr: to pronounce the formula *Allahu Akbar,* God is very great (*EI*[1], s.v.).

Tarāwīḥ: special prayers recited during the night in Ramaḍān (*EI*[1], s.v.).
Ṭaylasān: A kind of hood or scarf, worn over the head and shoulders or the shoulders only. In earlier times it was regarded as the distinguishing mark of the doctors of the Holy Law (Dozy, pp. 254 ff., 272 ff.).
Timar: see *sipāhī.*
Ṭirāz: a word of Persian origin meaning embroidery, hence embroidered or brocaded robes, and then the workshop, usually state-controlled, in which these were manufactured. *Ṭirāz* was often embroidered with suitable inscriptions. The wearing of *ṭirāz* and the granting of *ṭirāz* to other persons were royal prerogatives (*EI*[1], s.v.).
'Ulamā': plural of *'ālim,* a scholar, specifically in religious subjects. The term *'ulamā'* is used to describe the class of professional men of religious learning who form the nearest Muslim entity to a clergy (*EI*[1], s.v.).
Ulema: an Anglicized Turkish form of the Arabic *'ulamā'* (q.v.).
Umm walad: literally mother of a child; a slave-women who has born her master a child and thereby acquired certain legal rights (*EI*[1], s.v.).
Umma: an Arabic term meaning approximately "community," used of both religious and ethnic entities. The two were not clearly differentiated, although the religious meaning usually predominated. The term was commonly used for the religio-political community of Islam as a whole; it was also used for non-Muslim entities, both religious (for example, the Christians) and, less commonly, ethnic (for example, the Franks). It was not normally used in medieval times for ethnic groups within Islam.
'Ushr: tithe; a tax imposed by the Holy Law on Muslim-owned property for charitable and other purposes (*EI*[1], s.v.).
Vizier: see *wazīr.*
Walī: a term with several distinct meanings, derived from the Arabic root *waliya,* to be near, to be friends, to rule, to take charge, or to control. In the religious sense it means something like saint or holy man, that is, a friend of God. In law it denotes a guardian or legal tutor. In political and administrative usage

it means the authorized holder or executant of an office, a function, a duty, or a privilege.

Waqf: a form of endowment or trust, of land or other income-producing property, the proceeds of which are assigned by the founder to a specific purpose. The endowment, which is irrevocable and permanent, may be either for some pious object, such as a mosque, school, or charity, or for the benefit of named persons, normally the founder's family (*EI*[1], "Waḳf").

Wāsiṭa: an officer of state under the Fatimid Caliphs, corresponding approximately to the *wazīr* (q.v.).

Wazīr: A high officer of state, usually a civilian. The power and status of the office varied greatly. In some periods, as under the early 'Abbasids, the *wazīr* was the head of the bureaucracy and virtually in charge of the day-to-day conduct of government. Under the Seljuq Sultans he was effectively head of the administration. At other times he was a relatively minor official. The Ottoman Sultans had several *wazīrs,* the chief of whom came to be known as the Grand Vizier (*EI*[1], s.v.).

Zakāt: the alms tax, one of the five basic duties of a Muslim. According to Islamic law it is collected from certain categories of property and assigned to certain specified purposes (*EI*[1], s.v.).

Zanj, Zanjī: a word of uncertain origin, used to designate the people of East Africa, and hence more loosely, blacks in general.

Zindīq: a word of uncertain, probably Iranian origin. At first it was applied to the Manicheans but was later used extensively to denote the holders of unpopular or heretical beliefs, particularly those regarded as dangerous to the state and society (*EI*[1], s.v.).

Zunnār: from the Aramaic *zunnārā* and ultimately from the Greek *zōnē,* a belt. In medieval Islam the name was used in particular for the distinctive belt or sash which non-Muslims were required to wear (*EI*[1], s.v.).

Index

74 75 76 77 78 79 80 12 11 10 9 8 7 6 5 4 3 2 1